# THE ⟨crest⟩ TIMES
# ENGLAND'S WORLD CUP

# THE ⟪crest⟫ TIMES

# ENGLAND'S WORLD CUP

## THE FULL STORY OF THE
## 2019 TOURNAMENT

EDITED BY **RICHARD WHITEHEAD**
FOREWORD BY **MIKE ATHERTON**

The
History
Press

First published 2019

The History Press
97 St George's Place, Cheltenham,
Gloucestershire, GL50 3QB
www.thehistorypress.co.uk

British Library Cataloguing in Publication Data.
A catalogue record for this book is available from the British Library.

ISBN 978 0 7509 9323 4

Typesetting and origination by The History Press
Printed and bound in Great Britain by TJ International Ltd.

# CONTENTS

# FOREWORD

## *By Mike Atherton*

The photograph used across the inside spread of *The Times* to accompany the report of the World Cup final must be one of the most remarkable ever taken at Lord's. It showed the scene in the immediate aftermath of what was surely the most astonishing one-day match played at the ground.

In the background the Pavilion was alive, teeming with MCC members who had thrown off their usual reserve, like schoolchildren released from the straitjacket of uniforms after exams. In the foreground, the England players were running this way and that, as if in Brownian motion, trying to catch up with the team-mate closest to them.

Bottom right, alone with his thoughts amid the mayhem, was Ben Stokes, lying on the ground in crucifix position, overcome by the enormity of what he had helped to achieve. Stokes was the driving force behind England's ultimate triumph, a man who refused to admit defeat even as victory seemed to be slipping inexorably away.

The accepted narrative in years to come will be that England's was a collective triumph, built on meticulous planning and four years' hard work. There is some truth to that: having endured a wretched World Cup in 2015, there was a determination to put things right. There was a telling shift of priorities.

One-day contracts were introduced. A coach, Trevor Bayliss, with an outstanding white-ball record was appointed. Players were encouraged to explore franchised T20 leagues. The goal, to win the World Cup for the first time, was set out clearly. Over a four-year period, England rose to the top of the world rankings.

Yet, despite the preparation and planning, would England have won without such a singular cricketer as Stokes in their ranks? Would they have won without the last-minute change in regulations that advanced Jofra Archer's qualification? Archer, of course, bowled the Super Over under intense pressure and added an extra dimension to the attack with his pace and clever variations.

These questions lie at the heart of the game with its hard-to-calculate balance between the individual and collective, the instinctive and the planned. Without the focus put in place by Andrew Strauss as Director of England Cricket, England's eventual triumph would not have happened. Equally, Archer's pace and Stokes' competitiveness are qualities for which no amount of preparation can provide.

The World Cup 2019 was the first in England for 20 years and will probably be the last in this country for that period of time, if not more. It felt, then, like a once-in-a-lifetime opportunity for this set of players and the game more generally. With the final attracting an audience of between 8 and 9 million, following Sky Sports' decision to use a free-to-air platform to televise the match, it received the kind of oxygen that cricket has not enjoyed for some time.

For a while, though, as England battled their nerves and the competition experienced some poor weather, such a denouement did not look likely. England lost three matches in the qualifying stages: to Pakistan at Trent Bridge; then, gallingly, to one of the weakest sides in the competition, Sri Lanka, at Headingley, and then to Australia at Lord's. The defeat to Sri Lanka, botching the kind of run chase that would have not inconvenienced them at all the build-up to the tournament, suggested some frayed nerves.

The weather aside, which had a destructive effect on some early matches in the West Country especially, England once again showed why it remains a fine place for a global tournament. Matches were heavily sold. Every team could boast a decent-sized following and the players enjoyed the compact nature of the travel. Bangladesh, in particular, enjoyed wonderful support – especially in London – and their players responded to it with some stirring performances.

The most talked about game of the initial stages involved, inevitably, India and Pakistan. There were almost 600,000 ticket applications for the match at Old Trafford and thankfully the threatened rain for the most part stayed away. The ground heaved. Corporate boxes swapped hands for many thousands of pounds. India won comfortably, so maintaining their unbeaten record against their most intense rivals in World Cup matches.

With England struggling to make qualification, India advanced to favouritism, despite a near upset against Afghanistan. Of the big guns, South Africa disappointed the most and were among the first to be eliminated along with Afghanistan. Whereas pundits had touted a high-scoring tournament, the reality turned out quite different, with slow, dry pitches (despite the early wet weather) countering the bullishness and adventure of the modern batsman.

England needed to beat both India and New Zealand in the qualifying stage, which they duly managed, having recovered their confidence. Australia's defeat to South Africa in the final group stage match meant an England–Australia semi-final at Edgbaston to follow an India–New Zealand semi in Manchester. By now England had their swagger back and their defeat of Australia was predictable and routine, while India's defeat to New Zealand was anything but.

Quite how England won the final will puzzle those who were there: with Trent Boult stepping on the boundary rope, having taken what would have been a match-winning catch; with boundary overthrows erroneously given to help England tie the match, it felt like a home win was preordained. Morgan and England finished the tournament with the trophy; Williamson and New Zealand won hearts everywhere with the grace they showed in defeat.

# LIST OF CONTRIBUTORS

Elgan Alderman

Elizabeth Ammon

Mike Atherton (Chief Cricket Correspondent, *The Times*)

Rick Broadbent

Josh Burrows

Rob Cole (*The Sunday Times*)

Matt Dickinson

Peter Game (*The Sunday Times*)

James Gheerbrant

Ian Hawkey (*The Sunday Times*)

Simon Hughes

Steve James

Owen Slot

Matthew Syed

John Westberby

Simon Wilde (Cricket Correspondent, *The Sunday Times*)

**Photographs by Marc Aspland and Bradley Ormesher**

THE ... T

Friday May 31 2019 | thetimes.co.uk | No 72861

# Hot property

**Where the chic are buying a second home**

## et to confront May over Huawei

security adviser, said that the US was prepared to accept "zero" risk in its federal telecoms network from Huawei and suggested that Washington was trying to convince its intelligence partners to follow suit.

Mr Bolton indicated that he did not believe that Britain had reached a verdict on whether to use the company in its next-generation mobile network,

despite reports that Mrs May favoured allowing it in "non-core" parts of 5G. "I'm not sure this decision has reached the prime ministerial level in final form," he said in London.

The US has banned Huawei from its federal network amid security concerns and has outlawed American companies from selling technology, goods and services to the company. It

tch as England opened their World Cup campaign with a 104-run victory

# e sport

**country**

## Tuition

## make history

England stars get letters from loved ones before World Cup
Football, pages 62-63

---

# England drop the ball

**Errors hand Pakistan win**
**Morgan may face ban**

Elizabeth Ammon

Morgan blamed England's ng for the 14-run defeat n at Trent Bridge that d the first setback of their Cup campaign.
n Roy dropped a simple to dismiss Mohammad , who went on to score 84, while England also gave 7 runs in misfields and ll wides. To add to their , captain Morgan may face two-match ban for a slow ed on page 67

---

## Murray will play at Que

Stuart Fraser Tennis Correspon

Andy Murray will make a c in a fortnight. The grand-slam champion has ente doubles draw at the Rev Championships at the Queen with Feliciano López, of Spa deeming himself ready to retur the hip-resurfacing surgery underwent in late January.

Murray, 32, told The Times two ago that he was "pretty certain would be able to make a comeb doubles and there have bee setbacks in training since to com him otherwise. On Saturday, he p a video on social media of hi serving on grass at Wimbledon.

The decision was taken by Mu yesterday to play with López, accomplished 37-year-old Spa left-hander who won the men's doub
Continued on page 60

## Chinese chase Aubameyang

Gary Jacob

Arsenal could face a battle to keep Pierre-Emerick Aubameyang after Chinese clubs again tried to sign the striker by offering to pay him nearly £300,000 a week.

Arsenal's failure to qualify for the Champions League and their need to cut costs has encouraged the clubs, thought to be Guangzhou Evergrande and Shanghai SIPG, to believe that Aubameyang could be tempted to China at the third time of asking. The Gabon international, who will be 30 in two weeks, was the Premier League's joint top scorer with 22 goals.

He joined Arsenal for £56 million from Borussia Dortmund in January last year, only weeks after a proposed £62 million move to Guangzhou Evergrande collapsed. Six months

ez at long-off with the Pakistan batsman on 14. He went on to score 84 as England were set a testing target of 349 that proved too much for them

rossword 27368

England batt

# THE BUILD-UP

**n London trip**

nation should affect it. A British official based in Washington said: "We will of course listen to what the president has to say about this. That will be an important part of our consideration, but we have to take a national decision."

Speaking in Washington yesterday Mr Trump praised Boris Johnson and Nigel Farage as two "big powers" in

Continued on page 2, col 3

---

THE TIMES

# Sport

**Royal Ascot 2019**
Rob Wright's tips and the best of the first day's action
Racing, 60-63

**England th**
Red card and
U21s after Fod
Match report, page

## The six machine

Captain Morgan breaks world record with 17 maximums in brutal innings of 148 as England beat Afghanistan

**Elizabeth Ammon**

Eoin Morgan led England to the top of the World Cup group table on a record-breaking day in Manchester as the hosts demolished Afghanistan by 150 runs. The England captain hit a career-best 148, including 17 sixes, that beat the record of 16 held by the West Indian Chris Gayle.

Morgan had recovered from the back spasm that he suffered during the win over West Indies in Southampton last week to play the innings of his life. "I would never have thought I could play a knock like that, I'm delighted," the captain, 32, said, adding that it felt "very weird" to have broken the record for number of sixes.

"It's something that I never thought I would do. It's a nice place to be but I'm probably just a target now for the other guys in our changing room to take down. The hundred I scored [off 57 balls] today is considered

our

---

Saturday June 15 20

## Hot streak

Root's second century of World Cup takes England to easy win, but Roy and captain Morgan suffer injury scares
Pages 2-5

Mark Wood, inset, comforts Roy as the opener leaves the field with a hamstring injury before Morgan suffered a back spasm while fielding

---

THE TIMES

# sport

Saturday June

---

to last 16

about me having a sub fielder, but the injury was genuine and I missed the final,' he says.

June 23, 1979 was the only time England's men competed in a World Cup final at home, something Eoin Morgan's team want to emulate this year. Without Willis, England relied on getting 12 overs out of Geoffrey Boycott, Graham Gooch and Wayne Larkins, a manufactured and costly solution, although, as Willis explains, West Indies were overwhelming favourites in any case.

'Viv Richards was just playing a completely different game. We had suffered in 1976, when he got two double hundreds against us. With the bat and in the field, he was on a different planet. Everyone else generally looked to bat normally for 35 overs and double their score in the last 25. There were no special tactics, often no sweepers in the field. We played it like a Test match, only shorter. There was an obsession with keeping wickets in hand, which cost us dearly in the final.'

With a target of 287, England had all ten wickets in hand after Mike Brearley and Boycott had put on 129, but the rate was climbing to the point where it was (at the time) out of control. All ten wickets then fell for 65 runs, amid a blizzard of Joel Garner yorkers. 'I don't remember any desolation in the dressing room afterwards,' Willis says. 'We didn't expect to win; we didn't win and we just dispersed after the game. It didn't really have the feeling of an event at all, given that we went home between matches and only played five games in all.'

# 1983 – England

## *Graeme Fowler*

The sense that the World Cup was a bit of an afterthought had not dissipated by 1983 when Fowler, an impish opener from Lancashire, played in his one and only World Cup. By this stage match fees had risen to £175 ('You made your money on petrol expenses') although the visit to the Palace ahead of the tournament went little better than for Hayes, his Lancashire colleague, eight years earlier.

'We were told to go and buy a suit – any suit – for the tournament and we turned up at Lord's for the photos and everyone else was in uniform and we looked a shambles. An utter shambles. Then we went to the Palace, my only trip, and the first thing the Queen asked me was why were we in different outfits. Embarrassing. The TCCB [Test and County Cricket Board] didn't give a shit about one-day cricket then.

'I don't remember any hype. It was on telly, of course, BBC, so background noise. Always there. No hype, like now. Beefy [Ian Botham] was in his Tim Hudson [Beefy's agent] phase and so he'd turn up in stripy blazers, leather trousers and dyed blond hair. He was like a God then.

'It was amateurish, really. We played our group games in about 11 days and we got into a routine: play, get pissed, travel, repeat. I remember we played New Zealand in Birmingham and both teams were staying on the Hagley Road. There was a nightclub and we all ended up there. Had we been breathalysed the next day going to the ground we'd all have been over the limit. That's how it was. Pandemonium. We looked on it as a bit of fun rather than a serious competition.'

That said, England, under Willis, played seriously and rather well, looking as good as anyone in the group stages, winning five out of their six games against New Zealand, Pakistan and Sri Lanka (all played twice) at grounds that now included Taunton and Royal Tunbridge Wells, among others. Fowler, partnered by none other than Chris Tavaré ('Tav gets a bad rap because of his Test performances, he could destroy bowlers in one-day cricket') was one of England's in-form batsmen and ended the tournament with more runs than anyone bar David Gower and Richards.

Then came semi-final heartbreak again, this time against India. 'The semi was at Old Trafford, my home ground, and the pitches then were shit heaps. I was in good form – I had scored four consecutive fifties – and I felt that I knew the pitch better than everyone, so I felt I had to get the runs. I top-scored but only got 30-odd and it was the biggest disappointment of my career. I felt I had failed. We were very confident going into the game, maybe too confident. The final? I can't remember thinking it was particularly significant at the time when India won, although it was in hindsight.'

# THE SHIFT EAST

## 1987 – India and Pakistan

### Paul Downton

In the history of the World Cup, no event has had more significance than India preventing West Indies winning for the third consecutive time at Lord's on June 25, 1983. Not only did it bring to an end West Indian dominance of the competition, it enthused a country approaching a billion people who hitherto had been tied more strongly to Test cricket. More than that, it encouraged administrators from the subcontinent to explore ways of exporting the World Cup out of England for the first time.

Although Downton, the Kent wicketkeeper, had not been a part of England's triumphant romp under Mike Gatting in Australia in 1986-87 – they beat Pakistan to win the Benson & Hedges Challenge and Australia in the finals of the World Series Cup – the nucleus of the World Cup squad had been and Downton recognised the confidence in the group that resulted as they gathered in Gujranwala, Pakistan, in October 1987, for the first match of a competition that remained limited to eight teams but was now played over 50 rather than 60 overs for the first time.

'The tactics were simple really,' Downton recalls. 'You'd look to bat first. Anything around 235 you felt in the game; anything over 250 meant you were favourites. We played a lot of one-day cricket in England and we weren't intimidated by anyone. Sri Lanka weren't a force, there was no South Africa and we felt we were one of the favourites. The team had played well under Gatt in Australia and we were very confident.' It was a confidence undented by the absence of the stars, Botham and Gower, both of whom were undergoing MOTs.

In the group stage, England beat everyone bar Pakistan, including West Indies twice. In the semi-final in Mumbai, they beat India by 35 runs. 'Goochie played one of the great innings, sweeping us to victory on a turner and with India and Pakistan getting beat, it was the final, us against the Aussies, that no one really wanted.'

England lost by seven runs with Gatting famously getting bowled reverse-sweeping when in a winning position. 'Losing the final was the worst moment of my career,' Downton says. 'I had this overwhelming feeling that it was a one-off opportunity and that we'd got ourselves into a winning position and messed it up. It was a terrible feeling in the dressing room afterwards.

'My wife and I were expecting our first child and the three or four of us who weren't involved in the Pakistan tour to follow flew home. Lamby [Allan Lamb] got us upgraded to first-class on BA.'

# 1992 – Australia and New Zealand

## *Derek Pringle*

With coloured clothing, floodlights, the arrival of South Africa and fielding restrictions in the early overs, the 1992 World Cup was the first to have a modern feel. Not that the players were remunerated in that way, recalls Pringle. 'The ICC was supposed to be paying for extras and I remember we had been told that we'd have to wash our own coloured clothing.

'Goochie [the captain] was unimpressed by the thought of going to the launderette, telling Bob Bennett, our manager: "You wouldn't get Joe Montana doing his own washing before the Super Bowl." So we managed to get the TCCB to cough up.'

Once again, England qualified with ease from the group stage, playing the best one-day cricket that Pringle can recall as an international player. The semi-final is remembered for the rain rules that scuppered South Africa's late charge – their target of 22 runs from 13 balls became 22 from one – but Pringle has little sympathy for their complaint. 'We'd been similarly caught out against them in the group stages and we knew the rules were bonkers.'

Having been a mere squad member in 1987, and having missed out on the final, Pringle was not about to let a niggling side strain prevent him from playing in England's second consecutive World Cup final on a balmy night in Melbourne on March

Strauss] blocked Tillakaratne Dilshan at the start, Trotty [Jonathan Trott] got 80-odd and said the pitch was tricky and 230 would be competitive. We were still of the opinion that 250 wins you 80 per cent of the games. [Sri Lanka] just came out and smashed it. We still had players in our team who were there because they were high-class Test players.'

# 2015 – Australia and New Zealand

## *James Taylor*

That warning should have been enough but England's selectors passed up the opportunity to take the road less travelled, when they appointed Alastair Cook to the one-day captaincy next, doubling down on their error by then sacking him on the eve of the 2015 tournament in favour of Eoin Morgan.

Taylor did not know it when he walked out to bat against Australia in Melbourne on February 14, aged 25 and in his prime, but the end of his career would be only 14 months away. At least, in a tournament of horrible lows, the first match at MCG gave him an individual career highlight when he made a thrilling unbeaten 98 in a losing cause.

'I remember Eoin taking me into the back room on the eve of that first game and my heart sank. I thought he was going to tell me I'd been dropped but it was to tell me I'd be moving down the order to No. 6. I hadn't done very well in the tri-series against Australia in the build-up, so when I came in, they were full of chirp. They brought Mitchell Johnson back on to bowl, we were in trouble and I looked around and there were slips and gullies and a short leg and I thought, "Hang on, I thought this was one-day cricket." It was so satisfying though to hear them gradually go quiet with me. I felt I'd begun to earn their respect. As always, I felt while I was at the crease that we could win the game, although that wasn't to be.'

That eve-of-match change highlighted some of the uncertainty. England brought in Gary Ballance at No. 3 when they could have selected Alex Hales, and Taylor moved down the order into Ravi Bopara's position. Twenty-four hours before the first match, Taylor found himself going to the nets to practise a completely different kind of role from the No. 3 position he had been occupying until then.

Bad defeats followed against New Zealand, Sri Lanka and Bangladesh, which meant England did not qualify for the knockout stages. The defeat by New Zealand in Wellington was particularly hard to take, coming as it did before the floodlights had time to be switched on. 'I've played in a lot of embarrassing defeats as a cricketer but that was the worst. We got booed off when we got bowled out cheaply; booed again by supporters when we had to come out to field for a short period before the lunch break, and booed off again at the end.'

Through it all, though, and despite the hospital pass Morgan received on the eve of the tournament, Taylor recognised real leadership qualities in England's one-day captain. 'He's a natural leader, the way he commands the dressing room and the way he talks to the players, which is a skill in itself. It was too late for him to put his stamp on the team in that tournament, but it's not surprised me to see how he's done since.'

Until his heart condition brought a tragically premature end to his career, Taylor was part of the renaissance immediately after the 2015 competition. 'I've never known a bunch of players enjoy each other's success more,' he says of the present squad. 'When we scored 400 against New Zealand at Edgbaston, I was carrying the drinks. You shouldn't really enjoy carrying the drinks as a professional cricketer but I loved watching that performance. Jason Roy was out first ball but we still powered to 400.'

In that first completed match after the 2015 World Cup, England did power to 408, with hundreds from Joe Root and Jos Buttler, a sign of what was to come. Of that team, seven will form the nucleus of England's challenge now, in a tournament that is a far cry from the inaugural two-week affair in 1975. Taylor is a selector now and if the boos are replaced by jubilation in the final on July 14, he will feel he has played his part still and nobody will be happier. It is, after all, about time.

So, here we are: World Cup, 2019. Ten teams, format similar to 1992, prize money totalling £10 million, England favourites. What can possibly go wrong?

# EOIN MORGAN PROFILE

JOHN WESTERBY

There are two defining features of the patch of ground where Eoin Morgan played much of his earliest cricket that tell us much about the way he has since developed. On a modest housing estate in the small town of Rush, 20 miles up the Fingal coast from Dublin, Morgan first learnt the game with his three brothers and two sisters on a narrow strip of concrete at the end of the terrace on the cul-de-sac where his family lived, with a large expanse of open grass beyond.

The Morgans lived in the second house on the terrace so they were only a few strides away from their makeshift cricket ground and, with two adults and six children in a three-bedroom house, there was every incentive to get out and about. The concrete pathway that became their pitch ran directly up against the pebble-dashed wall of their next-door neighbours' garage, meaning there was one drawback: the batsman could score on only one side of the wicket.

As a result, Morgan's scoring options, as a left-hander, were limited to the leg side. Speak to those who have monitored his progress since and his punchy, idiosyncratic strokeplay has always been marked by an ability to lift the ball off his stumps, high and long into the leg side, his bottom hand dominant. The England captain, 32, whose side begin their World Cup campaign against South Africa tomorrow, was doing much the same in his explosive innings of 76 against Pakistan in Leeds earlier this month, dislodging tiles from Headingley's pavilion roof. 'It probably wouldn't be the way you'd teach a lad to play,' Matt Sheridan, his junior coach at Rush Cricket Club, says. 'But from an early age Eoin hit the ball so cleanly through the leg side.'

Follow the path of one of those blows from the concrete strip and you come across the other striking feature of the Morgans' field of dreams: a vast, pillared, stone portico. In these otherwise humble surroundings, such a grandiose structure looks utterly out of place, as though it has landed from outer space.

The portico is all that is left of Kenure House, a stately home that fell into disrepair and was demolished in 1978, one of a number of grand houses scattered around the Fingal district.

It was the owners of these houses, with their English links, who introduced cricket to the area and, unlike other landowners, encouraged their staff to take part. 'It wasn't seen as a foreign imposition,' Eoin Sheehan, the secretary of Rush CC, says. 'Among the workers, cricket never seemed to have the social stigma of being a foreign sport that it would have had elsewhere.'

Even at the height of anti-British feeling, around the time of the War of Independence, from 1919 to 1921, cricket endured in the Fingal area, despite the Gaelic Athletic Association (GAA) ban on members playing foreign sports. 'I heard

THE TIMES
# CRICKET WORLD CUP 2019

WEDNESDAY MAY 29 2019

# England expects

**Morgan's men aim for historic first title**

In association with
sky sports cricket

about a grand-uncle of mine, who was very involved in the republican side of things during the war, yet he kept playing cricket,' Sheridan says. 'He'd look down the barrel of a gun at a British soldier, but he still wanted to play cricket.'

Morgan grew up in a family steeped in this culture, defined by a tough, uncompromising style of play on the pitch and a caring, family-based feel around the boundary edge.

'There's no doubt about it, Eoin and his family definitely show the traits of that Fingal culture,' Ed Joyce, the former Ireland and England batsman, who hails from south of Dublin, says. 'There's a stubbornness, a single-mindedness, they're comfortable in their own skin.'

The walk from that terraced house on the St Catherine's Estate to Rush Cricket Club, where Morgan spent much of his childhood, takes about 15 minutes. This was a journey with which Morgan became so familiar that, at the age of three, knowing that his father, Jody, was out playing cricket, he set off from home on his own and made it all the way to the cricket club, only to be told when he arrived there that his father was playing an away game. Friends at the club transported Morgan back to his worried mother.

On most occasions, he would arrive at the Skerries Road ground accompanied by his father and siblings. Dragging his bat, Morgan would head for the nets tucked neatly away behind the tea room, housed in the gate lodge of the former Kenure House estate.

The playing area at Rush is compact and bordered on three sides by walls, sitting adjacent to the St Maur's housing estate. As in Morgan's day, the junior section remains strong, for boys and girls, and All-Ireland titles have been won at under-11, under-13 and under-15 levels in recent years, testament to the club's place in the heart of the community and its ability to attract gifted juniors from the local estates.

On a Saturday, after a senior game, the outfield will be filled by children playing until dusk, often with parents and grandparents. 'The talent comes to us from over the wall,' Eddie Scanlan, the club president, says. 'But we keep working at it, going into the schools, because we're a minority sport, and in every small town and village in Ireland, the GAA are the main sports for getting young talent.'

Morgan played Gaelic football and hurling until he was 12, but has played down the impact of hurling on his batting, particularly the potent reverse-sweeps that he has developed. From an early stage, having played for Ireland's under-13 team from the age of 11, his focus was firmly on cricket and his reputation was growing. 'He would be the star batsman in every game he played,' Sheridan says. 'In pairs cricket, he'd often bat for four overs with Gwen, his younger sister. He'd hog the strike and jog a single last ball. Most games, I don't think Gwen got to face a single ball.'

The difficulty for Rush, having reared so many promising cricketers, can sometimes come in hanging on to them, with the lure of Dublin so close at hand. This was the case, eventually, with Morgan's family after Jody transferred jobs, from local landscape gardening work to become a groundsman at Trinity College in the centre of Dublin. The family relocated into town and Morgan moved to play at Malahide Cricket Club. It was around this time, too, that he was offered a scholarship to Catholic University School (CUS), a private school just off St Stephen's Green.

'It wasn't something that had been done before,' Stephen Tonge, head of sport at CUS, says. 'But it was clear that Eoin was going to be something special. Since then, we've had several lads from Rush at the school on scholarships.'

Just how special the new batsman could become was clear in an early game, when he struck a double-century for the school in a 20-over match. 'I just remember these balls disappearing constantly over the leg-side boundary,' Tonge says. 'It was extraordinary to watch.'

The school would later provide opportunities for Morgan to broaden his horizons, with exchange visits to a school in Durban, South Africa, and at Dulwich College in south London. By that time, though, Morgan, in conjunction with his father, had already taken a decision that would have far-reaching consequences for Irish and English cricket. 'He would only have been 13, we were standing in a classroom at school,' Tonge says. 'I asked Eoin, "Where do you want to take your cricket?" He answered straight away, "I want to play Test cricket for England."'

It was in making this choice – with such conviction, at such a young age – that Morgan demonstrated the steely ambition that remains his hallmark. Even before he made his debut for Ireland's senior team, aged 16, he had informed Adrian Birrell, the national coach, that he saw his long-term future in England.

There was no first-class cricket in Ireland at the time, but such a bold statement of intent was inevitably going to attract scorn from certain quarters. 'Back then, there was an inferiority complex in Irish cricket about England, so it was unusual for someone to be so upfront about his ambitions at such a young age,' Joyce says. 'There certainly wasn't an inferiority complex where Eoin was concerned.'

By the time he was 17, Morgan was playing regularly in the second team for Middlesex, where Joyce was a member of the first team. He would go on to appear in 23 one-day internationals for Ireland, playing in the 2007 World Cup and helping them to qualify for the 2011 tournament. But his county commitments would soon take priority and his time with Ireland ended on an unsavoury note when Phil Simmons, the coach, reduced him to carrying the drinks and lambasted him in the dressing room over his eagerness to return to Middlesex after the World Cup qualifiers.

'It was a little uneasy for people around me,' he has said of his far-sighted decision. 'At the time, Irish cricket was completely amateur, a million miles away from turning professional. You may get called cocky or overconfident. But there's no harm in shooting for the lights.'

Whatever the stage of his career, Morgan has never been afraid of taking the unconventional route. It may be said that he arrived in county cricket at an opportune time, ready to surf the swelling wave of Twenty20. He was in the vanguard of the movement, though, his powerful forearms enabling him to transform reverse-sweeps into full-blooded strokes.

He developed the priceless knack, rare at the time, of hitting yorkers hard and straight from deep in the crease and, as ever, retained the ability to hit destructively through the leg side. Once he was established in the Middlesex first team, the sheer variety of his strokeplay quickly began to attract wider attention. 'I remember one 50-over game at Lord's when we were playing against Somerset [in 2007] and Andy Caddick was bowling fairly sharp,' Joyce says.

'There was a short boundary to the Mound Stand and Moggie kept picking up length balls off middle stump over mid-wicket and into the stands. It was quite something to see this little ginger Irish guy taking on a huge former England bowler, with so much composure. I was sitting next to Andrew Strauss [their Middlesex team-mate] on the balcony and we both knew we were watching a pretty unusual talent coming through.'

Fast-forward eight years and Strauss would be present again at another seminal moment in Morgan's career, having been appointed director of England cricket in the wake of the team's disastrous performance at the 2015 World Cup. Morgan had been captain for that tournament and Strauss had to decide how much responsibility the captain bore. Was a clean slate required?

But Morgan had assumed the captaincy from Alastair Cook late in the piece and he did not carry full responsibility for England's woefully outdated approach. Strauss, with a determination to shift English cricket's priorities farther towards the white-ball games, with the home World Cup of 2019 in mind, was certain that Morgan was the right man to implement the required changes.

That shift in priorities was one that Morgan had already made himself, when the Test career he had long desired proved frustratingly short-lived and ended three years earlier. Once again, as he had done with his desire to move away from Ireland, as he had done batting on that concrete strip back in Rush, Morgan had seen one route blocked off and resolved decisively to make the most of another. He had dedicated himself instead to becoming one of the world's best limited-overs batsmen and, in a period when it was largely frowned upon in English cricket, he had unapologetically taken the chance to play in the Indian Premier League, where many of the most innovative white-ball strategies were being honed.

Now, with the opportunity to stamp his own mark on the team, he set about instilling a new fearlessness in England's 50-over team, pushing them ahead of the curve instead of playing catch-up. The results, incredibly, were instantaneous. A thrilling series at home to New Zealand saw England pass 400 for the first time, at Edgbaston, and then chase a target of 350 at Trent Bridge with six overs to spare.

Paul Farbrace, the interim head coach at the time, recalls a moment from that Trent Bridge run chase that encapsulated Morgan's impact on the side, leading by example. 'We were well ahead in the run chase and Rooty [Joe Root] had hit seven from the first three balls of the over, then Morgs came on strike,' Farbrace says. 'We were having a chat on the balcony about whether, as we were so far ahead, we should take it steadier and Jos Buttler said, "There's our seven for the over, that will do us for now." To the next ball, Morgs came down the pitch and flat-batted [Matt Henry] over extra cover for six. That gave us the answer to our question.'

The tone had been set for England's four-year project and they arrive at the World Cup as the No.1 side in the world. This is Morgan's team and there is an awe in the way that team-mates speak of his firm but fair leadership. 'Ask anyone who's played under him for England in the last few years,' Joyce says. 'They'll tell you there's no doubting who's the boss.'

As it happened, it was back in Fingal a few weeks ago that Morgan was required to demonstrate the quality of his leadership one final time before the World Cup. England were playing Ireland at Malahide, on the ground where Morgan had played his later club cricket, and they had arrived with the storm over Alex Hales' demotion for failing a drugs test looming over them.

In a short but impassioned speech, Morgan told of how Hales had shown 'complete disregard' for the team's values and, as a result, had lost the trust of his team-mates. From a man who has built a career on containing his emotions, he was now letting the old Fingal fire come pouring through.

Morgan will be shooting for the lights again over the next six weeks and, once his mind is set on something, woe betide anyone that gets in his way.

# TOURNAMENT PREVIEW

MIKE ATHERTON,
CHIEF CRICKET CORRESPONDENT

England is not the rightful home of the World Cup – the competition has long since spread its geographical wings after its humble beginnings here in 1975 – but it remains the best place for the pinnacle of one-day cricket to be held. Quite apart from the glory of an English summer, with its warm, long evenings, there are practical and logistical reasons why an English World Cup, the fifth to be held in this country, will be well received by players and fans alike.

Although more recent immigrants to England from Eastern Europe will have little impact on, or association with, cricket, the postwar waves of immigration from, first, the Caribbean and then South Asia will ensure that every team have widespread support, which is often not the case elsewhere. Second and third-generation British Asians often stay true to their parents' or grandparents' cricketing loyalties, and the large numbers of Australians and South Africans in London will ensure that the event has a very global feel. England will enjoy some home advantages, but their supporters may well be outnumbered from time to time.

At the time of writing, grounds are 94 per cent sold out, a higher figure than any in World Cup history, although clearly those figures bear little comparison with previous events, given the size of the grounds in India and Australia especially. Still it was the World Cup of 1999 here that belatedly made the authorities realise the strength of feeling for the game among the South Asian population. The recent demand for tickets for the India v Pakistan clash (almost 600,000 inquiries for a ground, Old Trafford, that holds fewer than 30,000) is further indication of that.

For that reason, the ECB looked at staging that match and the game between England and Australia at the Olympic stadium, until logistical difficulties and cost stymied its ambitions. So, the matches will be played at (mainly) historic cricket grounds, which will please the players who, too often, are asked to compete in soulless and sometimes empty stadiums in places such as the UAE and, more recently, the Caribbean.

Players will also enjoy the logistics of the seven-week tournament. The teams stay in relative proximity to each other; there is no need for air travel and coach journeys often help engender a strong sense of team spirit. Trips to England whet the appetite for touring teams like few other.

This will be the first World Cup here since 1999 and the first for a generation that England start as a fancied runner, given that Eoin Morgan's team have enjoyed a resurgence since an embarrassingly poor competition in Australia and New Zealand four years ago. Morgan, this inscrutable Irishman with a gambler's instinct hidden behind a veneer of cool calculation, has driven the project after being handed a hospital pass on the eve of the previous tournament when he replaced the deposed Alastair Cook as captain, and he intends to make amends for what he took as a personal humiliation down under.

Since then England have produced the best one-day cricket of any country, climbing to the top of the rankings and remaining unbeaten for more than two years in bilateral series. The blips in this period have been few and far between: there was a one-off defeat by Scotland last summer and defeat in the Champions Trophy, again in England, two years ago, when they lost to Pakistan in the semi-final, their nerve deserting them on a dry, holding surface. Unfancied Pakistan proved once again when beating India in the subsequent final that while form is important in the run-up to knockout competitions, it is not everything, an uncertainty that further increases the tantalising possibilities for this tournament.

The structure of this year's competition unashamedly apes the first of the 'modern' World Cups in Australia and New Zealand in 1992. One group, with all the teams playing one another and the top four playing off in semi-finals; 45 games in a little over five weeks before the knockout stages. It should ensure, if nothing else, that the best teams make the semi-finals, and from there it's anyone's game. On form it is hard to look past four of England, India, Australia, South Africa and New Zealand for those semi-final places.

There are bound to be surprises though. Afghanistan make another World Cup appearance and play with verve and courage and will turn someone over somewhere down the line. Bangladesh dumped England from the event in 2015 and have proved repeatedly that teams take them lightly at their peril. West Indies, having sneaked into the tournament by the skin of their teeth in qualifying, include some of their big guns, such as Chris Gayle, for whom this will be an international swansong. Pakistan, stung by ten consecutive defeats in ODI cricket have recalled the experienced seamers Mohammad Amir and Wahab Riaz and can never be discounted. Only Sri Lanka arrive with more questions than answers, and a need to rediscover competency out of chaos.

For players, the World Cup is still the greatest of stages, a platform to announce and express themselves before a global audience of hundreds of millions. The game's legendary players have often produced their best on this stage: think of Clive Lloyd's scintillating hundred in the 1975 final (the earliest cricketing memory for me); Viv Richards, brilliant with bat and in the field, in 1979; Wasim Akram responding to Imran Khan's urgings to 'fight like cornered tigers' in 1992, and Adam Gilchrist's swashbuckling hundred in Barbados in 2007. I could go on.

But as well as these legendary players, the World Cup is often a place where a younger player can announce himself and transform his life. Who will it be this year? Jofra Archer, late to England but filled with Caribbean flair? Shimron Hetmyer, the Guyanese firecracker? Rashid Khan, who has encapsulated Afghanistan's remarkable rise? Will Jasprit Bumrah and Kagiso Rabada rise to the occasion and, on behalf of a beleaguered bowling fraternity, show that pace, skill, accuracy and nerve can blossom even in these run-filled days? And who will take the game to the next level, with a revolutionary shot, a new delivery? Who will provide the tournament's iconic image as Jonty Rhodes did in 1992 with his flying run-out?

The possibilities are tantalising and endless. If the weather is kind, then a festival of top-class cricket is ensured. There will be a global audience but English cricket fans should relish each moment of it because it will be at least another two decades before it comes back to the cradle of the game again.

# THE SQUADS

## ENGLAND

| | | |
|---|---|---|
| Eoin Morgan (capt) | Tom Curran | Ben Stokes |
| Moeen Ali | Liam Dawson | James Vince |
| Jofra Archer | Liam Plunkett | Chris Woakes |
| Jonny Bairstow (wk) | Adil Rashid | Mark Wood |
| Joss Buttler (wk) | Joe Root | |

## AFGHANISTAN

| | | |
|---|---|---|
| Gulbadin Naib (capt) | Hazratullah Zazai | Rahmat Shah |
| Aftab Alam★ | Ikram Alikhil (wk) | Rashid Khan |
| Asghar Afghan | Mohammad Shahzad (wk)★ | Samiullah Shenwari |
| Dawlat Zadran | Mujeeb Ur Rahman | Sayed Shirzad |
| Hamid Hassan | Naijbullah Zadran | |
| Hashmatullah Shahidi | Noor Ali Zadran | |

★ *Ikram Alikhil replaced Mohammad Shahzad and Sayed Shirzad replaced Aftbab Alam*

## AUSTRALIA

| | | |
|---|---|---|
| Aaron Finch (capt) | Nathan Lyon | Marcus Stonis |
| Jason Behrendorff | Shaun Marsh★ | Usman Khawaja |
| Alex Carey (wk) | Glenn Maxwell | David Warner |
| Nathan Coulter-Nile | Kane Richardson | Adam Zampa |
| Pat Cummins | Steve Smith | |
| Peter Hanscomb | Mitchell Starc | |

★ *Peter Hanscomb replaced Shaun Marsh*

## BANGLADESH

| | | |
|---|---|---|
| Mashrafe Mortaza (capt) | Mithun Ali | Rubel Hossain |
| Abu Jayed | Mohammad Saifuddin | Sabbir Rahman |
| Liton Das (wk) | Mosaddek Hossain | Shakib Al Hasan |
| Mahmudullah | Mushfiqur Rahim | Soumya Sarkar |
| Mehidy Hasan | Mustafizur Rahman | Tamim Iqbal |

# INDIA

| | | |
|---|---|---|
| Virat Kholi (capt) | Ravi Jadeja | KL Rahul |
| Bhuvneshwar Kumar | Kedar Jadhav | Vijay Shankar |
| Jasprit Bumrah | Dishesh Karthik (wk) | Rohit Sharma |
| Yuvendran Chahal | Mohammed Shami | Kuldeep Yadhav |
| Shikhar Dhawan★ | Hardik Pandya | |
| MS Dhoni (wk) | Rishabh Pant | |

★ *Rishabh Pant replaced Shikhar Dhawan*

# NEW ZEALAND

| | | |
|---|---|---|
| Kane Williamson (capt) | Martin Guptill | Henry Nicholls |
| Tom Blundell (wk) | Matt Henry | Mitchell Santner |
| Trent Boult | Tom Latham (wk) | Ish Sodhi |
| Colin De Grandhomme | Colin Munro | Tim Southee |
| Lockie Ferguson | Jimmy Neesham | Ross Taylor |

# PAKISTAN

| | | |
|---|---|---|
| Sarfaraz Ahmed (capt/wk) | Hasan Ali | Mohammad Hasnain |
| Asif Ali | Imad Wasim | Shabad Khan |
| Babar Azam | Imam-ul-Haq | Shaheen Afridi |
| Fakhar Zaman | Mohammad Amir | Shoaib Malik |
| Haris Sohail | Mohammad Hafeez | Wahab Riaz |

# SOUTH AFRICA

| | | |
|---|---|---|
| Faf du Plessis (capt) | Aiden Markram | Kagiso Rabada |
| Hashim Amla | David Miller | Tabraiz Shamsi |
| Quinton de Kock (wk) | Chris Morris | Dale Steyn★ |
| JP Duminy | Lungi Ngidi | Rassie van der Dussen |
| Beuran Hendricks | Andile Phehlukwayo | |
| Imran Tahir | Dwaine Pretorius | |

★ *Beuran Hendricks replaced Dale Steyn*

# SRI LANKA

Dimuth Karunaratne (capt)

Dhananjaya de Silva

Avishka Fernando

Suranga Lakmal

Lasith Malinga

Angelo Mathews

Kusal Mendis (wk)

Jevan Mendis

Kusal Perera (wk)

Thisara Perera

Nuwan Pradeep★

Milinda Siriwardene

Lahiru Thirimanne

Isuru Udana

Jeffrey Vandersay

★ *Nuwan Pradeep was withdrawn*

# WEST INDIES

Jason Holder (capt)

Fabian Allen

Carlos Brathwaite

Darren Bravo

Sheldon Cottrell

Shannon Gabriel

Chris Gayle

Shimron Hetmyer

Shai Hope (wk)

Evin Lewis

Ashley Nurse

Nicholas Pooran

Kemar Roach

Andre Russell

Oshane Thomas

# UMPIRES

Aleem Dar (Pakistan)

Kumar Dharmasena (Sri Lanka)

Marais Erasmus (South Africa)

Chris Gaffaney (New Zealand)

Michael Gough (England)

Ian Gould (England)

Richard Illingworth (England)

Richard Kettleborough (England)

Nigel Llong (England)

Bruce Oxenford (Australia)

Ruchira Palliyaguruge (Sri Lanka)

Sundaram Ravi (India)

Paul Reiffel (Australia)

Rod Tucker (Australia)

Joel Wilson (West Indies)

Paul Wilson (Australia)

# MATCH REFEREES

David Boon (Australia)

Chris Broad (England)

Jeff Crowe (New Zealand)

Ranjan Madugalle (Sri Lanka)

Andy Pycroft (Zimbabwe)

Richie Richardson (West Indies)

# THE GROUNDS

## COUNTY GROUND, BRISTOL

**Capacity:** 11,000
**Ends:** Pavilion End and Ashley Down Road End
**2019 World Cup:** Three matches
**Previous World Cups:** 1983 (one match), 1999 (two matches)

## COUNTY GROUND, TAUNTON

**Capacity:** 8,000
**Ends:** Somerset Pavilion End and River Tone End
**2019 World Cup:** Three matches
**Previous World Cups:** 1983 (one match), 1999 (two matches)

## EDGBASTON

**Capacity:** 24,500
**Ends:** Pavilion End and Birmingham End
**2019 World Cup:** Five matches, including semi-final
**Previous World Cups:** 1975 (three matches), 1979 (two matches),
1983 (three matches), 1999 (three matches, including semi-final)

## HEADINGLEY

**Capacity:** 18,350
**Ends:** Kirkstall Lane End and Football Stand End
**2019 World Cup:** Four matches
**Previous World Cups:** 1975 (four matches, including semi-final),
1979 (three matches), 1983 (three matches), 1999 (three matches)

# LORD'S

**Capacity:** 28,500
**Ends:** Pavilion End and Nursery End
**2019 World Cup:** Five matches, including final
**Previous World Cups:** 1975 (two matches, including final),
1979 (two matches, including final), 1983 (three matches, including final),
1999 (three matches, including final)

# OLD TRAFFORD

**Capacity:** 23,000
**Ends:** Brian Statham End and James Anderson End
**2019 World Cup:** Six matches, including semi-final
**Previous World Cups:** 1975 (two matches), 1979 (three matches,
including semi-final), 1983 (three matches, including semi-final),
1999 (three matches, including semi-final)

# THE OVAL

**Capacity:** 25,000
**Ends:** Pavilion End and Vauxhall End
**2019 World Cup:** Five matches
**Previous World Cups:** 1975 (three matches, including semi-final),
1979 (three matches, including semi-final),
1983 (three matches, including semi-final), 1999 (three matches)

# SOPHIA GARDENS, CARDIFF

**Capacity:** 15,200
**Ends:** Cathedral Road End and River Taff End
**2019 World Cup:** Four matches
**Previous World Cups:** 1999 (one match)

# THE RIVERSIDE, CHESTER-LE-STREET

**Capacity:** 14,000
**Ends:** Lumley End and Finchale End
**2019 World Cup:** Three matches
**Previous World Cups:** 1999 (two matches)

# ROSE BOWL, SOUTHAMPTON

**Capacity:** 17,000
**Ends:** Pavilion End and Hotel End
**2019 World Cup:** Five matches
**No previous World Cup matches**

# TRENT BRIDGE

**Capacity:** 17,000
**Ends:** Pavilion End and Radcliffe Road End
**2019 World Cup:** Five matches
**Previous World Cups:** 1975 (two matches), 1979 (three matches),
1983 (three matches), 1999 (three matches)

Friday May 31 2019 | thetimes.co.uk | No 72861

# Hot property

### Where the chic are buying a second home

## ...et to confront May over Huawei

...ington

...dent
...ed to
...pany
...k, a
...al

security adviser, said that the US was prepared to accept "zero" risk in its federal telecoms network from Huawei and suggested that Washington was trying to convince its intelligence partners to follow suit.

Mr Bolton indicated that he did not believe that Britain had reached a verdict on whether to use the company in its next-generation mobile network,

despite reports that Mrs May favoured allowing it in "non-core" parts of 5G.
"I'm not sure this decision has reached the prime ministerial level in final form," he said in London.

The US has banned Huawei from its federal network amid security concerns and has outlawed American companies from selling technology, goods and services to the company. It

has has al...
ban the c...
works.

A Down...
the govern...
Trump to r...
was 'genui...
published as...
the source s...
minister did...

...tch as England opened their World Cup campaign with a 104-run victory over

## ...e T...    sport

...country

...ment electi...
...support dro...
...r of voters...
...general ele...
...poll found...
...n tied on P...
...n 8 per cent...
...r two chan...
...op places...
...according...

...es that...
...ween tho...

...Tuition

...ans to eu...
...lion feel...
...e: 4 2019

...ake history

England stars get letters from loved ones before World Cup
Football, pages 62-63

# England drop the ball

### Errors hand Pakistan win
### Morgan may face ban

Elizabeth Ammon

...in Morgan blamed England's ...lding for the 14-run defeat by ...kistan at Trent Bridge that ...rked the first setback of their ...rld Cup campaign.
...ason Roy dropped a simple ...nce to dismiss Mohammad ...feez, who went on to score 84, ...14, while England also gave ...y 17 runs in misfields and ...led 11 wides. To add to their ...cerns, captain Morgan may ...e a two-match ban for a slow ...tinued on page 67

## Murray will
## play at Que

Stuart Fraser Tennis Correspon...

Andy Murray will make a c...
in a fortnight. The thre...
grand-slam champion has ente...
doubles draw at the Fev...
Championships at the Queen...
with Feliciano López, of Spai...
deeming himself ready to retur...
the hip-resurfacing surgery t...
underwent in late January.
Murray, 32, told The Times two...
ago that he was "pretty certai...
would be able to make a comeb...
doubles and there have bee...
setbacks in training since to com...
him otherwise. On Saturday, he po...
a video on social media of hi...
serving on grass at Wimbledon.
The decision was taken by Mu...
yesterday to play with López,...
accomplished 37-year-old Spa...
left-hander who won the men's doub...
Continued on page 60

## Chinese chase
## Aubameyang

Gary Jacob

Arsenal could face a battle to keep Pierre-Emerick Aubameyang after Chinese clubs again tried to sign the striker by offering to pay him nearly £300,000 a week.
Arsenal's failure to qualify for the Champions League and their need to cut costs has encouraged the clubs, thought to be Guangzhou Evergrande and Shanghai SIPG, to believe that Aubameyang could be tempted to China at the third time of asking. The Gabon international, who will be 30 in two weeks, was the Premier League's joint top scorer with 22 goals.
He joined Arsenal for £56 million from Borussia Dortmund in January last year, only weeks after a proposed £62 million move to Guangzhou Evergrande collapsed. Six months
Continued on page 64

# England bat

...afeez at long-off with the Pakistan batsman on 14. He went on to score 84 as England were set a testing target of 349 that proved too much for them

...s Crossword 27,368

# THE GROUP GAMES

Saturday June 15 20

THE TIMES

## Sport

**Royal Ascot 2019**
Rob Wright's tips and the
best of the first day's action
Racing, 60-63

**England th**
Red card and
U21s after Fode
Match report, page

# The six machine

Captain Morgan breaks world record
with 17 maximums in brutal innings
of 148 as England beat Afghanistan

**Elizabeth Ammon**

Eoin Morgan led England to the
top of the World Cup group table
on a record-breaking day in
Manchester as the hosts
demolished Afghanistan by 150
runs. The England captain hit a
career-best 148, including 17 sixes,
that beat the record of 16 held by
the West Indian Chris Gayle.
Morgan had recovered from the
back spasm that he suffered
during the win over West Indies in
Southampton last week to play the
innings of his life. "I would never
have thought I could play a knock
like that, I'm delighted," the
captain, 32, said, adding that it felt
"very weird" to have broken the
record for number of sixes.
"It's something that I never
thought I would do. It's a nice
place to be but I'm probably just a
target now for the other guys in
our changing room to take down.
The hundred I scored [off 57 balls]
today is considered

Saturday June

# Hot streak

Root's second century of World Cup
takes England to easy win, but Roy and
captain Morgan suffer injury scares
Pages 2-5

Max Wood, inset, comforts Roy as
the opener leaves the field with a
hamstring injury before Morgan
suffered a back spasm while fielding

THE TIMES

## Sport

to last 16

# ENGLAND v SOUTH AFRICA

*Thursday, May 30*

*The Oval*

**England 311-8** (50 overs) (Roy 54, Root 51, Morgan 57, Stokes 89; Ngidi 3-66)
**South Africa 207 all out** (39.5 overs) (De Kock 68, Van der Dussen 50; Archer 3-27)
*England (2pts) won by 104 runs*
**Toss** *South Africa*

MIKE ATHERTON,
CHIEF CRICKET CORRESPONDENT

There needed to be a very good reason for England to change their qualification regulations in the months before the World Cup, as well as for them to change a settled squad on the eve of the tournament, and in Jofra Archer there was one very obvious reason to do both. Few England players have enjoyed such a hyped build-up in recent years, and few have made such an immediate impression on their first World Cup appearance. The hype was justified.

After a batting performance that was workmanlike rather than, as has become the expectation, scintillating, Archer's explosive new-ball burst went a long way towards settling the opening match in England's favour. More than that, he put top-order batsmen everywhere on notice that, while modern one-day cricket may be a batsman' game, it remains a challenging one when he has a new ball in his hand. The sight of a genuinely fast bowler is always an electrifying one, and the capacity crowd at the Oval were roused by what they saw.

Opening matches in big tournaments can be nervy, fraught occasions and, while England's batting never quite hit the heights, it is a measure of how far they have come in the past four years that a score of more than 300 felt a little underwhelming. Still, having been asked to make the fourth-highest chase in World Cup history to win, South Africa rarely threatened.

On a potentially tricky day, the scale of the victory by 104 runs was more than Eoin Morgan could have hoped for and his team can stride on from here confidently, although the refrain of 'It's Coming Home' that sent England from the field moments after the final wicket may have been a little premature. Receiving his 200th England ODI cap from Andrew Strauss before play and passing 7,000 ODI runs during a fluent half-century, Morgan enjoyed a good day and can look forward to a relaxed round of golf at The Grove hotel today.

With Archer completing the side, all things are possible. Not only did his opening spell bring the key wickets of Aiden Markram, caught at slip, and Faf du Plessis, hooking to fine leg, it sent Hashim Amla from the field, head spinning after being hit on the helmet by a rapid bouncer. While Amla may not be quite the batsman that he was, that this great player was so late in trying to hook a bouncer is a measure of the pace that Archer generates from apparently little effort. For any batsman, that is disconcerting.

# THE  TIMES

Friday May 31 2019 | thetimes.co.uk | No 72861

£1.80 Only £1.10 to subscribers

## Hot property
### Where the chic are buying a second home

**Caitlin Moran's Celebrity Watch**
**I've got a crush on the royals** Times2

# Trump set to confront May over Huawei risks on London trip

Lucy Fisher Defence Correspondent
David Charter, Boer Deng Washington
Oliver Wright

Donald Trump will confront Theresa May over the security risk posed to Britain by the Chinese company Huawei during his visit next week, a senior aide to the president has said.

John Bolton, the American national security adviser, said that the US was prepared to accept "zero" risk in its federal telecoms network from Huawei and suggested that Washington was trying to convince its intelligence partners to follow suit.

Mr Bolton indicated that he did not believe that Britain had reached a verdict on whether to use the company in its next-generation mobile network,

despite reports that Mrs May favoured allowing it in "non-core" parts of 5G. "I'm not sure this decision has reached the prime ministerial level in final form," he said in London.

The US has banned Huawei from its federal network amid security concerns and has outlawed American companies from selling technology, goods and services to the company. It

has also put pressure on its allies to ban the company from their 5G networks.

A Downing Street source said that the government fully expected Mr Trump to raise the issue. The review was "genuinely ongoing" and would be published as soon as it was completed, the source said, adding that the prime minister did not believe that her resig-

nation should affect it. A British official based in Washington said: "We will of course listen to what the president has to say about this. That will be an important part of our consideration, but we have to take a national decision."

Speaking in Washington yesterday Mr Trump praised Boris Johnson and Nigel Farage as two "big powers" in Continued on page 2, col 3

Rising to the occasion **Ben Stokes** took a spectacular catch as England opened their World Cup campaign with a 104-run victory over South Africa at the Oval yesterday. He had earlier scored 89. **Pages 69-72**

# Poll surge puts Lib Dems on top

## Pro-Remain party most popular in country

Oliver Wright Policy Editor
Henry Zeffman Political Correspondent

The Liberal Democrats have surged into first place ahead of the Conservatives, Labour and the Brexit Party, a poll has revealed.

The pro-Remain party topped the Times/YouGov survey poll with 24 per cent, the first time the party has been in the lead since 2010 under Sir Nick Clegg's leadership.

The Brexit Party, which came first in

the European parliament elections on 31.6 per cent, saw its support drop back. Twenty-two per cent of voters would support the party if a general election were held now, the poll found. The Tories and Labour were tied on 19 per cent, with the Greens on 8 per cent.

It is unprecedented for two challenger parties to take the top places in a voting intention poll, according to Anthony Wells of YouGov.

The findings add to signs that the electorate is fracturing between those

who support a no-deal Brexit and those who want to reverse the 2016 referendum. The poll found nearly 70 per cent of voters believed Brexit was the most important issue facing the country.

Yesterday Philip Hammond, the chancellor, became the first cabinet minister to suggest that the Brexit impasse could only be resolved by a second referendum. "If we do get to the point where parliament does admit that it cannot resolve the situation, then it will have to be remitted back to the

people," he told the Today programme on BBC Radio 4. "I am not sure that a general election can resolve the question for the simple reason that both the main political parties are divided on the issues."

Mr Hammond also warned that he could bring down a government whose leader was determined to pursue a no-deal Brexit. "I am very clear that the national interest trumps the party interest," he told Sky News.

Jeremy Corbyn, the Labour leader,

held talks yesterday with Leo Varadkar, the Irish prime minister, in Dublin. Labour sources said that Mr Varadkar had pushed Mr Corbyn for details of how a no-deal Brexit could be stopped by parliament in the face of a new Conservative prime minister determined to walk away from an existing agreement.

A spokesman for Mr Varadkar said that the pair shared their "serious concerns" about a no-deal scenario and its "inherent dangers, including the Continued on page 6, col 1

## IN THE NEWS

**GP surgery closures**
More than half a million patients were forced to change their GP surgery last year as closures hit a record high. Smaller practices were worst affected. **Page 4**

**Rollercoaster fall**
A boy aged 6 was airlifted to hospital after allegedly falling up to 30ft from a rollercoaster. A witness said that the boy's mother was "screaming hysterically." **Page 5**

**Tuition fee reform**
Plans to overhaul university tuition fees have been criticised by economists who claim that the reforms would most benefit the richest graduates. **Page 12**

**Danube disaster**
Rescuers said there was little hope of finding survivors from a tourist boat after it collided with a cruise ship on the Danube. Seven people were confirmed dead. **Page 30**

**Uber loses £1 billion**
Uber, the world's largest taxi-hailing company, has posted a loss of $1 billion in the first results since its disappointing flotation on the stock market this month. **Page 35**

**Sarri: I want to stay**
Maurizio Sarri, the Chelsea head coach, will tell the club that he wants to remain at Stamford Bridge next season if they are prepared to give him their full backing. **Page 72**

Amla came back eventually at No. 8 and did so, wouldn't you know it, in the middle of Archer's second spell, which accounted for Rassie van der Dussen, caught as Du Plessis had been, mishooking a bouncer. Demonstrating that he has a fast bowler's mentality at heart, Archer gave Amla a short ball as a greeting. It was an uncomfortable day all round for a man who, at 36, offers little in the field these days, and, with David Miller warming the bench, South Africa have some tricky selection decisions ahead.

If Archer's efforts formed the centre-piece of a near-perfect performance in the field (marred only by a drop from Jos Buttler standing up to Moeen Ali), the high point was an astonishing catch in the deep by Ben Stokes in the 35th over, as South Africa's slide acceler-ated. Slightly out of position as Andile Phehlukwayo swung Adil Rashid into the leg side, Stokes backpedalled rapidly, arched himself backwards, stretched out his right hand and plucked the ball from the air in front of a disbelieving crowd. Even Stokes shook his head and looked as though he could scarcely work out how he had done it – and the tournament has an early contender for its most cherished moment.

If that summed up the sharpness of England's out-cricket, there was plenty more to admire as they tightened the noose in the second half of the game. Partnering Archer with the new ball, Chris Woakes maintained a tight line to the super-talented Quinton de Kock so that, despite claiming a breezy half-century, De Kock was never quite able to break free and dominate at the start as he likes to do.

When De Kock, frustrated by Liam Plunkett's maintaining of the line that Woakes had set, eventually swung one into the trap at fine leg, South Africa's main hope was gone. Four overs later, they were five down and with the rate climbing, the game was done.

Stokes wrapped things up with two late wickets to complete a triumphant day for him, which also included a half-century that shepherded England to a comfortable total. All told, with wickets, runs and a headline-making catch, this was a return to the kind of attention-seeking cricket that Stokes was routinely known for, before attention-seeking of a different kind knocked his career off the right trajectory for a while.

As morning cloud gave way to bright sunshine, and the last of the formalities faded quickly from memory, Du Plessis, the South Africa captain, had sprung the first surprise of the tournament. Not by electing to field first – with a 10.30am start, a tinge of green on the pitch and against a team who love chas-ing, that much was obvious – but by throwing the ball to Imran Tahir, the oldest man in the tournament, to open the bowling, instead of Kagiso Rabada.

No doubt this move was aimed at Jason Roy, who likes pace on the ball, but instead it was Jonny Bairstow who got England's campaign off to the worst possible start when he pushed tentatively at his first ball, the second of the match, and edged to De Kock, allowing Tahir, 40, one of his trade-mark, extravagant celebrations, arms splayed wide, hair desperate to escape the limitations imposed by the now standard hairband.

If this was an earlier-than-hoped-for 'here we go again' moment, then Roy and Root quickly doused those fears by bringing up 50 in the ninth over, with no further alarms, doubling that tally by the 17th over. Quickly into his stride with three boundaries flush out of the middle of the bat, including one gorgeous drive through extra cover, Root looked in fine touch, while Roy's eagerness, which initially resulted in two miscued drives, quickly gave way to greater fluency so that Roy actually pipped Root (56 balls) to his half-century, the Surrey man's coming in five fewer balls.

Both fell within three deliveries of each other, leaving the stage to Morgan, first of all, who gave notice of his good form with a run-a-ball half-century that included three mighty sixes, and then Stokes. With South Africa's bowlers cleverly varying the pace later in the innings, and the fielders catching well in the deep, the hoped-for acceleration never quite came. It meant that Stokes had to play intelligently, rather than extravagantly, occupying the crease between the 20th and penultimate overs of the innings.

As man of the match, Stokes will generate today's headlines. Archer's performance with the new ball, though, was more significant.

PLAYER OF THE MATCH:
*Ben Stokes (England)*

## WHAT THEY SAID

'If I had been in the right position it would have been a regulation one, but it's one of those that either sticks or it doesn't. The crowd's reaction behind me was pretty awesome. I just tried to take that in as much as I could.'

Ben Stokes

'He's had a full day out. When he does that it's extremely entertaining. It's great for the game.'

Eoin Morgan

'He is a bit nippier than you think when he hits the crease. It will take time for international teams to get used to his action.'

Faf du Plessis on Jofra Archer

## KEY NUMBER

### 200

Eoin Morgan made a landmark appearance for England

# PAKISTAN v WEST INDIES

................................................

*Friday, May 31*

*Trent Bridge*

**Pakistan 105 all out** (21.4 overs)
(Holder 3-42, Thomas 4-27)
**West Indies 108-3** (13.4 overs)
(Gayle 50; Mohammad Amir 3-26)
*West Indies (2pts) won by seven wickets*
**Toss** *West Indies*

ELIZABETH AMMON

The World Cup organisers have been forced to issue full refunds for about 2,000 tickets after spectators missed the majority of yesterday's match between West Indies and Pakistan due to long queues at the ticket office.

Those who had not received tickets in the post were faced with queues of up to two hours and many missed almost the entire first innings, in which Pakistan were bowled out for 105 in only 21.4 overs.

Full refunds will be issued to everyone who did not have their ticket printed at the ticket office before the start of play. The organisers are now allowing spectators for future matches to print their tickets at home, something that they had not previously sanctioned to try to stop tickets falling into the hands of third-party resellers or touts.

West Indies knocked off Pakistan's paltry total in 13.4 overs for the loss of three wickets, meaning that the match was over by 2pm. Even fans who got into the ground on time saw about a third of the play in a normal one-day international.

Steve Elworthy, the World Cup managing director, said: 'I sincerely apologise to every single fan who was affected by the queues today. It is certainly not what we want their first experience of what is already proving to be a fantastic Cricket World Cup to be.

'We have delivered over 700,000 tickets but not all tickets were successfully delivered and as such we have seen a higher volume collecting at the venue. It is only right that we refund these fans by way of an apology.'

Having lost the toss and been asked to bat on an atypical Trent Bridge pitch, Pakistan were blown away by some hostile West Indian seam bowling.

The second match of the tournament was an altogether less memorable occasion than the opening game between England and South Africa on Thursday. Much was expected of matches at Trent Bridge given that it is the highest-scoring ODI ground in the country.

This was a masterclass in short-ball bowling from Jason Holder, the West Indies captain, who took three for 42, and the imposing Oshane Thomas, who took four for 27, exposing Pakistan's weaknesses against aggressive short-pitched bowling.

Their total of 105 was their second-lowest at World Cups. Their lowest score of 74 came in 1992, when they went on to lift the trophy. They would not have reached three figures had it not been for Mohammad Amir and Wahab Riaz, who put on a tenth-wicket partnership of 22. Put simply, they were unable to cope with a pitch offering seam and bounce and a bowling attack blessed with height and pace. It was a very encouraging performance by West Indies, who have been inconsistent in the build-up to the tournament. Early signs are that the pitches may not be as good as expected and, with the 10.30am starts, bowling first may generally be a good option for West Indies with their seam-bowling attack.

Andre Russell was particularly aggressive, with 15 of the 18 balls that he sent down short of a length. He picked up two top-order wickets for four runs before an injury fielding at fine leg curtailed any further bowling from him. Holder was relatively relaxed about Russell's injury, though, because West Indies have a break of six days before their next match.

Chris Gayle broke the back of the small chase, blasting his way to a 52nd ODI half-century from only 33 balls before appearing to tweak something in his back.

He was caught at point after an unconvincing heave and walked gingerly off the pitch, leaving Nicholas Pooran (34 runs from 19 balls) and the rising star Shimron Hetmyer to finish off the job.

Only Amir could make any impact with the ball for Pakistan. He missed the series against England before the World Cup with illness but picked up all three of the West Indies wickets, getting some notable movement off the seam.

This was a horrible way for Pakistan to start their campaign and offers other teams a template for how to bowl at them: short, short and shorter.

......................................................

PLAYER OF THE MATCH:
**Oshane Thomas (West Indies)**

## WHAT THEY SAID

'We just want to be aggressive even if we give up a few runs up front, trying to take wickets. If you're not taking wickets, you're going to struggle.'

Jason Holder

'Andre Russell led the way, bowling aggressive and fast. The Pakistani guys didn't like it. So I just picked up where he left off really.'

Oshane Thomas

'We were aware of the West Indies fast bowlers, and that they bowl 90-plus. We had practised a lot. It is just that in the first ten overs, our shot selection was not good and we lost wickets.'

Sarfaraz Ahmed

## KEY NUMBER

# 105

Pakistan made their second lowest World Cup score

# JOFRA ARCHER AND THE IMPACT OF PACE

MIKE ATHERTON,
CHIEF CRICKET CORRESPONDENT

Against expectations, fast bowling has been the main talking point of the first two matches of the World Cup. General predictions, based around recent history and trends, were for a run-fest. So far, early days though these are, that has not materialised after England's defence of a good score against South Africa and West Indies' demolition of Pakistan in quick time at Trent Bridge yesterday, which was a welcome reminder of their potency.

Cricket enthusiasts should welcome these promising signs. At its best, the game is a multifaceted one, and the longer the format the more chance there is that the broadest range of skills can surface.

Quick bowling is as exhilarating a sight as anything in the game and young hopefuls in England, the Caribbean and elsewhere need to see the occasional evidence that bowlers are not simply there to be flogged in one-day cricket, for the game to remain healthy and balanced.

The physical threat inherent in fast bowling has always been a part of the game and, while no one wishes to see batsmen get hurt, the evidence presented by the shattering blows to the helmet grilles of Hashim Amla in the first match, courtesy of Jofra Archer, and Fakhar Zaman, courtesy of Andre Russell in the second, was a welcome reminder that bowlers can be aggressors too, even in one-day matches when batsmen generally are on the front foot. There may be a bit more wariness from openers from here on in.

The link between those first two matches, and in the fast bowling offered by England and West Indies, comes in the shape of Archer, of course. Born to an English father and presenting an British passport, and therefore with a right to play here after the recent change in regulations, his cricket is all West Indian in character. He grew up not far from Oistins on the south coast of Barbados, attended the Christ Church Foundation school, the alma mater of one of the great fast bowlers of an earlier era, Joel Garner, and learnt the game there.

As it happens, I found myself chatting to another great fast bowler, Jason Gillespie, on the eve of England's first match. Having taken more than 400 wickets across formats for Australia, and being the coach of Sussex, Archer's county side, Gillespie was well-placed to offer insight.

The gist of it? If you think that Archer, 24, is good in one-day cricket, just wait until you see him with a red Dukes in hand in first-class cricket. Gillespie was convinced that not only would Archer make an impression in the World Cup but that an Ashes berth will be a formality later in the summer.

Gillespie was also one of those fast bowlers who had the priceless gift of being able to bowl a ball that appeared to gather pace from the pitch. That much, the scientists say, is an impossibility but any batsman will tell you that some bowlers seem to be able to nip the ball and hurry it off the surface.

Amla was certainly very late on the shot when hit by Archer, a deception that, South Africa's captain Faf du Plessis said would worry batsmen in this tournament. Like Andy Roberts of an earlier generation, Archer seems to possess a lethal bouncer that comes from nowhere, and there is nothing that nags away at the back of a batsman's mind more than that.

Where does the ability to bowl quickly come from? There are natural reasons, of course, the physiological gifts and the fast-twitch muscle fibres that separate the few who can and the majority who cannot. But technique matters too and Archer shares two key characteristics with Gillespie, who was not as quick but who was still a great bowler.

The first is a braced (or stiff) front leg at delivery; compare Archer's leg position with, say, Liam Plunkett, who bends (collapses) his front leg and loses pace as a result. Archer's is braced, as most genuinely quick bowlers' front legs are, which acts as a springboard for the body to come over the top, and the hips to drive through, creating the momentum and speed in the delivery.

Second, is a superb wrist position. It is flexible, cocked and pointing almost backwards, in an east-west, rather than north-south, position, so that is snaps forward at the point of release.

Barring injury, Archer will play in the Ashes and, suddenly, England's future after James Anderson and Stuart Broad looks bright. His, and England's, great challenge over the next few years will be workload and stress on the body, given that he will be an all-format cricketer. In recent years, Broad, 32, and Anderson, 36, have had their bodies protected to some degree by not playing one-day cricket. Archer will be sought after not just in all three formats of the international game but in franchised competitions too. Bowling fast, as Michael Holding, the great West Indies fast bowler says, is impossible seven days a week.

Genuinely fast bowlers are rare and precious, rarer and more precious still in English cricket. Remember too that England can yet look to strengthen their World Cup team with the inclusion of Mark Wood, another with an electric yard of pace, in place of Plunkett. Wood, who has just recovered from an ankle injury, has to strain to bowl rapidly in a way that Archer does not, and his return is one to relish as well as being a cautionary tale where Archer is concerned.

While bowling fast is the most exhilarating aspect of this great game, it is also the most punishing. Sometimes, like Frank Tyson, thought to be England's quickest-ever bowler for a brief period in the 1950s, they burn brightly but briefly. England will be hoping that Archer's flame is a long-lasting one.

# NEW ZEALAND v SRI LANKA

*Saturday, June 1*

*Sophia Gardens, Cardiff*

**Sri Lanka 136 all out** (29.2 overs)
(Karunaratne 52 not out; Henry 3-29,
Ferguson 3-22)
**New Zealand 137-0** (16.1 overs)
(Guptill 73 not out, Munro 58 not out)
*New Zealand (2pts) won by ten wickets*
Toss *New Zealand*

SIMON WILDE, *SUNDAY TIMES*
CRICKET CORRESPONDENT

Sri Lanka's cricketers got their World
Cup off to the worst of starts with an
utterly abject performance in Cardiff.
Unable to handle the speed or movement of the New Zealand pacemen,
they were dismissed for 136, a total
that openers Martin Guptill and Colin
Munro eclipsed in just 16.1 overs.
Shortly before 3pm, the Sri Lankans left
the field to boos from their supporters.

Dimuth Karunaratne, their captain, who alone deserves exoneration,
having carried his bat for 52 through
his side's abysmal innings, was left to
make apologies. 'Everyone wants to
see a good match,' he said. 'They [the
supporters] have come far from Cardiff
and spent their money [to do so]. We
need to give it a chance. Losing doesn't
matter but we need to give a good
fight, that's the main thing. One hundred and thirty-six runs is no game. We
need to give a good show.'

One suspects his players lost their
appetite for the fight on seeing an
emerald-green pitch first thing in the
morning. If they thought it might receive
another trim from the mower before the
start, they were disappointed. It was reminiscent of something you might see in
Christchurch rather than Colombo.

What they would also not have
enjoyed was sitting square to the wickets, as happens given the position of the
dressing-rooms at Sophia Gardens, and
seeing just how fast Lockie Ferguson
was bowling. Statistics show that
Ferguson's average speed in ODIs this
year is 145kph and his nearest rival,
Jofra Archer, stands well behind at just
below 140kph.

Once Sri Lanka lost the toss, the die
was cast.

Remarkably, New Zealand's bowlers
ran amok despite Tim Southee being
unavailable because of a calf problem
and Trent Boult not being at his best.
Boult received an early warning for running down the line of the stumps and
did not get among the wickets until
what proved to be his ninth and last over.
He made up for it by fielding superbly.

Instead, Matt Henry, man of the
match only four days after going for 107
runs in nine overs in a warm-up match,
punched a hole in the Sri Lankan top
order with three wickets in his opening
spell, among them Kusal Perera, who
briefly counterattacked hard. Ferguson
also picked up three while coming
closest to removing Karunaratne.

The skipper, recalled to lead his
country at this World Cup having not
played ODI cricket for four years, displayed more grit than the rest of his
side put together, but even he struggled
to keep out Ferguson. He had scored

42 when a short ball took the shoulder of his bat, only to elude the flying leap of the keeper. Then, to the final delivery before last man Lasith Malinga had his stumps rearranged, Karunaratne appeared to be caught low in the deep by Mitchell Santner, but he was reprieved by a third-umpire review.

'He was fantastic,' Henry said of Ferguson, who claimed the wicket of David Warner in his first over of international cricket in December 2016. 'He's been bowling with good pace for the last couple of years. He hit his length beautifully. It's brilliant to have someone who bowls with those kinds of wheels in your team. He was accurate as well and bowled some really good bumpers.'

As for the helpful surface, Henry added: 'You don't get too many one-day wickets like that.'

Three Sri Lankans were out for ducks and five others also failed to make double figures. Even Thisara Perera, who can hit a long ball and stayed for enough time to share in a stand of 52, the biggest of the innings, played his first ball from somewhere near square leg and later shoveled a ball off his ribs from Ferguson while in a crouching position. He got out to the spinner, which doesn't look so bad.

Karunaratne became only the second man to carry his bat through a completed World Cup innings, after Ridley Jacobs, of West Indies, against Australia in 1999. There was also another instance of the zing bails failing to leave their grooves when Lahiru Thirimanne cut a ball from Boult on to the outside edge of off stump.

Sri Lanka are in a mess.

They have left one of their best players, Dinesh Chandimal, at home and Angelo Mathews is batting too low at No. 6. New Zealand may also come to review playing Munro as an opener, but here he had licence to slog and it came off. For New Zealand, who now play Afghanistan and Bangladesh, everything came off.

........................................

PLAYER OF THE MATCH:
*Matt Henry (New Zealand)*

## WHAT THEY SAID

'There's a limit to our capabilities, and if you compare us with some other teams, realistically we are a side with limited talent. But there's no reason why we can't win with what we've got.'

Dimuth Karunaratne

'There's some variety there – and you want a balanced attack going into any surface. It is important that you have that to have aggressive options for different occasions.'

Kane Williamson on his seam attack

## KEY NUMBERS

### 12

New Zealand's victory was the 12th ten-wicket win in World Cup history

### 12

Dimuth Karunaratne was the 12th batsman to carry his bat in a One-Day International, and the second at a World Cup.

# AFGHANISTAN v AUSTRALIA

........................................................

## Saturday, June 1

## County Ground, Bristol (day-night)

**Afghanistan 207 all out** (38.2 overs) (Najibullah Zadran 51; Cummins 3-40, Zampa 3-60)
**Australia 209-3** (34.5 overs) (Finch 66, Warner 89 not out)
*Australia (2pts) won by seven wickets*
*Toss Afghanistan*

ELIZABETH AMMON

David Warner is not always known for being sensible but he carried his bat in an uncharacteristically watch-ful innings of 89 from 114 balls which helped Australia to start their World Cup campaign in convincing style with a seven-wicket win over Afghanistan.

It could not have been a worse start for Afghanistan, who chose to bat. Mitchell Starc began Australia's 2019 World Cup in the same way he did their 2015 winning one, with a wicket in the first over. Four years ago it was a yorker to remove Brendon McCullum, yesterday it was a similarly full delivery that rattled into off-stump to dismiss hard-hitting opener Mohammad Shazhad.

In the next over Pat Cummins had Hazratullah Zazai caught behind to leave the 10th ranked team in the world reeling at five for two, but a rally from the middle order stopped the innings from imploding.

Gulbadin Naib, Najibullah Zadran and Rashid Khan took on Australia's fast bowlers in courageous style, adding 109 runs between them, including an 83-run partnership between Naib and Khan who were happy to try to clear the relatively short boundaries at Bristol and did so with ease on a number of occasions.

Some late-order blows took Afghanistan from 166 for eight to a total of 207, something they could at least try to defend but it was always going to be short of a competitive total.

Leg-spinner Adam Zampa took three important wickets in his eight overs. The 27-year-old will have a significant role to play in this tour-nament and this was an interesting day for him, taking three wickets but being dispatched for 22 off one of his overs. Rashid Khan, batting at eight, took a liking to the bowling of Marcus

Stoinis, scoring 21 of his 27 runs off one of his overs.

The chase was completed efficiently in 34.5 overs. Aaron Finch and Warner started breezily, putting on 55 in the powerplay. It was not chanceless though: Warner edged just past slip in the sixth over and the opening bowlers beat the bat on a couple of occasions. The opening pair were building a good platform until Finch miscued to Mujeeb at deep extra cover for 66, having hit six fours and four sixes.

Australia's second wicket was that of Usman Khawaja, who came into the tournament in such bad form that there were questions about whether he was going to be selected for the squad. This was an opportunity missed for him, as he made just 15 before not picking a Rashid Khan googly and being given out lbw.

Bristol rang out with boos as Smith walked to the crease to replace him with Australia needing 51 to win. He very nearly got Australia over the line, making a solid-looking 18 before being caught at point with his side still needing three more runs to win.

Glenn Maxwell, with one eye on his strike rate, hit his first ball for four to seal a straightforward confidence-boosting win for Australia. 'It is good to be back,' said man of the match Warner. 'I did have a few nerves getting back into the camp and getting back into the full intensity of it but I was more relaxed once Finch started going. For us it was about getting past this first victory.

This team is a different one to our winning one in 2015 but there is a great energy within the squad.'

Afghanistan may struggle to post imposing totals but it must be remembered that it is just 13 years since they first toured England, and that tour included matches against Hoddesdon, Ditchling and the Royal Military Academy. Here in 2019, they may not be in with a shout of a World Cup final but this a team with some fine cricketers who are here to compete. You feel they are capable of gaining a couple of wins in the group stages.

While this was mostly a walk in the park for Australia, there is a lot to admire about how Afghanistan played.

Their bowling, particularly in the spin department, may be their strongest suit but the flair shown by the middle order of Gulbadin Naib, Najibullah Zadran and Rashid Khan illustrates a team who have come a long way and are entertaining to watch.

They now move on to Cardiff where they play Sri Lanka on Wednesday in their second group match, a very winnable game given how poor Sri Lanka seem.

Australia head to Trent Bridge to play West Indies on Thursday. It should be an intriguing battle between two teams with strong seam attacks and aggressive, powerful batsmen.

...........................................................

PLAYER OF THE MATCH:
*David Warner (Australia)*

## WHAT THEY SAID

'Playing Twenty20 cricket over the last sort of 12 to 14 months – I hadn't really moved my feet at all. So to get back into rhythm out there, start moving in the right direction, getting my head over the ball – that was just great to get out there and do that.'

David Warner

'I think he was struggling for the first half of his innings there. He struggled to time the ball and his feet weren't really going, so the fact that he kept hanging in there and hanging in there... you always have to remember that it's going to be harder for a new batter to come in.'

Aaron Finch on Warner

# BANGLADESH v SOUTH AFRICA

*Sunday, June 2*

*The Oval*

**Bangladesh 330-6** (50 overs) (Shakib Al Hasan 75, Mushfiqur Rahim 78)
**South Africa 309-8** (50 overs) (Du Plessis 62; Mustafizur Rahman 3-67)
*Bangladesh (2pts) won by 21 runs*
**Toss** *South Africa*

JOSH BURROWS

If there is one thing that Bangladesh love, it is the big stage. South Africa, not so much. In the best game of the World Cup so far, the world's No. 7-ranked ODI team strangled South Africa at the Oval, winning by 21 runs. On paper this was an upset but such was Bangladesh's superiority that it did not feel like it.

England face Mashrafe Mortaza's men on Saturday. On this evidence it will be one of the toughest fixtures of the group stage. Minnows they ain't.

'I'm extremely disappointed,' Faf du Plessis, the South Africa captain, said. 'All formats of our game aren't firing. It's not good enough. Bangladesh batted really well. They took calculated risks and paced their innings. They showed us how to set up a big score. They were 30 runs better than us.'

South Africa were well off full pace – literally. Without Dale Steyn, who is still recovering from a shoulder injury, they lacked sting. Kagiso Rabada has not yet found his quicksilver best and, worryingly, Lungi Ngidi bowled four expensive overs before leaving the field with a hamstring strain.

When Ngidi departed, heads dropped and South Africa started going through the motions, hoping that Bangladesh would not cause too much trouble.

The game started leaking away during a high-class third-wicket partnership between Shakib Al Hasan, the world's top-ranked all-rounder, and Mushfiqur Rahim, the tiny wicketkeeper.

None of South Africa's seamers could complete an over without offering a boundary ball.

Imran Tahir finally broke the 142-run partnership when Shakib tried to sweep a ball that was too full. Briefly South Africa exercised some control only for discipline to desert them in the final five overs; Chris Morris was particularly wild as Mahmudullah and Mosaddek Hossain carved the ball time and again to the big square boundary.

Chasing 330 successfully would have set a World Cup record but South Africa stood little chance after their innings got off to a messy start. Quinton de Kock, their most destructive batsman, was dropped behind only to be run out when called through by Aiden Markram for an imaginary single. Markram, not a natural player of spin, was deceived by an arm ball from the superbly skillful Shakib. Du Plessis and David Miller were rebuilding until the former ran past a flighted delivery from the excellent Mehedi Hasan.

On a tired pitch, this was the difference: Bangladesh's strangulation specialists outperforming South Africa's seamers.

Misfields disrupted Bangladesh's momentum but Mehedi eventually clung on to a sharp chance at backward point off Mustafizur Rahman, whose cutters and slower balls earned him three wickets, one of them Miller. The wicket of Rassie van der Dussen – bowled for 41 slogging – turned the game back to Bangladesh. There were minor contributions down the order but pyrotechnics were needed and South Africa had been damp squibs all day. Du Plessis' side are already in deep trouble. Having lost to England last week, they play India next. Lose that and their World Cup hoodoo will grow larger still.

. . . . . . . . . . . . . . . . . . . . . . . . . . . . . . . . . . . . . . . . . . .

PLAYER OF THE MATCH:
**_Shakib Al Hasan (Bangladesh)_**

## WHAT THEY SAID

'It is one of our best performances because we are away from home, and I loved the way we played today. We know that it won't happen every day but we will take this win any day.'

Mashrafe Mortaza

'I have to believe that we can still win the World Cup. I wouldn't be South African if I said no.'

Faf du Plessis

## KEY NUMBER

# 330
Bangladesh's highest one-day international total

# BEN STOKES PROFILE

SIMON HUGHES

It is a warm March night in Jaipur, India, and Rajasthan Royals are having a practice in the middle the day before their first match of this year's Indian Premier League. Ben Stokes and Steve Smith send white balls arcing endlessly into the night sky with drives, pulls and slog sweeps.

It is like being at a fireworks display.

Every time that Stokes miscues one, he berates himself and bangs the bat on the ground in annoyance, then takes his irritation out on the next delivery. This carries on for an hour and a half. He and Smith almost have to be dragged from the crease.

'Don't you get bored?' I ask Stokes afterwards. 'No, I could have carried on for at least another hour,' he replies.

Stokes had a disappointing IPL. He averaged 20.50 with the bat and didn't make a fifty, while his bowling was expensive. Partly as an apology for his low output, he gave some of his £1.4 million salary to an Indian charity.

You could not fault his work ethic. He pushed himself incredibly hard. In fact, that was the problem. He practised so intensely that he was almost spent when he came into a match.

England's mission this summer has been to 'tame the beast', as they privately describe it. It is a delicate balance because they don't want Stokes to sacrifice any of his natural competitiveness or exuberance.

Fast forward to the Oval last Wednesday. England are practising before their first World Cup match against South Africa. Joe Root is in the first net, Eoin Morgan the second, Stokes the third. Root is having throwdowns from Paul Collingwood and Trevor Bayliss. Morgan is facing Adil Rashid and some other young spinners. Chris Woakes, Mark Wood and a tall Surrey academy lad are running in at Stokes.

Some batsmen prefer low-intensity practice sessions the day before a big game, or to work on specific skills. Not Stokes. He still wants everything full bore.

Wood, charging in hard, bowls him a fast bouncer. I estimate at close to 90mph. It would have clattered a few helmets. Stokes swivels with amazing speed and balance and pulls it powerfully over square leg. It would have gone for six.

'It's better to bowl short 'cos he can't hit that back at me,' Wood exclaims. 'Bloody dangerous bowling at him.' (That is borne out when the England physio Craig de Weymarn shows me his missing tooth and the metal plate in his jaw which was broken by a Stokes drive in a net session last year.)

Using a new ball, Woakes bowls a respectable delivery on off stump, good pace. Stokes drives it smoothly over extra cover. There is a lovely flow to the shot. Wood tries another short ball, chest high; pulled over mid-wicket.

He shrugs. Back at the end of his mark, he says, 'I'll get him this time.' He tries a slower ball from round the wicket. It is perfectly pitched, on a length hitting middle and off, a bit of movement off the pitch. A good ball. Clearing his front leg slightly, Stokes launches it clean over an imaginary long off. He leans on his bat contentedly.

Gamely, Wood changes tack. 'Third man, long leg up,' he shouts from the end of his mark. 'Deep cover, long off, three out on the leg.'

Before setting off, he tells me, 'I'm going for his toes, a yorker just outside leg. If it's on the stumps he can hit it over wide mid-on or he'll ramp me.'

He charges in, gets the line right but it is a full half-volley, not quite a yorker. Stokes flicks it nonchalantly over deep square leg. Wood kicks the ground in frustration. 'Wide yorkers is what it's got to be,' he says. The next delivery is a fast, low full toss almost on the return crease. Pretty hard to hit. Stokes toe-ends a drive without much timing. He nods an acknowledgment to Wood.

Root and Morgan have finished their practice but Stokes continues for a while longer, smacking balls in all directions. He is not slogging, but using his remarkable versatility, brilliant reflexes and considerable strength to play an appropriate shot for each ball. He looks to be enjoying himself.

Suddenly the session is over. In almost an hour of batting he has barely played a false stroke. Noticeably when he did, however, he did not curse or berate himself.

England's backroom staff have placed much emphasis on scaling back all the players' training as a match approaches. 'High intensity but low volume,' is how the trainer Phil Scott explains it. Quality rather than quantity, in other words.

'One set of weights is sufficient the day before a game. It makes sure they are fit but not fatigued,' Scott says. 'It breeds consistency.'

Stokes has heeded the advice. The penny has dropped. His preparation has been focused but measured rather than obsessive. When Scott suggests that he does not need to do much in the gym today, he listens.

His scores since returning to the England team from the IPL have been 37, 71 not out, 21, 20 and a match-winning 89 on Thursday, containing some really smart manipulation of the field rather than just muscular hitting. Coupled with his sensational fielding and two wickets, it was a command performance.

Back in India, at the Rajasthan children's charity that he supported, he was approached by a small boy, who asked: 'Sir, as an all-rounder, how do you manage to do everything you need to? How do you fit it all in?' It is a good question.

He gets his zest and uncompromising commitment from his father, Ged, who was with him that day. With his slicked-back hair, chiselled jaw and heavy tattoos, Ged Stokes could look like a character out of *Breaking Bad*. But he was a very tough, highly successful rugby league forward for Canterbury and New Zealand, and later a popular coach.

A story from 1982 lays down the Stokes family legacy. Ged badly dislocated his middle finger early on in his last game in New Zealand before heading to England, where he had been signed by Workington Town. The Canterbury physio told him to come off the field and get his finger sorted but Ged knew that would jeopardise his trip to England, so he elected to strap it up and continued playing.

He flew to England shortly after and played the entire rugby season with the two middle fingers on his left hand taped together. After the last game, it was discovered that his middle finger was now so damaged it was beyond repair. So it was amputated at the knuckle.

He returned to Workington twice more as a player and then, 20 years later after he had retired, he was hired as club coach. By then he had a 12-year-old son, Ben, who had exceptional sporting talent – he was always playing junior provincial rugby – but who ended up playing cricket for the Cumbrian club Cockermouth. A year later, in 2004, Stokes was playing for Cumbria Under-13 and leaving rugby behind. Durham snapped him up two years later.

It is not stretching the imagination too far to say that had Ged Stokes not come to England in 1982 with his badly damaged finger, they may never have come to the UK and his son may have ended up as an All Blacks rugby player rather than an England cricketer.

Ben pays homage to this every time he sits for a team photo, doubling over the middle finger of his left hand as he rests it on his knee. And, if he carries on performing like he did last Thursday, he may be able to do the same around the World Cup trophy.

# ENGLAND v PAKISTAN

.........................................

*Monday, June 3*

*Trent Bridge*

**Pakistan 348-8** (50 overs) (Babar Azam 63, Mohammad Hafeez 84, Sarfaraz Ahmed 55; Woakes 3-71, Ali 3-50)
**England 334-9** (50 overs) (Root 107, Buttler 103; Wahab Riaz 3-82)
*Pakistan (2pts) won by 14 runs*
**Toss** England

MIKE ATHERTON,
CHIEF CRICKET CORRESPONDENT
Cricket remains an endlessly fascinating and puzzling game. How to explain things?

This was the team that does not lose at home against a team on an 11-match one-day international losing streak; the tournament favourites against a team who had been humbled in an opening match that had lasted little more than three hours. A loss, somehow, for the team that had just beaten their opponents 4-0 in a series a fortnight ago and that were returning to their most favoured ground of all, where they had set two world records.

The answer lies in the unpredictable nature of sport, of course, and the mercurial, maddening nature of the Pakistan team, this collection of highly talented cricketers who, no matter how badly they have been playing, always remain a threat. With a leg spinner and two skilful left-armers in their ranks, lifted by batsmen who showed the

World Cup their best face at last and with a proud history and fanatical support to help them through, how could they not be a threat?

More than that, there was an obvious desperation to Pakistan's cricket. They knew that they had let their supporters down in the defeat by West Indies last Friday and they returned to how they play at their best; with carefree abandon, aggressive with bat and ball, so that, despite hundreds for England's classiest batsman, Joe Root, and their most destructive, Jos Buttler, the match was always on a knife-edge.

Teetering on it, England slipped the wrong side when Root and then Buttler carved to short third man with time ticking away, the latter the ball after bringing up his hundred, so that the tail was left with too much to do.

This was a very different Pakistan line-up from the one that England had beaten heavily last month. Back to stiffen the bowling ranks were Mohammad Amir and Wahab Riaz, the former stymied by chickenpox recently, the latter by the feeling that Pakistan had younger hopefuls but who, after a brilliant month in the Pakistan Super League, had been recalled at the last minute. There was the leg spinner, Shadab Khan, who had been suffering with hepatitis during the one-day series but who was fit enough yesterday to take the new ball, dismiss Jason Roy with it and lift Pakistan in the field.

Afterwards, Eoin Morgan thought that his team were outfielded, and that the 15-20 runs they gifted Pakistan through fumbles and overthrows, as well as through the simple skier put down at long-off by Roy when Mohammad Hafeez had 14, were the difference between the teams. It was a fair summation, despite four catches for Chris Woakes, two of them excellent dives in the deep. Hafeez made a breezy 84, pushing Pakistan's total to the point where England needed a World Cup record to win.

With Bangladesh beating South Africa on Sunday, England overturned here and Pakistan resurgent, there may be much about this tournament that will be hard to predict. At least Morgan's decision to field at the outset was predictable enough, given his team's strength in chasing at home and given the nature of the pitch, which was as flat as the two on which they had posted world-record scores. Mind you, chasing 349 in a largely irrelevant one-day series is different from chasing in a World Cup match with consequences in defeat.

There were many aspects to Pakistan's revival but a key one, the opening partnership between Fakhar Zaman and Imam-ul-Haq, will probably go unacknowledged. Yet, with England unleashing Mark Wood alongside Jofra Archer, and given how meekly Pakistan had succumbed to West Indies' quick bowlers on a pitch just ten yards away, their partnership of 82 for the first wicket settled the inevitable nerves in their dressing room.

Fakhar is a dangerous player who looks like one to take to the trenches, strong and fearless in his approach and clearly willing on the big occasion. Imam, batting in glasses, looks the more studious type but they combined well, marking a half-century together within

eight overs and setting a solid base on which Pakistan's talented middle order could build.

First among equals in that regard is Babar Azam, a batsman with nine ODI hundreds in only 64 innings and a player who, like Root, always seems to have 20 on the board in no time, so busy is he from the off. Babar was helped considerably by Hafeez, an experienced performer at 38 years of age but who yesterday batted with the dash of a youngster. He charged at his first ball, thrashed it over the off side and rolled back the years after that, his half-century coming in a rollicking 39 balls.

Although Moeen Ali enjoyed the strong cross-breeze to pick up three wickets, the rest of England's outcricket felt below par. Archer endured a more difficult day than his World Cup debut at the Oval, conceding 79 runs from his allocation. No bowler finds life easy at Trent Bridge, with the flat, grassless pitch and the boundaries that have been shaved at the corners presenting a tricky combination, and England as a result began their run chase with optimism.

Once again, though, an early wicket fell to leg spin as Roy swept at a ball that was too full and departed with a volley ringing in his ears from Pakistan's fielders. Even though Jonny Bairstow and Root, dashing between the wickets, added 48 for the second wicket it always felt that Pakistan's attack were offering more threat than a month ago, a point reinforced when Bairstow edged a lifter from Wahab.

Morgan, briefly, looked unsettled by the short ball and after Ben Stokes had edged a cut behind, the stage was left to Root and Buttler who, gloriously, added 130 for the fifth wicket. Root, seemingly, has made peace with how he plays now in one-day cricket, gliding, caressing and placing the ball rather than looking to clout it in the manner of Stokes or Buttler. His 15th ODI hundred, and his second in World Cup matches, was the finest expression of his particular way of playing.

When he and Buttler were together, England did not look like losing. Such is Buttler's presence these days at the crease, it was almost impossible to see England losing while he was there. His innings was a rapid but controlled affair: 34 balls for his first 50 runs and just 75 balls for his hundred in all, nine fours and two sixes hit with that combination of power and timing, with the ball often flying to unorthodox places; one ramp shot off Wahab was staggering in its audacity.

With the run chase not out of control, if not under control, Root slashed a quicker ball from Shadab into Hafeez's hands at short third man and, when Buttler carved Amir to the same position six overs later, it felt as if the decisive blows had been made. England required 61 from 33 balls when Buttler was dismissed and, with Hasan Ali's assortment of slower balls and bouncers too much for Ali to handle, suddenly the equation was 38 off three overs, 29 off two, allowing Wahab to stroll through the last over off a short run.

An early blip for England, and a reminder that the burden of chasing in knockout tournaments can weigh down the mightiest of teams.

PLAYER OF THE MATCH:
*Mohammad Hafeez (Pakistan)*

## WHAT THEY SAID

'We have gone from probably one of our best performances in the field to one that, whilst not extremely bad, has cost us probably 15-20 runs, which is a lot in the one-day game.'

Eoin Morgan

'The most important thing now for us as a group is not to panic. We know what works for us as a formula and as a team, but other sides are allowed to play well.'

Joe Root

## KEY NUMBER

# 9

Jos Buttler scored his ninth one-day international hundred, his first at a World Cup

# Sport

**Go and make history**
England stars get letters from
loved ones before World Cup
Football, pages 62-63

# England drop the ball

- Errors hand Pakistan win
- Morgan may face ban

**Elizabeth Ammon**

Eoin Morgan blamed England's
fielding for the 14-run defeat by
Pakistan at Trent Bridge that
marked the first setback of their
World Cup campaign.

Jason Roy dropped a simple
chance to dismiss Mohammad
Hafeez, who went on to score 84,
for 14, while England also gave
away 17 runs in misfields and
bowled 11 wides. To add to their
concerns, captain Morgan may
face a two-match ban for a slow
Continued on page 67

Roy drops Hafeez at long-off with the Pakistan batsman on 14. He went on to score 84 as England were set a testing target of 349 that proved too much for them

## Murray will play at Queen's

**Stuart Fraser** Tennis Correspondent

Andy Murray will make a comeback
in a fortnight. The three-times
grand-slam champion has entered the
doubles draw at the Fever-Tree
Championships at the Queen's Club
with Feliciano López, of Spain, after
deeming himself ready to return from
the hip-resurfacing surgery that he
underwent in late January.

Murray, 32, told *The Times* two weeks
ago that he was "pretty certain" he
would be able to make a comeback in
doubles and there have been no
setbacks in training since to convince
him otherwise. On Saturday, he posted
a video on social media of himself
serving on grass at Wimbledon.

The decision was taken by Murray
yesterday to play with López, the
accomplished 37-year-old Spanish
left-hander who won the men's doubles
Continued on page 60

## Chinese chase Aubameyang

**Gary Jacob**

Arsenal could face a battle to keep
Pierre-Emerick Aubameyang after
Chinese clubs again tried to sign the
striker by offering to pay him nearly
£300,000 a week.

Arsenal's failure to qualify for the
Champions League and their need to
cut costs has encouraged the clubs,
thought to be Guangzhou Evergrande
and Shanghai SIPG, to believe that
Aubameyang could be tempted to
China at the third time of asking. The
Gabon international, who will be 30 in
two weeks, was the Premier League's
joint top scorer with 22 goals.

He joined Arsenal for £56 million
from Borussia Dortmund in January
last year, only weeks after a proposed
£62 million move to Guangzhou
Evergrande collapsed. Six months
Continued on page 64

---

## Times Crossword 27,368

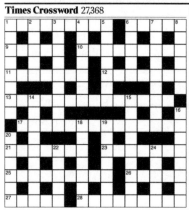

**ACROSS**

1 Decay beginning to show in
hideous couple (9)
6 Cheat cold seeping into unfinished
dwelling (5)
9 Figure of one stone, perhaps, with
front obscured (5)
10 Greeting crew members with fish
(9)
11 An aspiration to entertain
ambassador in Californian city (7)
12 Interpreter for example appearing
in late summer in France (7)
13 Rock festival featuring Queen? (7,7)
17 Complaint in sheikdom — unease
to spread (10,4)
21 Expert thus securing a flat (7)
23 Flighty African needs daily
porridge (7)
25 One allowed carrier in kit:
something for soap etc (6,3)
26 Confuse theologian introduced to
beer (5)
27 Yankee, ridiculously idle, has to
give up (5)
28 Fanatic to survive bracing term at
sea (9)

**DOWN**

1 Detective Inspector Morse
ultimately tough on southern
reactionaries (8)
2 Disgraceful mark time erased in
letter to Greeks (5)
3 Course incomplete with reason
given in confidence (5,4)
4 Embarrassed because news boss
engages amateur (7)
5 Little man with money recited
poem (7)
6 Leader abandons modest
expedition (5)
7 One to blend in drink with
energy-packed fruit (9)
8 Small study about headless sheep
in northern kingdom (6)
14 Brute concealing old record is to
put things straight (9)
15 Hint Tunisian criminal gave at last
(9)
16 Boring race gives no decisive result
(4,4)
18 Carriage cutting horse in two — it's
gruesome (7)
19 Understanding current things
differently (7)
20 Eating too much, mole covered in
pimples (6)
22 Up to each person (5)
24 Lemur visible in thin drizzle (5)

**Yesterday's solution 27,367**

Check today's answers by ringing 0906
7577189 by midnight. Calls cost 80p per minute plus your telephone company's network
access charge. SP: Spoke 0333 202 3390.

Buying The Times: Austria €4.00; Belgium €4.50;
Cyprus €4.50; North Cyprus 11.35; Denmark DKR33;
France €4.50; Gibraltar £2.70; Greece €4.50; Italy €4.50;
Luxembourg €4.50; Malta €4.50; Netherlands €4.50;
Portugal €4.50; Spain €4.50; Switzerland CHF6.80;
Turkey TL 25

9 771742 498622

## ANALYSIS

STEVE JAMES

Jos Buttler did not have a particularly good day at the Oval in England's opener against South Africa: only 18 runs and a rather scruffy performance behind the stumps.

Even in victory this did not go unnoticed. This is one of the downsides of the sort of excellence, mixed with moments of scarcely credible genius, in which Buttler routinely deals.

So when he was spotted doing extra training in the rain during England's allotted practice time at Trent Bridge on Sunday, running furiously around the boundary edge on his own before doing some intense catching practice with Bruce French, the wicketkeeping coach, it was assumed that this was some sort of reaction.

It wasn't. Buttler always does that. He trains like a maniac. There is no more committed and dedicated player in the England side. Maybe Ben Stokes, but only maybe. They needed Buttler at his best yesterday and it is a measure of Pakistan's astonishing turnaround after 11 consecutive one-day international defeats, allied to some sloppiness from the hosts, that he was somewhere near that level and yet England lost.

First, he did his job with the gloves. He made a smart stumping off Moeen Ali to get rid of Fakhar Zaman. There was only one bye, and that was rather unfortunately conceded early on when a ball from Jofra Archer bounced in front of him.

England's fielding woes were elsewhere, started by Eoin Morgan, the captain, who let through a four off the fourth ball of Pakistan's innings. Buttler had improved from the Oval; many of the rest had declined sharply after such a slick effort there.

Buttler then scored his ninth ODI century and it was only the second time in those nine that he has been on the losing side. The other occasion was when he made 121 in vain against Sri Lanka at Lord's in 2014.

He and Joe Root played so well for their hundreds yesterday that it seems inconceivable that England lost, but that is what happens when you leave yourself a record World Cup chase, lose both openers in the powerplay and your captain looks under pressure against the short ball.

Buttler joined Root with England's score at 118 for four in the 22nd over. A colleague mentioned that Buttler could get a hundred and England may not make the 349 required. Your correspondent chuckled. Surely not. Buttler was soon hitting Shoaib Malik over mid-off for four. Then he pulled Mohammad Hafeez over deep midwicket for six. It even tempted Root, who is deliberately trying not to ape his more muscular batting partners, to hit the same bowler over long-on for six.

No Buttler innings is complete without a ramp and he played that shot expertly down to fine leg off Wahab Riaz. When Buttler eased Shadab Khan's leg spin through extra cover for four, you sensed this was his day.

Cue a vital moment. On 33, Buttler played forward to Shadab and there was a huge appeal. It was turned down but Pakistan decided to review. The ball was shown to be going over the stumps, the slight sponginess of the surface working in Buttler's favour. Surely this really was his day now, a point reinforced first by an edged four past the wicketkeeper Sarfaraz Ahmed off Wahab and then by Asif Ali's inability to stop another pulled shot to deep midwicket.

The resultant six, with Asif requiring some medical treatment having landed awkwardly, took Buttler past 50 off 34 balls. He cruised from there. There were a couple of consecutive off-side boundaries off the left-arm pace of Mohammad Amir and Buttler seemed so comfortable in unison with Root. That Root went for 107, with 101 required off 11.1 overs, was a blow but with Buttler there all appeared possible.

Could he cope? He went to his hundred with a four off Amir hit flat to the left hand of mid-off. My colleague, Mike Atherton, has always maintained that opposing captains should position their mid-offs much wider to Buttler but they do not seem to be listening.

Four it was and a century it was, off 75 balls. That it was England's fastest World Cup century goes without saying, again emphasising the strides this England side have made and how dangerous they can be.

The very next ball, Buttler was gone, slashing Amir's cutter to short third man. Sixty-one were now needed off 33 balls. Without Buttler, it was over. He had had a good day this time but, being the consummate team man, you know that he would much have preferred the Oval scenario and a team win.

# AFGHANISTAN v SRI LANKA

......................................................

*Tuesday, June 4*

*Sophia Gardens, Cardiff*

**Sri Lanka 201 all out** (36.5 overs) (Kusal Perera 78; Mohammad Nabi 4-30) **Afghanistan 152 all out** (32.4 overs) (Malinga 3-39, Pradeep 4-31) *Sri Lanka (2pts) won by 34 runs, DLS Method* Toss *Afghanistan*

ELGAN ALDERMAN
Sri Lanka won the battle of the World Cup's two least-fancied sides, beating Afghanistan by 34 runs yesterday.

There was ardent support for both countries in an official crowd of about 8,800, of which 3,000 were local schoolchildren.

How were Afghanistan chasing only 187 from 41 overs? A combination of the Duckworth-Lewis-Stern system after rain disruption and a remarkable batting collapse. Afghanistan conceded a tournament-high 79 runs in the first powerplay and extras finished on 35, the second-top score of the innings. 'We did not bowl in the right areas [at the start] – the seamers did not bowl well,' Gulbadin Naib, the Afghanistan captain, said.

Sri Lanka were 144 for one when Mohammad Nabi changed the complexion of the match. He bowled Lahiru Thirimanne and had Kusal Mendis and Angelo Mathews caught in the space of five balls. Hamid Hassan then beat Kusal Perera with two back-of-a-length beauties and had Dhananjaya de Silva caught behind.

Perera, promoted to opener, cut prodigiously and made 78 before he gloved a reverse-sweep behind off Rashid Khan. Returning after a three-hour rain delay, Sri Lanka were all out for 201 and Afghanistan's target was reduced by 15.

Would-be Afghan heroes came and went. Hazratullah Zazai crunched boundaries through mid-wicket and flicked yorkers through his legs before falling to Thisara Perera's low, diving catch at fine leg. Nabi was the fifth man out, bowled by a ball from Thisara that seamed in, with 57 runs on the board.

Najibullah Zadran and Gulbadin put on 64 before the latter was one of four wickets for Nuwan Pradeep. Afghanistan's hopes lay with Najibullah and the innings lasted only four more balls after he was run out for 43.

PLAYER OF THE MATCH:
*Nuwan Pradeep (Sri Lanka)*

## WHAT THEY SAID

'We really needed a win. We haven't got much success lately. We need this badly.'
Sri Lanka coach Chandika Hathurusingha

## KEY NUMBER

# 9

Successive defeats for Sri Lanka against Full Members before this win

# INDIA v SOUTH AFRICA

........................................

*Wednesday, June 5*

*Rose Bowl, Southampton*

**South Africa 227-9** (50 overs)
(Chahal 4-51)
**India 230-4** (47.3 overs)
(Sharma 122 not out)
*India (2pts) won by six wickets*
**Toss** *South Africa*

RICK BROADBENT

India arrived fashionably late for the World Cup yesterday while South Africa continued to make for the exit with unseemly haste. JP Duminy had suggested that the Proteas look themselves in the mirror after their opening defeats to England and Bangladesh. He scored three and they lost by six wickets. The mirror cracked.

This is the first time in World Cup history that South Africa have lost three successive matches. They may yet save their skins, but apart from an eighth-wicket stand of 66 between Chris Morris and Kagiso Rabada, and an outstanding catch from Quinton de Kock, it was low-grade lethargy at the Ageas Bowl. 'It's pretty simple,' said Morris, who was economical with the ball and then the truth when suggesting South Africa were only a few half-chances away. 'We need to win every game from now on. The guys know what needs to be done. They are disappointed and a little bit angry. We'll sort that out in our heads tonight and when the sun comes up we'll go again.'

Chasing 228, India were patient and always comfortable, winning their opening game with 15 balls spare. Rohit Sharma was the standout performer with an unbeaten 122, but the bowlers had done the damage with Jasprit Bumrah claiming two wickets before the spin of Yuzvendra Chahal bagged four for 51.

Virat Kohli managed only 18, thanks to that De Kock moment, but he did not look unduly bothered at not making a century in his opening game at a World Cup for the first time. The skipper called the performance professional and praised Bumrah for rendering batsmen 'clueless'.

'He will bounce people, york people with the new ball and if you're not on top of your game it can be trouble,' Kohli said. 'If you play well against him in the nets you walk out with more confidence. He's going to be a massive factor for us here.'

Quite why India were allowed to be so rested after the Indian Premier League, while South Africa were playing for the third time in a week, is mystifying, but some of South Africa's shot selection and fielding was equally baffling. 'It's a bit tough on the body and it's mentally draining losing three times,' Morris said. It looked it.

India, though, were greeted by a party feel. Long before the start, roads around the grounds were gridlocked. The Indian fans ditched their cars, wore Kohli masks and held 'Keep Calm and Trust Kohli' placards. Some had travelled from California. Harry Kane, England's football captain, even tweeted his admiration for Kohli. Not to be outdone Thomas Müller, the Germany player, did likewise, citing Kohli's unlikely affection for Bayern Munich as reason for the love-in. No footballer seemed willing to back South Africa.

When David Miller dropped the simplest of catches to reprieve Sharma who was on 107 at the time, it summed up this team, out of sorts and probably not far from being out of the competition. Needless to say Sharma hit the next ball for four. When Morris caught and bowled MS Dhoni, clattering over the wicket and dislodging middle stump as he held on, even the good bits came tinged with calamity.

The only downside from India's point of view were hundreds of empty seats at a 17,200 sell-out. It is a crying shame that many of the most vocal and vibrant fans in cricket should miss out presumably because sponsors had a better lunch elsewhere. Claire Furlong, the ICC's general manager of strategic communications, said there were a couple of thousand people milling around the concourse all day and that there was a resale platform so fans were not ripped off, but she added: 'If people who've bought tickets don't turn up there's only so much we can do.'

It was not flawless fare from India. They allowed the South African tail to wag and faced some early hostility from Rabada. Indeed, they could only match their opponents' tally of 34 from the first ten overs.

However the two-time winners have obviously got what it takes to add to this tournament on and off the pitch. Hardik Pandya forced Faf du Plessis to have treatment on an injured finger – 'still attached' was Morris' medical report – and Bumrah caused them all manner of discomfort. Bumrah ended with two for 35 off ten overs. With his straight-arm action and short run up, he stands out anyway, but this effort suggests he could be an enduring star of this World Cup.

PLAYER OF THE MATCH:
*Rohit Sharma (India)*

## WHAT THEY SAID

'In my opinion this is by far his best ODI innings because of the kind of pressure the first game brings from a World Cup point of view.'

Virat Kohli on Rohit Sharma

'We're trying to make sure that we keep fighting, but we're still making mistakes all the time.'

Faf du Plessis

## KEY NUMBER

# 3

For the first time at a World Cup, South Africa lost three successive matches

# BANGLADESH v NEW ZEALAND

......................................................

*Wednesday, June 5*

*The Oval (day-night)*

**Bangladesh 244 all out** (49.2 overs)
(Shakib Al Hasan 64; Henry 4-47)
**New Zealand 248-8** (47.1 overs)
(Taylor 82)
*New Zealand (2pts) won by two wickets*
*Toss New Zealand*

JOSH BURROWS

So much for the boundary bonanza, the summer of sixes, the World Cup where 400 would not be enough. With nine matches completed the average first-innings score is 234. And first-innings batsmen are averaging just 26.03 – the lowest since 1979.

Bowling is very much not dead just yet – as proved last night in a nailbiter under the lights between New Zealand and Bangladesh. So much for the potential thrill of watching one team hit 500: this was a match with fewer than 500 runs in total, and it was all the better for it.

Chasing 245 for victory, New Zealand were cruising while Kane Williamson and Ross Taylor were at the crease, dabbing and jogging their way to a century partnership.

Then, out of nowhere, Williamson made a wildly uncharacteristic error of judgment, not quite reaching the pitch of a Mehedi Hasan delivery and lofting a catch to mid-wicket.

When Tom Latham recklessly followed five balls later in almost identical fashion, the green and red army in the stands suddenly woke up again – and they were on their feet when Taylor was caught behind for 82, feathering the ball down the leg side.

Fifty-four runs left to score on a pitch offering grip to Bangladesh's spinners, darkness closing in around the Oval. Game on.

Colin de Grandhomme and Jimmy Neesham briefly restored order until De Grandhomme was cleverly winkled out by a Mohammad Saifuddin slower-ball bouncer, superbly caught behind by Mushfiqur Rahim.

Now New Zealand really did need calm. Instead Neesham unleashed chaos when he needlessly chipped Mosaddek Hossain into the hands of long off.

Twenty-seven needed from 39 balls with two tailenders at the crease. But even then Matt Henry and Mitchell Santner looked to have things in hand until, with just eight runs needed, Saifuddin clean bowled Henry with a full toss.

Finally New Zealand limped over the line – the margin of victory just two wickets, with 17 balls remaining.

The 2015 finalists will look back and wonder how it ever got this tense, especially after conceding just 244. Line was key. With the new ball, Henry, Trent Boult and Lockie Ferguson starved the top order of width, using the short ball with precision, not profligacy.

When they returned at the death, they targeted heads and toes, rarely gifting Bangladesh the length balls and long hops they were gasping for.

The best on show, however, was Santner, the unglamourous slow left-armer, whose economy rate was only dented when his final ball was heaved for six. On a breezy afternoon and greenish pitch, his variations of flight and pace looked very much at home.

At the end of the game it was Santner who struck the winning runs too, driving the ball through the covers as if to prove that it may yet be bowlers, not batsmen, who have the final say at this World Cup.

PLAYER OF THE MATCH:
*Ross Taylor (New Zealand)*

## WHAT THEY SAID

'The run out of Mushfiqur while batting was the turning point. Again, Shakib and Mithun had their partnership broken when they were putting it together. If any of those two partnerships had gone into eighties or a hundred, things would have been different.'

Mashrafe Mortaza

'Credit to Bangladesh, their supporters came out – it felt like Dhaka or Chittagong.'

Ross Taylor

# AUSTRALIA v WEST INDIES

*Thursday, June 6*

*Trent Bridge*

**Australia 288 all out** (49 overs) (Smith 73, Coulter-Nile 92; Brathwaite 3-67)
**West Indies 273-9** (50 overs) (Hope 68, Holder 51; Starc 5-46)
*Australia (2pts) won by 15 runs*
**Toss** *West Indies*

JOHN WESTERBY
The early stages of this World Cup have been illuminated by the raw aggression of West Indies' quick bowling, but the outcome of this wonderfully fluctuating game was finally settled yesterday by the more clinical pace of Mitchell Starc. When Australia won the World Cup on home soil four years ago, Starc, the left-arm fast bowler, was the player of the tournament and he made a decisive late intervention yesterday when West Indies were homing in on his side's total of 288.

With five overs left, and four wickets in hand, West Indies needed 38 to win with Jason Holder well set and Carlos Brathwaite looking menacing. Starc had already taken the valuable wickets of Chris Gayle and Andre Russell and conceded only one run from the first two balls of the 46th over. His third ball was slower, a low full toss that enticed Brathwaite to loft high to mid-on.

Holder failed to score from the next two balls, the mounting burden of a run chase beginning to weigh that little more heavily on his capable shoulders and, when he attempted a hurried pull to Starc's next ball, he could only cuff it to short fine leg. One run had come from the over, two wickets had fallen and West Indies' chase was over. Before he was done, Starc would splinter the stumps of Sheldon Cottrell to complete a game-changing burst.

West Indies had given so much to the game, too, from the explosive early efforts of their pace bowlers, which had clearly rattled Australia's top order, to an extraordinary catch from Cottrell and innings of classy composure from Holder and Shai Hope.

Their pursuit had begun in bizarre fashion when Gayle was given out three times off Starc by Chris Gaffaney, the umpire. The first two, one for a caught behind – that actually clipped off stump but did not dislodge the bail – and one for leg-before both in the third over, were successfully reviewed by Gayle. The third, in Starc's next over, was shown to be clipping leg stump and was given out on umpire's call. Yet there was a further twist. Replays showed that Starc's previous ball had been a front-foot no-ball, so Gayle should then have been facing a free hit. 'Every time we get hit on our pad the finger goes up,' Brathwaite, the West Indies all-rounder, said. 'When we hit the opposition on their pad, the finger stays down.'

Holder went on to review two more leg-before decisions successfully as he built a 41-run stand with Hope. But once Hope had clipped a Pat Cummins slower ball to mid-on, the pressure

began to build and Starc intervened to end a brief assault from Russell, superbly caught running backwards at point by Glenn Maxwell. His jubilation signified that a finely balanced contest was tilting in Australia's favour. Starc's late burst then ensured it would stay that way. 'It was touch and go, but we always felt we were only a couple of wickets away,' Starc said.

After being asked to bat, Australia's innings had been revived from the perilous position of 79 for five in the 17th over, first by a stand of 68 between Steve Smith and Alex Carey, then by a more substantial alliance Smith forged with the unlikely figure of Nathan Coulter-Nile. In 18 previous ODI innings, Coulter-Nile had never made more than 34 and was averaging 12. But he had the gumption to hang around and, gradually, gain a degree of fluency.

Smith was never at his most expressive, but his wings had been clipped by the lack of top-order support. Booed sporadically in pantomime fashion after his ball-tampering ban, Smith reached a low-risk half-century from 77 balls, while Coulter-Nile eventually found his range, flicking Russell over square leg for the first of his four sixes.

Their stand of 102 was ended by one of the finest catches seen at a World Cup, to dismiss Smith with an early contender to rival Ben Stokes' effort against South Africa a week ago.

Coulter-Nile eventually drove to mid-off for 92 from 60 balls, an unexpected contribution that lifted his side's total to a level just beyond West Indies' reach.

PLAYER OF THE MATCH:
*Nathan Coulter-Nile (Australia)*

## WHAT THEY SAID

'I enjoy bowling at the death. You're not going to win them all, and there's going to be times where you go the journey or where you don't quite get your team over the line. But I think that's what I enjoy about the challenge of that.'

Mitchell Starc

## KEY NUMBERS

### 1,000

Chris Gayle reached 1,000 World Cup runs when he made six

### 150

Mitchell Starc reached 150 ODI wickets in 77 matches by dismissing Jason Holder, the fastest to that landmark in history

### 92

Nathan Coulter-Nile's score was the highest score by a No. 8 in a World Cup match

# PAKISTAN v SRI LANKA

*Friday, June 7*

*County Ground, Bristol*

Match abandoned without a ball bowled. Pakistan (1pt), Sri Lanka (1pt)
*No toss made*

# ENGLAND v BANGLADESH

......................................................

## Saturday, June 8

### Sophia Gardens, Cardiff

**England 386–6** (50 overs) (Roy 153, Bairstow 51, Buttler 64)
**Bangladesh 280 all out** (48.5 overs) (Shakib Al Hasan 121; Archer 3-29, Stokes 3-23)
*England (2pts) won by 106 runs*
**Toss** *Bangladesh*

SIMON WILDE, *SUNDAY TIMES* CRICKET CORRESPONDENT

Jason Roy and Jofra Archer had plenty of ground to make up going into this match. Neither had a good game in the defeat to Pakistan and both came away lighter in the pocket after being hit by the match referee for expressing frustration in the field. They could not have bounced back in greater style. Fines have given way to fanfares.

Roy's innings of 153 from 121 balls was brutal in its efficiency and his air of calm purpose as he butchered Bangladesh's bowling to all parts of Sophia Gardens' oblong-shaped field spread to the rest of the team as England turned in an exemplary performance. They needed to send a message that they remain the team to beat and their batting is still a beast to be feared. They did just that with a total of 386 for six that was their highest at any World Cup.

Just in case that didn't grab the attention of other sides at the tournament, Archer reprised the tenor of his spell against South Africa on the World Cup's opening day. Only this time, with a strong breeze blowing over his left shoulder, he touched 95.1mph while the average speed of his opening spell was 90.7mph, up on the 89.5mph he achieved at The Oval and the fastest in an ODI for England since records began in 2006.

If the most eye-catching sight was the ball with which he trimmed the top of Soumya Sarkar's off stump flying over the boundary rope 53 metres away without bouncing, there was more to Archer's spell than speed. He was supremely accurate and gave Bangladesh's left-handers in particular a torrid examination. Shakib Al Hasan, who would recover to score a wonderful 95-ball century, took an early blow in the ribs.

In fact, Archer did not even bowl the fastest ball of the day. That honour went to Mark Wood after he took over the down-wind end and reached 95.7mph in his third over. But Archer's figures of three for 29 from 8.5 overs brooked no argument: he was the best on show.

Neither Roy nor Archer has played Test cricket but both reaffirmed their credentials as Ashes picks later in the summer. But the Ashes can wait. England's World Cup mission is back on track and the only blemish on yesterday's outing was Jos Buttler doing himself a mischief as he struck a six into the River Taff off the back foot. Though he hobbled through the rest of his innings, he still managed to bludgeon 64 off 44 balls, but did not keep wicket in an effort to alleviate the tightness in his right hip. Seamlessly, Jonny Bairstow took over behind the wicket.

Bangladesh predictably opened up with spin but Roy and Bairstow were this time wise to the ruse. 'They looked for early wickets and we made sure we didn't give them any,' said Roy, overlooking an ugly swipe in Shakib's second over. With moisture around after Friday's rain, there was early movement for the seamers but Roy countered by walking down the pitch and soon settled into his best vein, with Bairstow not far behind.

By putting on 128 for the first wicket, their seventh century stand in their past 14 ODI innings in England and their eighth overall, they laid the kind of platform this team have become so adept at building on. A leading edge accounted for Bairstow, but there was no dislodging Roy, who motored to his hundred off 92 balls courtesy of a misfield in the deep.

Preoccupied with his moment of redemption, his celebratory jig led him to collide with umpire Joel Wilson, who was bowled off his feet but was unharmed. The next time Roy lost focus was after plundering three sixes at the start of the 35th over from Mehidy Hasan to take him to 153, five short of equalling England's best in a World Cup; attempting another maximum, he sliced high to cover. A double century was there for the taking.

Even without Moeen Ali – after being left out for Liam Plunkett he made his way home to join his wife, who is expecting their second child – there was no let-up in England's batting. When Buttler, Eoin Morgan and Ben Stokes fell in three overs, Chris Woakes and Plunkett were not content with living off scraps and hammered 45 from the final 17 balls of the innings.

Plunkett's contribution was as Tiggerish as Roy's and Archer's. He struck 27 from nine balls before giving Bangladesh a masterclass in what length to bowl at Cardiff through the middle overs and breaking a dangerous third-wicket stand between Shakib and Mushfiqur Rahim of 106. The catch at point was taken by the ubiquitous Roy.

With Mushfiqur gone and Mohammad Mithun soon dismissed by Adil Rashid, Shakib gave Bangladesh's passionate supporters something to cheer even though it was clear that the chase would be beyond them. He became only the second Bangladesh batsman to score a World Cup century after Mahmudullah before being bowled off his foot by Stokes, who finished with three for 23.

England's players left the field to feelings of relief and satisfaction. They had defended their proud record of not having lost back-to-back ODIs since January 2017. Their resilience is intact. So is their belief.

PLAYER OF THE MATCH:
*Jason Roy (England)*

## WHAT THEY SAID

'The slow nature of the pitch made it more difficult. Shorter balls didn't fly through. On a quick-natured pitch it's easier to play or get out the way of. It follows you when it's slower so here it was ideal.'

Eoin Morgan

'They are the two quickest bowler in the World Cup. It was tough but I felt very happy the way I played them.'

Shakib Al-Hasan on Wood and Archer

## KEY NUMBERS

### 300

England scored 300 or more for the seventh successive one-day international

### 386

England's 386 was their highest World Cup score.
It was also the seventh-highest ever scored by any country

# AFGHANISTAN v NEW ZEALAND

........................................................

## Saturday, June 8

## County Ground, Taunton (day-night)

**Afghanistan 172 all out** (41.1 overs) (Hashmatullah Shahidi 59; Ferguson 4-37, Neesham 5-31)
**New Zealand 173-3** (32.1 overs) (Williamson 79 not out; Aftab Alam 3-45)
*New Zealand (2pts) won by seven wickets*
*Toss New Zealand*

PETER GAME

New Zealand needed only 32.1 overs to pass Afghanistan's inadequate total of 172 and record their third win of the World Cup.

In the first one-day international at Taunton for 20 years, Afghanistan started well but lost four quick wickets and were bowled out in 41.1 overs for 172. Hashmatullah Shahidi was their top scorer with 59 from 99 balls.

James Neesham, named man of the match, had the best bowling figures of the World Cup so far with five for 31, while Lockie Ferguson took four for 37.

New Zealand were 41 for two in the ninth over in reply but there was never any doubt that they would make the runs. Their captain Kane Williamson was top scorer, unbeaten on 79 off 99 balls.

Afghanistan have now lost three matches in a row and their captain Gulbadin Naib said: 'We started really well and then we didn't take responsibility. We missed out on length balls and gave away ugly wickets. All credit to the New Zealand bowlers. We are not playing according to the plan, especially the batsmen. We put a good total on at the start but missed out in the middle. Our fielding has to improve. There's a lot of work to do to go to the next level.'

Jeremy Coney, the former New Zealand captain, said: 'New Zealand are in a place where you would expect them to be. It was a nice gentle start to the competition for them. It is about to get tougher though and we'll find out in the next four matches whether they're going to reach the semi-finals.'

Those four games are against India, South Africa, West Indies and Pakistan.

PLAYER OF THE MATCH:
*Jimmy Neesham (New Zealand)*

## WHAT THEY SAID

'We did some bad shots, and we didn't play 50 overs. Our shot selection is not good.'

Gulbadin Naib

'Jimmy bowled beautifully. We've seen in our three games so far how our attack complement each other and it's great to see them all playing a part in wins.'

Kane Williamson

## KEY NUMBER

# 5

Jimmy Neesham became the fifth New Zealand seamer to take five wickets in a World Cup match

# AUSTRALIA v INDIA

*Sunday, June 9*

*The Oval*

**India 352-5** (50 overs) (Sharma 57, Dhawan 117, Kohli 82)
**Australia 316 all out** (50 overs) (Warner 56, Smith 69, Carey 55 not out; Kumar 3-50, Bumrah 3-61)
*India (2pts) won by 36 runs*
**Toss** India

JOSH BURROWS

Some very strange things happened to Australia yesterday: from Virat Kohli urging his supporters not to boo Steve Smith, to bails that won't budge, to a David Warner half-century so slow that it killed his team's chances of winning the game. This was World Cup cricket but not as we know it.

The first of those incidents came midway through India's formidable first innings, after Kohli won the toss and elected to bat. With a sluggish pitch and near universal support in the stands, the Oval bore more resemblance to the Wankhede than the Waca – and India were determined not to waste the opportunity.

At the top of the order Shikhar Dhawan and Rohit Sharma had brought up yet another century opening stand – the 16th of their careers and their sixth against Australia – and Kohli was well on his way to a silky 82.

So comfortable did the India captain feel that he found time to signal to the India supporters packed into the stands to stop booing Smith – following up

with a touch of hands for Australia's former captain, who has only recently returned to international duty after his ball-tampering ban.

'We've had issues in the past and we've had arguments on the field but you don't want to see a guy feeling that heat every time he goes out to play,' Kohli said. 'Because there are so many Indian fans here, I didn't want them to set a bad example.

'I felt bad because if I were in a position where something had happened with me, and I'd apologised and I came back and I was still getting booed, I wouldn't like it either. So I told him I was sorry on behalf of the crowd. In my opinion that's not acceptable.'

The sympathy didn't extend to India's batting, of course. Dhawan was calmly destructive in making 117 – his third century in five innings at the Oval – and Kohli was typically sublime. The platform that India laid allowed them to promote the all-rounder Hardik Pandya up the order, where he carved his way to 48 from 27 balls before Pat Cummins removed him.

Plenty of damage had been done, though, and each of Pandya's boundaries was a hammer blow to Alex Carey, the Australia wicketkeeper, who dropped a regulation diving chance from his first ball. Cameos from MS Dhoni and KL Rahul then took India past the 350 mark, the second team after England to score at more than seven runs an over at this World Cup.

Against India's crafty bowling, there are not many batting orders who would back themselves to chase such a commanding total. Usually Australia's line-up – studded with the likes of Warner, Aaron Finch and Smith – would be one, but this was a day full of surprises and the reply started so lethargically that they seemed complicit in their defeat.

That was strange, but odder still was when Warner chopped a delivery from Jasprit Bumrah on to his stumps only for the ball not to dislodge the light-up 'Zing' bails – the fifth time at this World Cup that the bails have failed to play ball. Both captains said afterwards that they were unimpressed with the technology.

'This is not something you expect at the international level,' Kohli said. 'We checked the stump and it was actually loose, so I don't know what's wrong with the stump. I have no idea if the stump is too thick or too rigid but no team wants to bowl a good ball, hit the stump and not get the guy out.'

Finch, the Australia captain, added: 'We were on the right end of it today but you'd hate to see something like that happen in a World Cup final.'

With Warner in such uncharacteristically sedate form, the incident did not affect the course of the game. He made a bizarrely slow 56 from 84 balls and contributed to the unnecessary run out of his captain on the way.

Smith was promoted up the order to No 3 but for a long time he struggled to get on top of India's bowlers, particularly the twin wrist spinners Kuldeep Yadav and Yuzvendra Chahal. Only Glenn Maxwell and Carey showed any signs of being able to keep up with the run rate but by that point it was far too late.

In racking up more than 350 against Australia and defending it with relative ease, India have set a new standard at this World Cup – in batting, bowling and, thanks to Kohli, in sportsmanship too.

...............................................

PLAYER OF THE MATCH:
*Shikhar Dhawan (India)*

## WHAT THEY SAID

'Davey didn't have his best day, but was able to stick it out rather than throwing his wicket away early. He was able to bat deeper for us, which is a key thing. Unfortunately, probably the first big risk he took he got out but another day he hits that for six and he's away.'

Glenn Maxwell

'We had a point to prove to beat this side. They are playing really good cricket in the two games. We came with intent. The opening partnership was outstanding. It was the perfect game for us. We were very professional again and that pleases you as a captain.'

Virat Kohli

## KEY NUMBER

# 352

Australia conceded their highest total bowling first in a World Cup match

## ANALYSIS

MIKE ATHERTON

Making your way to the Pakistan Room in the great stand opposite the pavilion at the Oval, you do so down a narrow corridor framed with glorious old photographs, many reflecting the ground's rich history. One such shows street urchins in the 1930s giving each other a leg up to peer at the cricket over the wall on the Harleyford Road side of the ground. It is a beautiful if elegiac photograph of a time when the game was more a part of the national conversation than it is now.

As the biggest game of the World Cup so far began, a similar scene was taking place. Well, almost similar. A large group of Indian supporters were not keen on the leg up, but they were massed outside the gates that break up the bricked wall framing the Oval, peering for a glimpse of their heroes. With queues snaking around the ground, Richard Gould, the Surrey chief executive, could be seen chivvying supporters to an entrance where the waiting time to gain admittance was less problematic.

As a contest between two fierce rivals who have won the World Cup seven times between them, it felt like the grandest of occasions, and with more than 80 per cent of the tickets sold to Indian supporters, an Indian occasion

at that: the crowd was a sea of blue, with not much canary yellow on show, beyond 11 Australians on the field. They must have felt lonely out there, although when Virat Kohli exhorted India's supporters to clap rather than boo Steve Smith, when the Australia batsman was moved to the boundary edge, it appeared they had one ally in the ground.

So, there was no need for those ticketless spectators outside the ground to try to peer through the gates, all they had to do was listen. Every India boundary and wicket brought an explosion of noise, puncturing the constant drums and chanting, the first such coming in the fifth over, when Shikhar Dhawan leant on a cover drive from Pat Cummins for his first four. It was an early sign that it may be Dhawan's day and the opener did not disappoint.

Batting first, Kohli allowed us an opportunity to measure Australia's weakness. The new-ball pair of Mitchell Starc and Cummins are serious operators – Australia only sneaked out of a hole against West Indies at Trent Bridge because of Starc – but the drop-off in quality thereafter is significant. The absence of the overlooked Josh Hazlewood and the injured Jhye Richardson means that teams will eye the medium pace of Marcus Stoinis and the wrist spin of Adam Zampa, as India's batsmen did after a deliberate start.

With his flowing blond locks held in place by a black hairband, Zampa looks miscast as a sportsman. The 27-year-old had looked a little fragile under pressure against Afghanistan in Australia's opening match and his first two overs cost 18 runs yesterday, 50 coming from the six overs he was allowed. All told, these two conceded 112 runs in 13 overs with little threat until Stoinis strangled two wickets when the slog was on. Expensive yesterday, Starc shoulders a heavy burden in this team: if he does not take wickets with the new ball, Australia will be put under considerable pressure.

India's perceived weakness is in the middle order, but this was negated by the opening stand of 127 between Dhawan and Rohit Sharma. Instead, when Dhawan fell, heaving into the deep in the 37th over, Hardik Pandya was thrust up the order, much as England often do with Jos Buttler. Bristling with intent, the brutality of his hitting was startling and twice he nearly decapitated an Australia bowler on the follow-through. His hard-running, hard-hitting partnership with Kohli, worth 81 in 8.5 overs, was modern Indian cricket through and through – dynamic, powerful and showy.

The game, you sensed, once David Warner (enjoying an outrageous piece of fortune when his first ball from Jasprit Bumrah hit the stumps hard without dislodging the bails) and Aaron Finch had negotiated the new ball, would be decided by the contrast between Australia's change bowlers

and India's. Could Kuldeep Yadav and Yuzvendra Chahal, the wrist spinners, hold the line where Australia's had struggled? When Steve Smith, Australia's best player of spin, replaced Finch who was run out taking two to the deep, the game was on.

Kuldeep, the left-arm wrist spinner, was introduced in the 11th over, Chahal, the leg spinner, in the 18th. Bowling slightly quicker than when last seen in England last summer, Yadav's first five overs were economical enough, but it was Chahal, having switched ends after an exploratory three overs, who broke the partnership as a subdued Warner lifted a leg spinner into the deep. The rate was climbing. At the halfway mark, Australia needed almost nine runs an over and India's spinners had 11 overs remaining.

Kuldeep returned in the 30th over, with the run-rate a little under ten an over, which is just where any wrist spinner likes it. Conceding just two singles on his return, it kept climbing. With the spinners operating in tandem, India enjoyed a combination of control and threat that Australia lacked, and although both spinners were expensive in their final overs, by the time Bumrah, the No. 1 ranked ODI bowler, returned with six overs in the tank, the run-rate was almost out of control. It was time for that blast of noise again as Smith and Stoinis fell within three balls of each other, leaving Maxwell and Alex Carey too much to do.

Halfway through the second week, the competition has started to take shape. After India's belated entrance, all teams have now played at least two games and the four semi-finalists will come from England, India, Australia, New Zealand, Pakistan and West Indies. With Australia too reliant on their four champions – Smith, Warner, Starc and Cummins – India look a more powerful all-round side, with fewer weaknesses, and they remain the main threat to England. As the Oval rocked and swayed to thunderous noise, more than ever cricket felt like an Indian game.

## SOUTH AFRICA v WEST INDIES

*Monday, June 10*

*Rose Bowl, Southampton*

**South Africa 29–2**
*Match abandoned. South Africa (1pt), West Indies (1pt)*
**Toss** *West Indies*

## BANGLADESH v SRI LANKA

*Tuesday, June 11*

*County Ground, Bristol*

*Match abandoned without a ball bowled. Bangladesh (1pt), Sri Lanka (1pt)*
*No toss made*

# AUSTRALIA v PAKISTAN

.........................................

*Wednesday, June 12*

*County Ground, Taunton*

**Australia 307 all out** (49 overs) (Finch 82, Warner 107; Mohammad Amir 5-30)
**Pakistan 266 all out** (45.4) (Imam-ul-Haq 53; Cummins 3-33)
*Australia (2pts) won by 41 runs*
*Pakistan won toss*

JOHN WESTERBY

The previous time that David Warner had raised his bat on reaching three figures for Australia had come on the first day of the Ashes Test in Melbourne on Boxing Day 2017. Back then, he was the team's vice-captain to Steve Smith and opening the batting with Cameron Bancroft, a few months before all three were implicated in the ball-tampering scandal in Cape Town that would send a nation into a tailspin of soul searching, with Warner cast as the villain of the piece.

So yesterday, when he reached his first hundred since returning to the side after the expiry of a one-year ban from international cricket, a huge outpouring of emotion was uncorked. After edging Shaheen Afridi between the wicketkeeper and slip for four, Warner ran immediately towards the changing room – the players who had welcomed him back – kissed the badge on his helmet and glanced briefly to the skies. This was a moment he had feared – during his darkest periods,

the times of tearful apologies – that he would never experience again.

'There was always that in my mind,' the 32-year-old said of his absence. 'That's what drove me, to keep being fit, to keep scoring runs in T20 tournaments. Going through those tough times to put myself in the best position to come back to international cricket, I did everything I could.'

On a pitch tinged with green, in front of a raucous crowd dominated by Pakistan fans, his innings was key to Australia's third victory in four matches, an opening partnership of 146 in 22 overs with Aaron Finch paving the way to a total of 307, which would prove too many for Pakistan's skittish batsmen.

Warner's innings provided a swift riposte to concerns aroused during the previous game, his side's defeat by India on Sunday, that the need to curb the more combative elements of his personality may be compromising his aggression with the bat. His sluggish half-century at the Oval had put his side behind the clock, an accusation seldom levelled at Warner.

Yesterday, having worked with Justin Langer, the coach, and Ricky Ponting, the assistant, the crispness in his strokeplay had returned. There was an indication that his culpability in the run-out of Finch against India had played a part in the excessive restraint he had shown. 'He was really honest after the Oval, said he was playing more timid than normal,' Pat Cummins, the pace bowler, said. 'I know that run-out with Finchy knocked him around a bit.'

An indication, then, that Warner is desperate not to let down the team-mates who have readmitted him. 'We were so pumped for him,' Cummins said.

Along with the gratitude to his teammates, Warner reflected on the long months of his ban and paid tribute to his wife, Candice, who will arrive in the UK today with their two daughters. She is due to give birth to a third daughter on English soil later this month. 'The thing that kept me going was my wife and kids,' Warner said. 'She's disciplined, selfless, she got me out of bed a lot in those first 12 weeks, got me back running and training hard. I'm looking forward to seeing the kids and my wife.'

Unlike Smith and Bancroft, Warner chose not to give choreographed television interviews during his suspension. 'That was my thing,' he said. 'What was said was said back in those press conferences. I was just focused ahead.'

Warner was quickly into his stride, swivelling to pull from short of a length as Pakistan's pace bowlers failed to exploit the juice in the pitch.

Finch profited, too, from Pakistan's slapdash fielding, dropped at slip by Asif Ali off Wahab Riaz when he had made 30, going on to reach 82 from 84 balls before slicing Mohammad Amir to cover.

Warner, on 102, was also dropped by Asif, at third man, but that miss was less costly as he soon miscued to cover.

Amir, another player who knows about the perils of returning from a long ban, after his involvement in the spot-fixing scandal in 2010, bowled with greater penetration on his return to the attack, and his figures of five for 30 are the best of the tournament. Australia's reliance on Warner, Finch and Smith was clear again, as they slipped from 242 for three to 304 all out.

In their pursuit, Pakistan lost Fakhar Zaman early, upper-cutting to third man off Cummins, but Imam-ul-Haq consolidated, first in tandem with Babar Azam, then alongside Mohammad Hafeez. At the halfway point, Pakistan were 136 for two and set fair, needing a manageable 172 from the last 25 overs. But Pakistan's cricketers have a singular ingenuity for self-destruction.

Fifteen balls later, the game was as good as gone. Three wickets had fallen and their worryingly weak lower order was about to be exposed. Imam began the slide by gloving a short ball down the leg side from Cummins.

The next over was to be bowled by Finch, with his part-time left-arm spin, which had previously yielded the grand total of three wickets in 112 ODIs. The final ball of his over was a slow knee-high full toss on middle stump. Hafeez's eyes lit up like Zing bails and he dispatched the ball straight to deep square.

Cummins then made a quick ball jag back off the seam, taking Shoaib Malik's inside edge, and suddenly Pakistan were 147 for five. There was a highly entertaining late flurry from Wahab, but a clinical late burst from Mitchell Starc settled the issue, to the disappointment of Pakistan's voluble fans. The noise they made in Taunton, though, was merely a clearing of the throat before the meeting with India at Old Trafford on Sunday. They travel north in sore need of points, after one win from four games, if they are to retain hopes of making the semi-finals.

PLAYER OF THE MATCH:
*David Warner (Australia)*

## WHAT THEY SAID

'We made some runs and got starts but we've got to convert them and go long. If you want to win matches your top four must score runs.'

Sarfaraz Ahmed

'There's no doubt Australia batted well, but in the first 10-15 overs, we weren't able to pitch the ball up as consistently as we needed to. I think that might have been the difference between a score of 250-260, and the 300 plus they ended up getting.'

Mohammad Amir

'We don't really hear the boos when we're out there. We're out there to do a job. It's water off a duck's back. I've heard it my whole career. It eggs us on a lot and makes us knuckle down and try to score more runs if anything.'

David Warner

## KEY NUMBER

# 5-30
Mohammad Amir's best one-day international bowling figures

# INDIA v NEW ZEALAND

*Thursday, June 13*

*Trent Bridge*

*Match abandoned without a ball bowled.*
*India (1pt), New Zealand (1pt)*
**No toss made**

# JOFRA ARCHER PROFILE

OWEN SLOT

West Indies' loss is quite clearly England's gain. This is the narrative that home fans hope to see played out on Friday in Southampton when one of the rising stars of the game opens the England bowling against the team for whom, it seems, he was born and bred. It is also the conversation on the boundary of Jofra Archer's cricket club in Barbados: how could we have let the boy go?

It is a Wednesday, late afternoon, at the Wildey Cricket Club and the team, one of the best on the island, are training in the middle. We are just outside Bridgetown, the shadows are lengthening and on the concrete steps of a small stand, the older generation – ex-players, coaches – gather to watch, to share a beer and some memories. Archer, 24, is the new young superstar of England cricket, of world cricket, perhaps, and yet he was born here and grew up here. You will struggle to find anyone without an Archer story: when they saw him do this or that great feat. His first nine-wicket haul. The time he hit 86 batting at No. 9 to get his school team promoted to the first division of senior cricket. The days when he would hit sixes into the graveyard behind the school cricket ground and they said that Jofra was waking the dead. England haven't worked out what a good batsman he is yet, they say here. And wouldn't it be great if he was doing all that for us?

'You always preferred playing a game with him rather than facing him in the nets,' Pedro Graves, his former captain, says, grimacing, laughing. 'What you see now is what he did then.' He means the short, easy run-up and then the surprising pace. 'Really deceptive. Facing him was a challenge.'

This is another of his coaches, Corey Yearwood, from his first club, Pickwick, remembering the time he let loose a 'small, bony' 16-year-old Archer on Shane Shillingford, a West Indies Test player, in the nets: 'Shane said to me afterwards, "It is unbelievable that his small frame could bowl that pace. This guy is going to play for the West Indies."' It wasn't only Shillingford who thought that. The young man smashing the ball about here in the middle of the Wildey pitch is Jerome Jones and when he is done, he recalls how the international dream was one that he and Archer shared.

Archer and Jones go back to their early teens as schoolmates at Christchurch Foundation School together. It wasn't just those two, though, they had an extraordinary group. The great Joel Garner was also at Foundation, four decades earlier, but the Archer generation was a real cohort of talent. Jones would go on to play for West Indies Under-19, another team-mate Aaron Jones, primarily a batsman, would go on to play for Barbados and then the United States. Two years below was Zachary McCaskie, who played for Barbados Under-19, and would open the batting for Foundation with Archer.

'He loved batting,' McCaskie says. He, too, is training here at Wildey, still trying to follow his old school-mate to the top of the game.

Foundation at that time was that special rare thing, a hotbed of talent, where a group of unusually gifted young men happened to coincide and spur each other on to greater things. They were the best school in the country. 'We won everything together,' Jones says. 'Won under-13s, under-15s, under-19s, the lot.'

It was only in their final two years, though, that Archer and Jones formed the deadliest bowling attack in school cricket. Until then, Archer could not get to the front of the attack. He bowled leg breaks, batted, kept wicket. Then, in their final two years as a pair, they just took off.

Together, they were selected for Barbados. In the under-19 regional tournament, against the other islands, they spurred each other on farther. 'When I saw him take a wicket,' Jones recalls, 'I'd be fired up: I've got to take one now.'

Jones relished Archer's aggression. 'As far as I can remember, every game we played in that regional tournament, he hit someone on the head, at least one player on every team. And if not the head, the toe,' he says.

'It really started kicking in when we both made that under-19 team, especially how well we bowled in tandem. In most games, after ten overs, we'd have at least three or four wickets down, not much more than 30 runs. We loved the chemistry between us. We always used to tell each other that we would play for West Indies together.'

Except Jones is here at Wildey and Archer is the latest star in a different country altogether.

How did he get there? There are three key turning points in the road.

# THE INSPIRATIONAL STEPFATHER

The first key turn was the one made by his mother, Joelle. His father, Frank, is English, which is how Archer gets his English passport. When Archer was nine, Joelle introduced into his life a cricket nut who would later become his stepfather.

This is Patrick Waithe. He is an accidents and complaints officer with the Barbados bus company, though his passion is still keeping wicket for his local team, Sunrise. He also coaches on the junior programme at Pickwick. In his schooldays, Archer would cycle almost every day after school to Pickwick for an extra nets session with Waithe. Even that wasn't enough, though, so the pair of them dug a wicket out of the rubble in the yard by their house so that they could carry on when they got home. Waithe reckons that Archer has played cricket, in some form, on most days of his life.

One thing almost everyone mentions about Archer is his very genuine love for the game. 'If you were playing cricket on the moon, he'd be there,' Dennis Osbourne, one of his school coaches, says.

Without particularly intending to, Waithe nurtured this appetite. 'Whenever I'd go to play,' Waithe says, 'I'd take him too.'

Archer would seek out games with other children outside the boundary ropes.

'He'd always bowl them out first,' Waithe says. That way, he had earned the opportunity to bat. And he'd often bat until the match was done.

You wonder, then, in which of the two the love of cricket runs deeper – the father figure or the stepson. Waithe is often tuned into BBC Radio Sussex to follow Archer's county games. Archer's debut for Sussex happened to be against Pakistan.

'I still have the videos of that game,' he says. 'They took five wickets in the first innings and Jofra got four of them.'

## BANNED FROM BOWLING FAST

The second turning point was Christ Church Foundation School and not just the standard of cricket there, or the elite peer group in which Archer happened to find himself but, primarily, because of the coaches who banned him from bowling.

Jones always knew that Archer had the arm to bowl pace. 'When we didn't have classes,' he says, 'we'd go on the hard court and play tapeball [a taped-up tennis ball] and Jofra used to bowl really fast.' To be accurate, the coaches did not completely ban him from bowling in matches, they just limited him to leg breaks. They wouldn't unleash his pace bowling because they thought he chucked it.

'Misery. Total misery' is how Nhamo Winn, the head coach, recalls Archer's initial response to the decision. 'Obviously he was frustrated because in his opinion he wasn't throwing, but in everyone else's opinion he was,' Jones recalls with some amusement. Archer would take out his frustration on his team-mates in the nets and they would rib him in return. 'We'd be, "Ah Jofra, you can only hit us because you are throwing."'

Winn set about coaching him out of it. 'Jofra listened,' Winn says. 'He was very coachable. We went through footage. We broke down his action and did a lot of remedial work, getting his arm coming over and keeping out the kink. We'd train four days a week. There was a lot of growth, very quickly.'

Archer is now widely admired for his smooth bowling action. This is where he was taught it. When he was 15, Winn finally felt confident enough to unleash his new pace bowler on the world. 'I'm not sure if it was the first or second time he did bowl pace,' Jones recalls. 'He took nine wickets.' And thus was the Jones–Archer bowling attack formed.

Together they blew away their contemporaries, first in Barbados and then on the opposing islands. In that under-19 regional tournament, when they led the Barbados attack, Archer was the highest wicket-taker in the competition. Together, again, they were then selected for West Indies Under-19 to play Bangladesh. From those highs came the third, crucial turning point in his career.

# A LIFE-CHANGING SNUB

After their success in the under-19 regional tournament, it was assumed that Archer and Jones would go to the 2014 Under-19 Cricket World Cup. There was general shock, then, when the squad was announced; Jones was selected and Archer was not.

'It was weird,' McCaskie says. 'The other fast bowlers weren't better than him. At the beginning, he really, really wanted to play for the West Indies. After being disappointed, his heart's desire changed and it became just a matter of playing international cricket.'

This sole selection decision changed the course of Archer's life. He had an offer to play in England, so he took that instead. Waithe says: 'Things weren't happening for him here so we said, "Give it two years in England and see how it works out."' He went to Sussex and played for Middleton-on-Sea. On days off, he would hang out with Akeem Jordan, another Wildey player, who was on a contract with Slinfold, another Sussex club. It became apparent that his sights had shifted.

'He used to say that if he got the opportunity, he would now play for England,' Jordan recalls. 'He'd been so confident that he was going to make the Under-19 World Cup team and when he didn't, it crushed him, you could see it, his whole face and emotions just changed.'

Yet it is not as though he arrived in England and the good times immediately rolled. His first two years at Middleton were hampered by a back injury, his contribution was severely limited and he was more of a batsman than a bowler. Waithe says: 'There were times when my wife and I would be lying in bed saying, "We just want him to have him a chance."' When he came home after the second Middleton season, he went so far as to pick up a form to stay in Barbados and go to university instead. 'He was bluffing,' Waithe says. What he really wanted was a third year in England. He persuaded his parents to let him go back one more time. Then, finally, it all happened; Archer started the season with Horsham and finished in the Sussex first-team. And here we are, now, his first England game versus West Indies only a few days away.

# THE ONE THAT GOT AWAY

Here on the boundary at Wildey, they all wish it was the other way round. Of course they do. Yet they do not begrudge Archer; they could hardly be prouder of him. Yes, there are some on this island who do begrudge him but they are hard to find. They have neither the temperament here, nor the media, to whip up antipathy.

When he came back to visit his old school one time, Osbourne remembers trying to persuade him to stick with West Indies because he would have a longer career.

'That was just my personal view,' he says, though he, too, is deeply proud of Archer, even if he did go the other way.

Osbourne also recalls the time that Archer returned after his first season away, to practise with the school team.

'He was switch-hitting the ball over this building,' he says. 'That was phenomenal because when he left school, he didn't have that in his repertoire. Then you realise: this boy is exposed to a professional set-up.'

This is also the conversation on the Wildey boundary. Here, the best players on the island are practising after work. They are on a single net constructed in the middle of the pitch and they have to stop when it gets dark because there are no floodlights.

Jones and McCaskie say that Archer is their inspiration, the evidence that they, too, can still reach the top. Yet if Archer had never gone abroad, would he still be here with them? Where would his game have gone if he had not had the opportunities that a different cricket economy can afford: full-time cricket, floodlights, indoor nets, the coaching? 'It's true what Jofra says,' Osbourne concludes. 'England is where he got his opportunity. England have done well for him.'

'It wasn't that he was turning his back on the West Indies,' Waithe says. 'It was more that he wanted to pursue a dream of playing international cricket. And this was an option.'

Waithe also says that the West Indies never actually tried to persuade him not to take it.

Their loss is England's gain.

# ENGLAND v WEST INDIES

..............................................

*Friday, June 14*

## *Rose Bowl, Southampton*

**West Indies 212 all out** (44.4 overs)
(Pooran 63; Archer 3-30, Wood 3-18)
**England 213-2** (33.1 overs)
(Root 100 not out)
*England (2pts) won by eight wickets*
*Toss England*

### STEVE JAMES

Another strong statement from England, a third victory from four matches, with the force of their message to the other teams diminished only slightly by injury concerns over Eoin Morgan, the captain, and, perhaps more worryingly, the opening batsman Jason Roy.

Morgan had a back spasm and Roy tightness in his left hamstring, but England still romped to victory with 16.5 overs remaining. That is a thrashing.

England were sharper at almost every juncture. Their bowlers – with Chris Woakes, Jofra Archer and Mark Wood outstanding – were far too smart and savvy for the one-dimensional West Indian batting. Then Joe Root, opening in place of Roy and having already taken two wickets, gave yet another one-day international batting masterclass with an unbeaten century as West Indies demonstrated equal inflexibility with the ball.

Woakes, who was promoted to No. 3 having never previously batted above No. 7 in an ODI, made a composed 40,

dismissed with 14 required for victory. It was a rather clear reminder of England's depth.

Roy was injured as early as the eighth over of the day, pulling up and grabbing the top of his hamstring after going to chase a Chris Gayle slap over cover. Morgan was just moving to back up a throw in the 40th over when he halted in obvious discomfort. Like Roy, he left the field immediately.

However, neither of these injuries disrupted England's progress. That blip of a defeat by Pakistan 12 days ago appears a distant memory. The top four in the table of New Zealand, England, Australia and India are beginning to establish themselves and pull away from the pack.

With all the rain that had fallen in Southampton in the game's build-up, it had been a good toss to win and Morgan had no hesitation in inserting West Indies.

Wood passed his late fitness test, meaning that England were unchanged from the victory over Bangladesh in Cardiff last Saturday and Moeen Ali missed out again.

Woakes was quite superb with the new ball, bowling two maidens in his five-over spell and dismissing the left-handed Evin Lewis with a yorker.

West Indies' innings was always going to be about Gayle. He made a slow start, with his side eight for one after five overs, but then decided to take on Archer, clubbing him for two consecutive fours. Archer responded by rapping the great man on the gloves with a quick short ball, and then on 15 Gayle was dropped by Wood at third man off Woakes.

Woakes is a mild-mannered man not prone to tantrums but this was probably as agitated as you will ever see him. Wood's effort in the end, diving bravely forwards, was commendable but he had not picked up the flight of the ball quickly enough and moved into position too late.

Gayle is not a man to whom second chances should be offered but here, for once, it did not matter, even though he did then strike Woakes for a glorious straight six. He had made 36 before he was unable to resist pulling a short ball from Liam Plunkett that landed in the hands of Jonny Bairstow at deep square leg.

Shai Hope, the No. 3, could not get going. His 11 runs occupied 30 balls before he was trapped leg-before by Wood. It needed a review but it was dead in front.

Wood's initial spell of four overs cost six runs before Nicholas Pooran and Shimron Hetmyer put on 89. Pooran looked the more certain of the two exciting left-handers, with Hetmyer swinging rather too often for too little reward before he succumbed to Root's off spin.

That it was Root's first ODI wicket since January last year says much but, with Adil Rashid still not quite himself, it was a wise decision by Morgan to use him. Even wiser when Root claimed a second wicket, from another return catch, this time from a knuckle ball that looked ugly and would have been a legside wide had Jason Holder not used his leading edge to gently lob the ball back to the bowler.

Andre Russell came in at No. 7 and slogged a few before being dropped by Woakes and then hitting Wood to the same fielder out in the deep on the leg side. Pooran's fine innings of 63 off 78 balls was ended when trying to avoid a wicked short ball from Archer that just flicked his gloves. Sheldon Cottrell was palpably leg-before first ball and then Carlos Brathwaite was out hooking at Archer too. Wood finished it off, bowling Shannon Gabriel, with five overs and two balls remaining of West Indies' innings.

England needed 213 and the West Indian plan was obvious and fairly primitive. England had used the short ball effectively too but they had also done some investigations on a good length.

West Indies did not do that. It was either short or full and Bairstow and Root enjoyed the challenge. They cut, pulled and then drove handsomely. A couple of cover drives from Root in particular were jaw-droppingly good. One Bairstow on-driven four off Oshane Thomas was simply gorgeous.

The running between the wickets was excellent too; indeed no English pairing run as well as these two Yorkshiremen.

After ten overs and the first powerplay England were 62 without loss, compared with West Indies' 41 for one at the same point, and it was the fourth time in four matches that England had passed 60 in that initial ten-over period.

Bairstow had a nasty moment on 27 when hit by a Russell bouncer. Both men, batsman and bowler, went down. Russell, so obviously not fit for this match with his long-standing knee problem, limped off, while Bairstow continued after the lengthy, mandatory concussion test.

The sun was shining by now, the dark cloud cover of the morning burnt off, and the pitch, devoid of its earlier moisture, looked a picture.

Ugliness descended upon the vista only when Bairstow first hoiked Gabriel away on the leg side for four and then to the next ball gave himself room to upper-cut but could do so only straight to third man. He was gone for 45.

Woakes entered at No. 3; a short leg was posted and the short/full stuff continued. He was not deterred, straight-driving Gabriel for four before a pulled boundary that was so dismissive it could have been played by Root himself.

Root passed his century, his second of this World Cup, off 93 balls. He is simply in supreme form, his balance and weight distribution so precise that he is batting with a fluency that is a joy to behold.

He is now the leading run-scorer in the tournament and England are looking like the leading side that their favourites tag suggests.

PLAYER OF THE MATCH:
*Joe Root (England)*

## WHAT THEY SAID

'Joe is the glue that holds everything together. He's such an important player for us, it's exceptional to watch.'

Eoin Morgan

'There were a few careless shots, if we had hung in a bit longer we could've gone deeper and got some more in the end.'

Jason Holder

## KEY NUMBER

### 2

Joe Root became the second England batsman after Kevin Pietersen to score two centuries in the same World Cup

# sport

## Hot streak

Root's second century of World Cup takes England to easy win, but Roy and captain Morgan suffer injury scares
Pages 2-5

Mark Wood, inset, comforts Roy as the opener leaves the field with a hamstring injury before Morgan suffered a back spasm while fielding

JAMES MARSH/BPI/REX

# England battle into last 16

Taylor scores to beat Argentina 1-0 and seal place in World Cup knockout stages Pages 6, 7

## ANALYSIS

MIKE ATHERTON

Only time will tell whether England have seen the last of Christopher Henry Gayle, Jamaica's master blaster and the self-styled Universe Boss. Unless these two teams meet in the knockout stage then they will not have the dubious pleasure of facing him again and on the evidence of West Indies' worryingly listless performance at Southampton, further progress for Jason Holder's team is highly unlikely.

If so, England's bowlers, as well as bowlers everywhere, will breathe a sigh of relief, this being Gayle's international swansong. He came into the match averaging a little over 50 in one-day cricket against England, having taken them for four hundreds over the years, so the bowlers will feel that they escaped lightly in the 13 overs that he lasted, his flame flickering all too briefly for West Indies to post a challenging score.

Unable to entertain for very long with the bat, Gayle was reduced to entertaining in other ways as the game drifted to an uncompetitive end, clowning around in the field and with the ball. By the time his gentle off spin was called upon, the game was over as a contest, with Joe Root showing again there is room in the 50-over game for touch and timing as much as there is for the brute force of Gayle and his ilk. Root played beautifully and is now the leading runscorer in the tournament, with 279.

On a disappointing day as far as the spectacle was concerned, the game was at its most competitive in the morning when Gayle was at the crease, threatening to cut loose and presenting an excellent test of Jofra Archer's temperament and skill with the new ball.

If it ended a score draw between them, then Archer had the last laugh, returning to take the wicket of the top scorer, Nicholas Pooran, before cleaning up the tail, having been brought back by Eoin Morgan with that very intention – Morgan's last act as captain before a back spasm cut short his day in the field.

Morgan's first act was winning the toss, an important one it was too, given the rain that had fallen in Southampton and the early cloud cover. As Gayle stood in the middle of the pitch visualising, as is his wont before the first ball, muscled and dreadlocked, it was a very different-looking batsman from the one who first appeared against England almost two decades ago in ODI cricket.

That was against an England team at Lord's in 2000 that included Alec Stewart, Graeme Hick, Darren Gough and Graham Thorpe, now England's batting coach. The game also included Corey Collymore, now West Indies' bowling coach, so Gayle's longevity has been remarkable and he is one of only two players in the competition who played international cricket before the turn of the millennium. The game has changed fundamentally since then, as has Gayle's batting and physique, although he wound back the clock for his first run, a sprinted single to mid-off after nine balls without scoring.

It was an eagerly anticipated contest between Gayle and Archer, who seemed to suffer no nerves playing against his countrymen. Archer let fly a rapid bouncer over Gayle's right shoulder that brought an involuntary flinch from the batsman, whose attempted pull shot to the next ball flew to the fine-leg boundary off an inside edge, the kind of error that quick bowling induces. Another rib tickler followed and Gayle sought refuge at the other end, where Chris Woakes presented a more traditionally English-style challenge.

Woakes ought to have dismissed Gayle in the seventh over, when an attempted smear through the leg side flew to third man, where Mark Wood spilt a catch diving forward. Woakes' reaction, unusually animated for him, reflected the importance of the wicket.

Gayle looked intent on profiting from Wood's error. In Woakes' next over, he carted a short ball for four and then showed his intelligence, gambling that Woakes would respond with a fuller-length ball. Woakes did; Gayle advanced and, with a straight bat, planted it half-a-dozen rows back into the crowd over long-on. His colleagues struggled to come to terms with the lively conditions early on, so that Gayle scored 33 of the first 41 runs in the opening ten overs.

It was the change to Liam Plunkett that brought England their most prized wicket. Plunkett has profited more than any other seamer since the 2015 World Cup in the middle phase of the innings, and often through banging the ball into the surface and encouraging the batsmen to play square of the wicket. That tactic is a profitable one at Southampton, with its long square boundaries, and was profitable again as Gayle's attempted pull shot reached only as far as Jonny Bairstow in the deep.

After Gayle was out, there was only one decent partnership for West Indies, that between the two young, dashing left-handers, Pooran and Shimron Hetmyer, the torch having passed from old to new. If either of them achieves a fraction of what Gayle has in international cricket, or lasts half as long, they may retire happy men.

# AUSTRALIA v SRI LANKA

......................................................

*Saturday, June 15*

*The Oval*

**Australia 334-7** (50 overs)
(Finch 153, Smith 73)
**Sri Lanka 247 all out** (45.5 overs)
(Karunaratne 97, Kusal Perera 52;
Starc 4-55, Richardson 3-47)
*Australia (2pts) won by 87 runs*
Toss *Sri Lanka*

SIMON WILDE, *SUNDAY TIMES*
CRICKET CORRESPONDENT

If the mark of a quality side is winning matches from difficult positions, then Australia are building up a formidable head of steam at this World Cup. They were staring down the barrel against West Indies and Pakistan before Mitchell Starc killed off their run-chases, and it was Australia's loping left-arm fast bowler who again did the business yesterday as Sri Lanka's brave pursuit of what would have been a record World Cup chase died a late death at The Oval. The result hoisted the holders to the top of the group table.

Starc finished with four for 55, giving him figures for the tournament of 13 wickets at 19.15 apiece. He was, lest we forget, the player of the tournament at the last World Cup, when he took 22 wickets at just 10.18. He is a master at targeting the stumps when batsmen are swinging from the hip in the closing stages.

Nonetheless, the fight shown by Sri Lanka made their official protests to the ICC last week about unfavourable pitch conditions in their earlier matches look a little foolish. But the stand-off continued last night after they refused to fulfil their media obligations. 'The ICC is taking up the matter with them,' a spokesman said.

Australia are probably the least popular team at this World Cup. It could be the sandpaper row, the fact that they are serial killers of other people's dreams of lifting the trophy, or the old-fashioned way they go about playing 50-overs cricket. But you cannot fault their resourcefulness. They have not even won a toss yet.

With both teams keen to bowl first, they posted a testing 334 for seven built around a monumental innings of 153 from 132 balls by their captain Aaron Finch, who thereby equalled the best score at this World Cup set by Jason Roy, a teammate of his at Surrey, and his personal best in this format. Even so, they needed a late burst of magic from Glenn Maxwell with 46 not out from 25 balls to lift them into what they would have considered safe territory. No side has won a World Cup match chasing more than 329.

Where would Australia have been without the stardust of the oft-marginalised Maxwell, with his runs, ten canny overs for 46 runs and sharp catch at backward point to remove Sri Lanka's captain and top-scorer Dimuth Karunaratne for 97? He should have had Karunaratne lbw on 50 but umpire Richard Illingworth turned down the appeal and Australia had already burnt their review. Replays showed it should have been out.

The game provided a wonderful climax to The Oval's involvement in the tournament – five games blessed with good weather, high scores, great drama and passionately engaged crowds. Sri Lanka's fans, frustrated by two washouts in Bristol, dug out their flags and rediscovered their voice.

Their team, who will go into the game with England on Friday in better spirits after this performance, had Australia rocking with the way they set off in pursuit of the target. Karunaratne and Kusal Perera propelled them to 87 at the end of the first power-play, the best by any side at the World Cup so far, and at the 30-over mark Sri Lanka were 176 for two. Australia were 159 for two at the same point. Even before Karunaratne fell in the 33rd over, Sri Lanka were losing momentum against a combination of Maxwell's spin and Jason Behrendorff's high-bouncing left-arm pace, a fact highlighted by Karunaratne hitting only two fours off the 65 balls he faced after reaching his half-century.

Sure enough, the pressure of needing 131 from the last 15 overs told on the later batsmen. Angelo Mathews was bounced out by Pat Cummins – no surprise there – and then Starc, already with the wicket of Kusal Perera in his pocket, returned to sweep aside three more batsmen in the space of six balls.

What do you say about Australia's innings? They are playing a style of ODI cricket that stubbornly flouts the modern conventions of ultra-aggression but so far it has worked despite the obvious limitations. David Warner laid another solid foundation with Finch but again batted without verve, a man unsure if the world has yet forgiven him. Dhananjaya de Silva's off-spin did most to keep them quiet, conceding 20 runs from seven overs before Finch saw to it that as many came from his eighth.

Usman Khawaja looked stodgily out of place at No. 3, so too Shaun Marsh at No. 6. Between their sclerotic contributions Finch, who brought up his 14th ODI hundred off 97 balls with a six in the 33rd over, shared a stand of 173 with the impishly busy Steve Smith that was the highest of the World Cup, and Australia were eyeing a total north of 350.

But as happened against Pakistan at Taunton, the final push for runs went off like a whoopee cushion. Finch and Smith departed within six balls of each other and although Maxwell then plundered 22 off the 45th over from Nuwan Pradeep, there were no further boundaries until Maxwell struck the last ball of the innings for four. Australia added only 32 runs after the 45th over; at Taunton they managed just 16. Both times, though, they won the game in other areas.

..................................................

PLAYER OF THE MATCH:
*Aaron Finch (Australia)*

# AFGHANISTAN v SOUTH AFRICA

......................................................

*Saturday, June 15*

*Sophia Gardens, Cardiff (day-night)*

**Afghanistan 125 all out** (34.1 overs)
(Morris 3-13, Tahir 4-29)
**South Africa 131-1** (28.4 overs)
(De Kock 68)
*South Africa (2pts) won by nine wickets (DLS Method)*
**Toss** *South Africa*

ROB COLE

He may be the oldest player to feature for South Africa in the ICC World Cup, but Imran Tahir continues to prove he is still one of their greatest one-day players.

The 40-year-old spin bowler did what his side's pace attack couldn't do in Cardiff and stun the Afghanistan batsmen in what was a decisive game for the Proteas. After three successive defeats, and a washed-out game against the West Indies, it was win or bust for the South Africans, and with Tahir leading the way they won by nine wickets to move on to three points after five games.

Skipper Faf du Plessis had talked coming into the game about not carrying 'the ghosts of the past with us'. Now, at least, they have something to shoot for over their next four matches.

The only problem is that even though there is plenty of optimism after breaking their duck it was against the only team below them in the table. Now they have to find a way to get past New Zealand, Pakistan, Sri Lanka and Australia if they are to reach the semi-finals.

It may be a long shot, but with the tormenting Tahir in their ranks they will at least have a potent weapon to use. Having become the first spin bowler to open the bowling in a World Cup game against England, he used his well disguised googly to take a wicket with his first ball and unleash his trademark long-run celebration.

After that there was no stopping him as he took four for 29 in seven destructive overs to rip the heart out of the Afghanistan batting line-up.

'We prepared well for this match, were really up for it and we are really pleased to have put out that performance. There is a lot of confidence in the side, but we have to show it in the middle,' said Tahir, voted man of the match.

'We know there are a lot of big games ahead, but we are really up for the challenge. We have to carry this form with us to Birmingham next week.'

Du Plessis won the toss and had no hesitation in putting in the Afghans on a wicket that had plenty of grass cover and was supposed to give his seamers plenty of assistance. But Kagiso Rabada and Beuran Hendricks weren't able to make the early breakthrough and Hazratullah Zazai and Noor Ali Zadran were able to put on 39 before the former fell to a catch in the deep off Rabada.

The 50 came up in 14 overs before Chris Morris trapped Rahmat Shah lbw for six. The score moved on to 69 for two from 20 overs before the second of two rain breaks set in.

The first hadn't upset the batsmen, lasting a mere 25 minutes, but the second delay forced the players off the field for more than an hour and reduced the game to 48 overs.

When they returned it was carnage. Three balls after the resumption Andile Phehlukwayo had Hashmatullah Shahidi caught at first slip before Tahir took centre stage.

He bowled the stubborn Noor Ali for 32 with his first ball and also sent back Asghar Afghan in his first over. The Afghans lost four wickets in 13 balls after coming back out and the game was virtually over there and then.

Rashid Khan steered his side into three figures with a cameo innings of 35, which featured 14 in five balls off Tahir before he holed out on the boundary with the final delivery of the over. Having been 69 for two in 20 overs, the Afghans were all out for 125, leaving South Africa to chase an adjusted winning total of 127.

It was never going to cause them too much trouble and Hashim Amla and Quinton de Kock worked their way to a century opening stand in 23 overs before De Kock was caught by Nabi on 68. That was 104 for one and Phehlukwayo (17 not out) helped the out-of-sorts Amla (41 off 83) complete a nine-wicket victory in less than 29 overs.

PLAYER OF THE MATCH:
*Imran Tahir (South Africa)*

## WHAT THEY SAID

'Today we put our pegs in the ground.'

Faf du Plessis

'We know we've lost, we haven't played our best cricket but the vibe has never changed. The vibe has been gun. It's a World Cup, so what aren't you happy about?'

Chris Morris

# INDIA v PAKISTAN

*Sunday, June 16*

*Old Trafford*

**India 336-5** (50 overs) (Rahul 57, Sharma 140, Kohli 77; Mohammad Amir 3-47)
**Pakistan 212-6** (40 overs) (Fakhar Zahman 62)
*India (2pts) won by 89 runs*
*(DLS Method)*
**Toss** *Pakistan*

JOHN WESTERBY

It is not every World Cup game in which a detailed game plan is laid out for a team by the nation's prime minister. This fixture is never just any old cricket match, though, and Imran Khan, as a former World Cup-winning captain, has rather more claim than most prime ministers to lend informed advice to the Pakistan captain.

Perhaps Sarfaraz Ahmed would have been wise, then, to follow the suggestion offered by his illustrious predecessor, made on social media before the game, to bat first upon winning the toss, rather than presenting India's gifted batsmen with the opportunity to indulge themselves on an excellent pitch. Pakistan's captain could only watch ruefully at close quarters, from behind the stumps, as Rohit Sharma purred his way to a wonderful 140, joining forces with KL Rahul and Virat Kohli to send their massed ranks of supporters into raptures. They guided India to 336 for five, well beyond the reach of their fierce rivals, retaining their unbeaten record in the tournament.

When Pakistan won the World Cup in 1992, they made a remarkable recovery from three defeats and a washout in their first five matches to win their next five games. The side led by Sarfaraz have made an identical start, but they look ill-equipped to stage a similar resurgence, their bowling over-reliant on Mohammad Amir, their batting and fielding scruffy.

Imran, it seems likely, will soon be able to turn his attention back to his attempts to resume talks with Narendra Modi, his Indian counterpart, to ensure that the fragile relations between the countries do not deteriorate further.

In the heaving stands at Old Trafford, the support was boisterously good-natured, a full house of 23,500 as colourful and passionate as expected, despite the sporadic breaks for rain. The blue shirts of India and the flags of green, white and saffron comfortably outnumbered the bottle-green and white of Pakistan, mirroring the balance of power out in the middle. India's ascendancy was clear from the early stages, once Sharma and Rahul, opening in place of the injured Shikhar Dhawan, had made a watchful start before going through the gears in an opening stand of 136 in 23.5 overs.

Sharma may not receive the Bollywood-style adulation afforded to teammates such as Kohli and MS Dhoni, but the broad-shouldered right-hander is an undisputed great of the one-day game. Batting in the most pressurised position in the team, he is a model of unhurried consistency, adding a century yesterday to previous innings in the tournament of 122 not out against South Africa and 57 against Australia. It said everything about his appetite for runscoring that he was disgusted with himself when he gave away his wicket on 140 with 11.4 overs remaining.

This hunger explains why, of the eight double centuries made in ODIs, Sharma has three of them. After reaching his 24th one-day century from 85 balls, he had designs on a fourth double hundred yesterday until he scooped Hasan Ali straight to short fine leg.

The anger upon his dismissal, smashing bat against pad, was partly because he had made a rare departure from his usual orthodoxy. In terms of his stroke-play and the manner in which he paces an innings, there is a reassuringly traditional look to Sharma's batting.

He was circumspect against the new ball, driving Hasan handsomely through mid-off to settle the nerves, then accelerating by pulling clinically from just short of a length and cutting one short ball from Hasan gloriously over point for six.

It did not hinder India's batsmen that two of Pakistan's most dangerous bowlers, Amir and Wahab Riaz, both left-arm seamers, were each given two warnings from the umpires for running on the pitch. Still, Pakistan played a large part in their own downfall, as so often, with some slipshod fielding.

They wasted a golden chance to end India's opening stand when Sharma and Rahul found themselves in the same half of the pitch, only for Fakhar Zaman to throw to the wrong end.

Once Rahul had driven to extra cover, Kohli soon found his fluency, driving with astonishing power through extra cover, and he too was eyeing a century when he departed in curious fashion, caught behind hooking at Amir. Although Kohli walked without waiting for the umpire's decision, television replays showed no sign of an edge. He later seemed to examine the possibility that the noise came from his bat handle.

Where India's batsmen had been so resolute and disciplined, Pakistan's frailty was soon revealed by the soft dismissal of Imam-ul-Haq. When Bhuvneshwar Kumar limped off after bowling four balls of his third over, Kohli threw the ball to Vijay Shankar to finish it off.

Shankar is no mug with the ball but he had taken only two ODI wickets before this unexpected chance to turn his arm over. Significantly slower than Kumar, his loosener was full and straight and somehow Imam played all around it, palpably leg-before.

Fakhar and Babar Azam then added 104 in 19 overs before Kuldeep Yadav highlighted another area of India's superiority. For Pakistan, Shadab Khan, the leg spinner, had taken none for 61, while Imad Wasim, the left-arm finger spinner, had been more economical but remains a defensive option rather than a wicket-taker.

In three balls Kuldeep, the left-arm wrist spinner, had bowled Babar by turning one sharply back between bat and pad, then had Fakhar caught at short fine leg from a top-edged sweep. When Mohammad Hafeez clipped Hardik Pandya to deep square leg and Shoaib Malik edged the next ball on to his stumps, the outcome was beyond doubt.

After seven attempts, Pakistan have still to beat their rivals in a World Cup contest and yesterday they did not even come close.

PLAYER OF THE MATCH:
*Rohit Sharma (India)*

## WHAT THEY SAID

'Whenever we play Pakistan, it's always like that, but we are here on a mission. Our focus is to make sure we accomplish that mission. All the outside talk will keep happening, but for us it's just a focus on the job.'

Rohit Sharma

'We're not playing well in all the departments; fielding, bowling and batting.'

Sarfaraz Ahmed

## KEY NUMBER

## II,000

On 57, Virat Kohli became the fastest man to score 11,000 one-day international runs

# BANGLADESH v WEST INDIES

*Monday, June 17*

*County Ground, Taunton*

**West Indies 321-8** (50 overs) (Lewis 70, Hope 96, Hetmyer 50; Mohammad Saifuddin 3-72, Mustafizur Rahman 3-59)
**Bangladesh 322-3** (41.3 overs) (Shakib Al Hasan 124 not out, Liton Das 94 not out)
*Bangladesh (2pts) won by seven wickets*
*Toss Bangladesh*

ELGAN ALDERMAN

After the greatest rainstorms in World Cup history has come one of its greatest knocks in one of its greatest chases. Shakib Al Hasan is regarded by many as Bangladesh's finest cricketer and an unbeaten 124 in his country's highest successful one-day international pursuit, completed with 51 balls to spare, has done nothing to dissuade them.

This was no chanceless innings. West Indies' short-ball tactics provoked risky shots from the Bangladesh batsmen. Shortly after he passed fifty, Shakib twice top-edged pull shots towards fine leg, one falling short of Shimron Hetmyer, the second landing between Shai Hope and Shannon Gabriel. West Indies were unlucky but not blameless, conceding 25 wides.

It may prove to have been a coming-of-age for Liton Das, 24, whose unbeaten 94 off 69 balls on his World Cup debut was vital. He and Shakib added an unbroken 189 for the fourth wicket from 135 balls. Shakib's near misses should not detract from an innings of nerve and class. Already the world's leading all-rounder in ODIs – he dismissed Evin Lewis and Nicholas Pooran with his left-arm spin – he is now the highest run-scorer in this tournament, having made 75, 64 and 121 in his first three matches.

West Indies were asked to bat and scored 321 for eight, 40 to 50 runs short according to Jason Holder, their captain. Chris Gayle and Andre Russell faced 15 balls between them without scoring, leaving Taunton's short boundaries uncharted; it was left to Hope's 96 off 121 balls and quickfire fifties from Lewis and Hetmyer to set a target.

'At the end of the first innings, in the dressing room, no one felt this would be tough – everyone was comfortable, everyone was chilling,' Shakib said. By the end of the match, he and Liton had their feet up with a cigar.

Soumya Sarkar was the aggressor as Bangladesh took 70 runs from the first powerplay. His departure brought together Tamim Iqbal and Shakib, Bangladesh's two highest run-scorers in ODIs. Tamim stood, Tamim delivered, not always – but usually and most beautifully – through cover. Shakib made backward point his own, though his wagon wheel showed a mastery of the entire ground.

They were well set at 121 for one in the 18th over when Sheldon Cottrell continued his reinvention as a world-class fielder. He gathered Tamim's straight drive off his own bowling and hurled it back, somehow missing the batsman and hitting the stumps with Tamim just short of his ground. Alongside his brilliant boundary catch to dismiss Australia's Steve Smith, Cottrell is compiling quite the World Cup portfolio.

Tamim's exit, followed by Mushfiqur Rahim's departure for one, made West Indies favourites but thereafter they were resigned to defeat. Russell had knee trouble, his team-mates seemed lost; they soon did. Shakib reached his hundred off 83 balls, Liton his fifty off 43 before hitting Gabriel for three successive sixes in the 38th over. West Indies' attack was understaffed: Darren Bravo had replaced Carlos Brathwaite and Russell could hardly move.

Bangladesh's fast start was at odds with how West Indies had begun the day. After Gayle was caught behind off Mohammad Saifuddin for a 13-ball duck, Hope and Lewis reached 32 for one after ten overs, the slowest opening powerplay of the tournament.

Hope picked up the pace throughout, falling four short of a century. 'It was good that he went deep but we probably could have asked him to show more intent,' Holder said. Others made contributions, strikingly Hetmyer, who deposited three sixes into the crowd en route to a fifty off 25 balls, the joint fastest of the tournament.

PLAYER OF THE MATCH:
*Shakib Al Hasan (Bangladesh)*

## WHAT THEY SAID

'Mindset is very important. At this level, in this atmosphere, mental strength is very helpful. Fitness is important too, but the more you can be courageous, everything clicks.'

Shakib Al Hasan

'We were probably 40-50 runs short. The wicket played really well but we could have been more disciplined with the ball and we let ourselves down in the field as well.'

Jason Holder

## KEY NUMBER

# 23

Shakib Al Hasan passed 6,000 runs in one-day internationals on 23

# ENGLAND v AFGHANISTAN

........................................................

*Tuesday, June 18*

*Old Trafford*

**England 397-6** (50 overs) (Bairstow 90, Root 88, Morgan 148; Dawlat Zadran 3-85, Gulbadin Naib 3-68)
**Afghanistan 247-8** (50 overs) (Hashmatullah Shahidi 76; Archer 3-52, Rashid 3-66)
*England (2pts) won by 150 runs*
**Toss** England

MIKE ATHERTON,
CHIEF CRICKET CORRESPONDENT

There comes a point in a player's career when he recognises the moment and senses his destiny. For Eoin Morgan, that time has come.

Given a hospital pass before the 2015 World Cup, England's resurrection in one-day cricket during the past four years carries Morgan's stamp above all, and he arrived at this year's competition determined not to miss what he sees as a once-in-a-lifetime opportunity to win the World Cup on home soil.

His determination has been plain to see. It was Morgan who cut through the nonsense surrounding Alex Hales on the eve of the tournament to say without equivocation that dropping the troubled Nottinghamshire batsman was the right thing to do. It is Morgan who continues to drive his team's vaulting ambition, scaling heights rarely seen when he eviscerated Afghanistan's

bowling attack with a blistering career-best one-day international hundred that included 17 sixes, more than anyone has hit in an ODI before.

To think that he came into the game under an injury cloud. It was still not certain shortly before the start of play that Morgan would be fit. He underwent a late fitness test for the back spasm that cut short his involvement in the last match, although there were no signs of discomfort when he arrived at the crease and set about dismantling Afghanistan's bowling.

It was the kind of situation – 164 for two with 20 overs remaining, time running out and wickets in hand – in which Jos Buttler has often been promoted up the order. Morgan may have felt that he had a point to prove to his own dressing room, to show them that the batsman who was once England's one-day outlier can still live with the power of the younger men.

The near-capacity crowd knew that they had witnessed something special when he walked off the ground a little over an hour and a quarter later having made 148 in 71 balls, and they roared him off as only an Old Trafford crowd can. Walking up the steps his poker face broke into the broadest of grins and he looked like a man who had not only enjoyed himself but surprised himself.

A measure of the brilliance of Morgan's innings could be seen in the glances, smiles and shakes of the head between the two men, Ben Stokes and Buttler, who were out in the middle. They are among the most destructive

# Sport

**Royal Ascot 2019**
Rob Wright's tips and the
best of the first day's action
Racing, 60-63

**England throw it away**
Red card and own goal cost
U21s after Foden's solo opener
Match report, page 66

# The six machine

## Captain Morgan breaks world record with 17 maximums in brutal innings of 148 as England beat Afghanistan

**Elizabeth Ammon**

Eoin Morgan led England to the top of the World Cup group table on a record-breaking day in Manchester as the hosts demolished Afghanistan by 150 runs. The England captain hit a career-best 148, including 17 sixes, that beat the record of 16 held by the West Indian Chris Gayle.

Morgan had recovered from the back spasm that he suffered during the win over West Indies in Southampton last week to play the innings of his life. "I would never have thought I could play a knock like that, I'm delighted," the captain, 32, said, adding that it felt "very weird" to have broken the record for number of sixes.

"It's something that I never thought I would do. It's a nice place to be but I'm probably just a target now for the other guys in our changing room to take down. The hundred I scored [off 57 balls] today is considered a slow one in our changing room. Guys talk about doing that all the time."

Describing the feeling of hitting
Continued on page 71

## Tour scare for Thomas

**Josh Burrows**

Team Ineos last night said they were optimistic Geraint Thomas would be fit to defend his Tour de France title next month despite crashing out of his final warm-up race, the Tour de Suisse.

The Welshman came off his bike shortly after an intermediate sprint on yesterday's fourth stage. Thomas's crash came less than a week after Chris Froome, his Team Ineos team-mate and one of the other favourites for the overall title when the Tour de France starts on July 6, suffered career-threatening fractures at the Critérium du Dauphiné, ruling him out of action for the foreseeable future.

Thomas, 33, was taken to hospital but Ineos said he had suffered only abrasions on his shoulder and a cut above his eye and the injuries were "unlikely" to keep him out of the Tour. Thomas
Continued on page 68

## Marler set for cup comeback

**Owen Slot, Alex Lowe**

Joe Marler could make a return to international rugby for this year's World Cup as he has been named in the England elite player squad for the summer.

Marler, 28, announced his retirement from the international game in September last year to considerable surprise. He had 59 England caps to his name and was regarded as essential to the team as one of the two best loosehead props in the country.

He said at the time that he was quitting international rugby due to the long periods of time he was required to spend away from home. However, the fact that he has been named in the elite player squad (EPS) confirms that he may yet make a comeback for the World Cup in Japan in the autumn. In
Continued on page 60

---

## Times Crossword 27,381

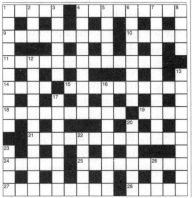

**ACROSS**

1 Seaman entering boozer to see what's afoot? (5)
4 Craftsman penning unlimited poems in rocker (9)
9 Small case for diamonds? (5,4)
10 Lustre perceived when heroin's injected (5)
11 Police officer probing one element of Labour opposition (13)
14 Party threatening to ditch leader (4)
15 Natural fibre, too much found in racket left on court (6,4)
18 Visual aids having setter long for correction? (10)
19 Pack animals to watch bears (4)
21 Dad recalled agent introducing one couple, fifty or so (13)
24 Senior retired Liberal in fashion again (5)
25 Almost complete backing for exhibit in church showing conversions? (9)
27 During many deliveries, Dr West stripped off outer garb (9)
28 Limit old women's fund (5)

**DOWN**

1 House group D? (10)
2 Exile's collar turned up (3)
3 Spanish fighter quickly ran mounted troops (6)
4 Canvasses on display, reputable Society taking the lead (6,3)
5 Matter bringing down temperature of the eye (5)
6 Campaigns fail, stopped by endless din from below (8)
7 Unorthodox vessel's link to betel nuts (5,6)
8 Regular payment slashed (4)
12 Don't stop English composer hiding for instance in Tyneside (5,3,3)
13 Comprehensive strike has support of illegitimate offspring (4-2-4)
16 Her vital statistics initially disrupted play (3,6)
17 Dazzling feature of church in India (6)
20 Departs, with inclination to wave (6)
22 Auditor's dealing with file at the appropriate time (2,3)
23 Island shot guards Down Under (4)
26 Rage following promotion (3)

### Yesterday's solution 27,380

of batsmen but they knew they were incapable of following that.

The final flourish, instead, came from Moeen Ali, whose brilliant 31 in just nine balls, including four sixes, lifted England to their highest World Cup score, beating the marker they set against Bangladesh in Cardiff ten days earlier. More records tumbled: the 25 sixes that rained down on spectators in the first half of the game were more than any team had hit in a one-day international before. And to think that bowling is Afghanistan's strength and in Rashid Khan they possess a bowler ranked third in ODI cricket.

It was a painful day for Rashid, who conceded 110 runs from nine overs, including 11 of those 25 sixes, more runs and sixes conceded than any other bowler in World Cup history. Held back until the 19th over to stem the charge, he had no answer, initially to Jonny Bairstow and Joe Root, who made fluent half-centuries and shared a second-wicket partnership of 120.

Rashid was given notice of the captain's intent almost immediately when, in the 36th over of the innings − Rashid's sixth − 18 runs came from Morgan's blade, although it included a dropped catch at deep mid-wicket by Dawlat Zadran. Morgan was on 28 at the time, a costly miss.

Once declared fit, it was a logical decision for Morgan to change his team's preferred habit by batting first instead of chasing. Afghanistan's best chance of causing an upset would have been by batting first, getting a score and hoping that their battery of spinners could cause some confusion under the pressure of a run chase and on a pitch already used during the India v Pakistan match. By opting to bat first, Morgan avoided that trap and offered his batsmen a golden opportunity on a warm day and a hard, dry surface.

These, then, were perfect conditions for James Vince to state his case for more permanent inclusion, given the absence of Jason Roy to a hamstring injury that may prove to be more problematic than he and England hope. It was an opportunity that Vince spurned in a fashion that was not surprising: having announced himself with two attractive boundaries against Dawlat, he was beaten by a bouncer that he looked to force off the front foot, only to top-edge the ball on to his helmet and into the hands of short fine leg.

Root, having a fine tournament, joined Bairstow, who had been a little subdued initially. Bairstow's half century in 61 balls was his slowest in England colours as an opener, largely because of Mujeeb ur Rahman's tidy concoction of off spinners, googlies and flickers with the new ball.

Unusually for England, the opening ten overs were the calmest of the innings, something quickly forgotten once Root got into his stride and Bairstow opened his shoulders. After Bairstow had hit a return catch to Gulbadin Naib, Root and Morgan combined for their 12th hundred partnership since the 2015 World Cup − the most of any combination − accelerating the run rate all the time, until Root, attempting to match Morgan, holed out at long-on.

Morgan's ball-striking was remarkable in its pureness and simplicity. There was none of the shots for which he was renowned in his early days – scoops, sweeps, paddles and reverse sweeps – rather there were withering straight hits between mid-off and midwicket, manufactured from a solid base.

He swung hard and straight and enjoyed the conditions that allowed him to connect easily through the ball. When he was done, the game was over as a competitive contest. To put his and his team's new aggression into perspective: they hit as many sixes here in the final 12 overs as they did throughout the entire 2015 World Cup. Morgan, off his own bat, hit nine sixes in his last 19 balls.

Afghanistan's bowling, while shredded, had been perfectly serviceable, although the ground fielding let them down badly. With the bat, they were more subdued and controlled in the absence of Hazratullah Zazai. With the pace of Jofra Archer and Mark Wood and the spin of Adil Rashid and Ali, England had a perfectly balanced attack for the conditions, the first three named sharing eight wickets. With the game won from the restart, it is sometimes difficult to maintain standards in the field, and Bairstow spilt two catches, one at slip and one at fine leg.

The most disconcerting moment was when Hashmatullah Shahidi was hit a shattering blow on the helmet by Wood. That he continued and topscored said much for his character. Afghanistan have never lacked character but they were simply outclassed here, and outmuscled by the remarkable Morgan.

......................................................

PLAYER OF THE MATCH:
*Eoin Morgan (England)*

## WHAT THEY SAID

'I would never have thought I could play a knock like that, I'm delighted.'

Eoin Morgan

'One of the reasons Morgs scored so quickly is I managed to give him so much strike. The reason I felt like I batted for the whole innings and only ended up on 88 is because I didn't have that much strike.'

Joe Root

'How they played was something special. Credit goes to Morgan – it was one of the best innings I've seen from him.'

Gulbadin Naib

## KEY NUMBERS

### 17

Eoin Morgan's sixes were the most by any batsman in a
one-day international innings

### 25

England's sixes were the most any team has hit in an ODI innings

### 110

Rashid Khan conceded more runs than any bowler in a World Cup innings

## ANALYSIS

STEVE JAMES

Jonny Bairstow was interviewed on television in between innings at Old Trafford. In truth he was not the man that everyone wanted to hear from, but he gave a nice snippet of the dressing-room view of Eoin Morgan's spectacular innings.

'Ridiculous knock,' he said. 'We were seriously entertained up there.'

Bairstow had been able to watch it all, as it had been his dismissal at the end of the 30th over that brought Morgan to the crease. With England 164 for two at the time and looking to kick on, there had been some consideration given to promoting Jos Buttler so it was not a bad decision for the captain to decide that he was the man to take England to an impregnable total.

And it had not been a bad innings from Bairstow. His 90 will easily be forgotten in the inevitable paeans that will accompany Morgan's innings but it was a sensible and well-judged contribution.

It was a surprise that Bairstow did not make a century. All the chat about Jason Roy's injury and Alex Hales' name being mentioned in terms of a replacement was to overlook Bairstow and his magnificent record as an opener. He likes to rise to the challenge in such circumstances, when he might feel a little undervalued. Remember how he responded to losing the Test wicket-keeping gloves last winter?

Since he began opening the innings in 2017, Bairstow has averaged 51.35 at a strike rate of 112.82. It is a quicker rate than Roy's overall one-day international strike rate of 107.06. Bairstow stands among the most feared of ODI openers right now.

And yet here he made the slowest (61 balls) of his ODI fifties as an opener.

The pitch was still a little tacky early on and the mystery variations of Mujeeb ur Rahman (six overs for 18 in his initial spell) demanded respect.

Bairstow played smartly. In the opening powerplay England reached only 46 for one (Afghanistan were 48 for one at the same point), their lowest score at that stage in this tournament, and their lowest score since they were 34 for four after ten overs against Australia on this ground last year.

Sometimes the calm of a measured beginning can be easily transformed into a torrent of runs, as Morgan proved rather well here, but so too did Bairstow to an extent in making his 90 from 99 balls. He accelerated excellently.

Bairstow had done his job, but James Vince will not feel quite so sated. With Roy absent, this was a huge opportunity for him. He made 26 from 31 balls. Was that a surprise? That is somewhere near his average (27.88) in ODI cricket.

He seems to specialise in middling scores. In his nine ODI innings only once has he been dismissed in single figures, but he has made only one fifty.

In T20 internationals it is a similar tale. In eight innings there has not been one single-figure score, but not one fifty either, and an average of 28.75.

Vince averages 24.90 from 22 innings in Test cricket with three half-centuries and no century, but he has only six single-figure scores.

It has become a cliché to say that he does not have the figures to match his talent. Most annoying of all is that he always looks comfortable on the international stage.

He never looks especially rushed or edgy, except perhaps when he was out here attempting to pull off the front foot, which is a technical bugbear of mine, a modern extension of the power-hitting position when the pull is always better played off the back foot, given the obvious advantages of more time and the greater ability to cope with the bounce. Youngsters should watch Joe Root's pull shot for reference.

This was not one of Vince's prettier innings but he was still into his stride quicker than Bairstow. He showed glimpses of what he can do. But he has been doing that for too long now.

He will have another chance, against Sri Lanka on Friday. He may have a few more chances if Roy's injury persists. He needs to start taking them. He is good enough to do so.

# NEW ZEALAND v SOUTH AFRICA

......................................................

*Wednesday, June 19*

*Edgbaston*

**South Africa 241-6** (49 overs)
(Amla 55, Van der Dussen 67 not out;
Ferguson 3-59)
**New Zealand 245-6** (48.3 overs)
(Williamson 106 not out,
De Grandhomme 60; Morris 3-49)
*New Zealand (2pts) won by four wickets*
Toss *New Zealand*

**Match reduced to 49 overs per side**

JOHN WESTERBY

There has been a retro feel about much of this World Cup, from England's shirts echoing the kit design from 1992, to old-school, nerve-gnawing pursuits of low(ish) totals, as witnessed in this engrossing contest, the tightest game of the tournament so far.

In the end, New Zealand triumphed on a sticky pitch thanks to an exceptionally responsible century from Kane Williamson, who guided his side past South Africa's total of 241 for six with three balls to spare.

It was a captain's innings, but the precise opposite of Eoin Morgan's effort for England against Afghanistan the day before. Where Morgan had pummelled sixes at will, Williamson dabbed endlessly to third man for singles, struggling throughout his innings for any fluency, but nudging and scuffing his way into the nineties with minimum risk as wickets fell at the other end. There are different ways to skin an opponent in this World Cup.

As the last over arrived with his side requiring eight, Williamson had barely hit a ball cleanly for an hour. But with seven needed from five balls, he dropped to one knee to slog-sweep Andile Phehlukwayo over mid-wicket and into the Hollies Stand for six. With that one blow, he reached his hundred from 137 balls, ensured that his side would remain unbeaten and made South Africa's elimination from the tournament almost certain. 'It's about committing to the team plan, rather than your own, and not getting caught up in what it looks like,' he said.

He had been exceptionally grateful, too, to the efforts of Colin de Grandhomme, who struck the ball more cleanly than any other batsman on either side, sharing a stand of 91 with his captain before driving the first ball of the penultimate over to long-off.

Incredibly South Africa might have dismissed Williamson for 77, but failed to review an appeal turned down for a catch behind. Williamson cut at the final ball of Imran Tahir's quota, drawing a loud appeal from the bowler, but nothing from Quinton de Kock behind the stumps. South Africa did not ask for a review but television replays showed a faint edge and Williamson survived.

From the 19th over onwards, when he lost Tom Latham to a fine ball from Chris Morris that bounced and left the left-hander, Williamson knew that his side's fortunes rested on his shoulders. From 72 for one, they had lost three wickets in 20 balls, Martin Guptill slipping on to his stumps and Ross Taylor caught behind down the leg side.

As long as Williamson was at the crease, though, New Zealand remained in control of their destiny. 'Kane played a great knock,' Faf du Plessis, the South Africa captain, said. 'It was probably the difference between the sides.'

South Africa's batsmen had struggled after being asked to bat first, coming into the game low on confidence after three defeats in their first five matches. De Kock's defences were breached by Trent Boult and Du Plessis' stumps were shattered by a spearing yorker from Lockie Ferguson.

But a succession of batsmen dug in, applying themselves to the task. Hashim Amla chiselled out a half-century before a lovely ball from Mitchell Santner, the left-arm spinner, on middle stump that turned to hit off. Aiden Markram and David Miller made thirties, and Rassie van der Dussen finished unbeaten on 67 from 64 balls, signing off with a flourish of ten off the last two balls of the innings.

They were helped by New Zealand's fielding – two dropped catches and a missed run-out – but the total always seemed within New Zealand's grasp.

PLAYER OF THE MATCH:
*Kane Williamson (New Zealand)*

## WHAT THEY SAID

'You can feel in the dressing room the guys are hurting. We left everything out there, and that's all I can ask for as a captain, that the guys fought.'

Faf du Plessis

'There were a number of contributions that were so vital. It was one of those surfaces that provides a great spectacle.'

Kane Williamson

## KEY NUMBERS

### I
Kane Williamson made his first World Cup century

### 8,000
On 24, Hashim Amla passed 8,000 one-day international runs

# AUSTRALIA v BANGLADESH

......................................

*Thursday, June 20*

*Trent Bridge*

**Australia 381-5** (50 overs)
(Warner 166, Finch 53, Khawaja 89;
Soumya Sarkar 3-58)
**Bangladesh 333-8** (50 overs)
(Tamim Iqbal 62, Mushfiqur Rahim
102 not out, Mahmudullah 69)
*Australia (2pts) won by 48 runs*
Toss *Australia*

JAMES GHEERBRANT

David Warner hit the highest score of the World Cup so far as Australia tamed the tigers of Bangladesh and moved closer to locking down a semi-final place.

Batting with a mix of the responsibility that has characterised his World Cup innings so far, and some of the brutal power-hitting that has more traditionally been his trademark, Warner made 166 off 147 balls to buttress an imposing total of 381 for five on a Trent Bridge pitch that was slightly trickier than pre-tournament prognostications of 500-plus totals had reckoned with.

Bangladesh had chased 322 so comfortably in their previous match against West Indies that thoughts of a thrilling chase were not entirely fanciful, but Australia took wickets regularly to undermine their pursuit, with Mitchell Starc picking up two to take his haul for the tournament to 15. In Warner and Starc, Australia have the leading run-scorer and wicket-taker, with Aaron Finch the third-most prolific batsman. There may be weaknesses in this team but outstanding individual contributions have underpinned their impressive progress so far.

What their top order lacks in explosiveness, it makes up for in consistency and heavy scoring. In an ominous sign for other sides, Warner and Finch are averaging 89.40 and 66 respectively. Asked about his relatively methodical approach, particularly to the opening ten overs, Warner said that he was looking to bat deep into the innings.

'I don't mean to go out and bat slow,' he said. 'At times you middle one and it goes full pace to the fielder, so you can't get off strike. Finchy kept on telling me to hang in there and bat deep and bat time. It must be a bit more maturity.' Told that he had equalled Adam Gilchrist's tally of 16 ODI centuries, Warner made a self-deprecating quip about being 'not as much of a dasher' as Gilchrist, a joke that would not have worked as well two years ago.

Finch won the toss for the first time all tournament and elected to bat, as Australia had in three of their four previous wins. Without quite shedding the suspicion that they are not operating in top gear, Australia have found a steady winning formula: a solid platform laid by the top order; late acceleration by the middle order (typified by Glenn Maxwell's cameo of 32 off ten balls); and wickets at crucial times with the ball. Finch's team have won 13 of their past 14 ODIs and deserve to be seen as a frontline contender for this trophy.

Bangladesh were left to rue leaking 50 runs too many with the ball, as their highest ODI total – and an excellent century by Mushfiqur Rahim – proved in vain. Mashrafe Mortaza's side have amassed scores of 330, 322 (off 41.3 overs) and 333 at this tournament but their bowling has let them down. They are fifth in the table and best placed of the outsiders to gatecrash the semi-finals but this was a result to crystallise the growing sense that Australia, England, India and New Zealand have the qualification places locked up. Even victory in their remaining matches against Afghanistan, India and Pakistan may not be enough to take Bangladesh through to the last four.

Barring an improbable combination of results, the final two and a half weeks of group games could play out as a series of matches of gradually dwindling significance. India, the fourth-placed side, have a two-point advantage over Bangladesh, with two games in hand, and the top four could be confirmed as early as Thursday, potentially leaving 11 dead rubbers. That would be a minor disaster for the sport's global showpiece and this may go down as the day that Australia not only sealed Bangladesh's fate, but also hammered the last nail in the coffin of a misconceived format.

PLAYER OF THE MATCH:
*David Warner (Australia)*

## WHAT THEY SAID

'A positive side is that we made 320-plus in our last two matches, and both were chases. The batsmen believe that we can chase around 320-330.'

Tamim Iqbal

'I was a bit down in the dumps after I hurt myself. And again now I'm back in the team and able to do my thing.'

Marcus Stoinis

## KEY NUMBER

# 16

David Warner made his 16th one-day international century,
joint third on Australia's all-time list

# ENGLAND v SRI LANKA

......................................................

*Friday, June 21*

*Headingley*

**Sri Lanka 232-9** (50 overs) (Mathews 85; Archer 3-52, Wood 3-40)
**England 212 all out** (47 overs) (Root 57, Stokes 82 not out; Malinga 4-43, De Silva 3-32)
*Sri Lanka (2pts) won by 20 runs*
Toss *Sri Lanka*

STEVE JAMES

The old adage is never to judge a pitch fully until both teams have taken their turn to bat on it, and this was as sharp a reminder of that as you can imagine.

What looked as if it should have been a stroll in the park for England turned into a depressing defeat – their second of the tournament after the loss to Pakistan at Trent Bridge – as their batsmen simply could not come to terms with a tricky surface, as well as the ageless Lasith Malinga, ending 20 runs short of Sri Lanka's 232 for nine.

It was incredibly harsh on Ben Stokes, who finished stranded on 82, having played one of his finest innings, but his colleagues let him down. Some of their decision-making with the bat was quite brainless.

England should now have had one foot in the semi-finals but instead they face their most difficult games, against Australia, India and New Zealand, with at least one win required.

At times, Sri Lanka's innings was so seemingly tedious – a reversion to how it used to be when we had the boring middle overs in this format – it would have been easy to conclude that it was a simple and dreadful advertisement for the state of cricket on their island. Maybe England were thinking that way. They certainly looked complacent.

Yes, Sri Lankan cricket is in a mess, but their batsmen had actually made a decent score (even if it was below par) in the circumstances. They had opted to bat, the obvious decision on what was a good-looking pitch, but the surface revealed itself as tacky and two-paced. There was some turn for the spinners. Batting was never straightforward.

Angelo Mathews had scored nine runs in three previous innings in the tournament, with two ducks, and, having taken an eternity to find any sort of touch, it appeared that his 85 not out from 115 balls had been too slow – he did not hit a six until the final over of the innings – but it was not as out of place as it first seemed.

A highlight of the Sri Lankan innings was the perky 49 made by the 21-year-old No. 3, Avishka Fernando. This was his first match in the tournament and only his seventh one-day international, but the right-hander provided some rare moments of early aggression, twice hooking Jofra Archer for six. His innings had occupied just 39 balls when, disappointingly, he upper cut Mark Wood straight into Adil Rashid's hands at third man.

Sri Lanka had lost both openers inside three overs, Dimuth Karunaratne edging Archer behind and Kusal Perera slashing Chris Woakes down to Moeen

Ali at third man. Recovery was not easy. Kusal Mendis laboured over 68 balls for his 46, Dhananjaya de Silva took 47 balls for his 29 and poor old Jeevan Mendis chipped a return catch to Rashid first ball.

That the last two balls of the innings went runless – there were 153 dot balls in the whole innings – emphasised the pitch's difficulties. In fairness England's bowling and fielding had been excellent. The pace of Archer and Wood was again incisive, with both bowlers claiming three wickets each.

The spinners Ali and Rashid had bowled well in tandem. Though wicketless, Ali conceded only 40 runs from his ten overs, without a boundary, and Rashid, who also took a superb diving catch at third man to dismiss Thisara Perera off Archer, looked as if he was returning to his best, unafraid to bowl the ball more slowly and being rewarded with two wickets.

England's reply began calamitously, however. To the second ball of the innings, Jonny Bairstow was out first ball for the second time in this tournament, adjudged leg-before to the 35-year-old Malinga and then not saved by technology upon review, with the call just siding with the umpire.

James Vince had just begun to get things moving when hitting Malinga for consecutive fours, through mid-off and midwicket, when he edged to slip off the same bowler. It was classic Vince. The length was not quite full enough but still he drove hard at it.

At the end of the opening powerplay England were 38 for two, their second lowest score after those ten overs in 49 home ODIs since the last World Cup. Sri Lanka had been 48 for two at the same point.

Joe Root never really found his timing, even if much of that was down to the fact that Nuwan Pradeep bowled superbly, maintaining an exemplary length in conceding only 12 runs in his six-over opening spell.

Malinga was a little more expensive initially, with 27 runs coming from his five-over opening spell but he had taken the first two wickets and returned to take two more. He bowled with the vigour of a much younger man.

Eoin Morgan, after his six-hitting spree in Manchester on Tuesday, may have hit his second ball for four but there were no sixes here and very little fluency before he was caught and bowled by the left-armer Isuru Udana.

England were 73 for three in the 19th over. This was getting a little jittery.

Root passed fifty in 78 balls – the second slowest half-century of his ODI career – and gradually Stokes found the pace of the pitch until he was able to hit two sixes, both down the ground, one driven and one rank long hop pulled, from an over of the leg spin from Mendis.

But then on 57 Root was gone. It needed a review from Sri Lanka but technology eventually revealed that he had got a tickle down the leg side to Malinga. Soon there was another review, this time Jos Buttler hoping his leg-before decision from Malinga's bowling was wrong. It was not. England were 144 for five in the 33rd over, with 89 required.

Ali had just hit De Silva for six when he foolishly attempted something similar to the next ball. He was caught at long-off. The game changed irretrievably from there.

Stokes passed fifty off 61 balls, but soon lost Woakes and Rashid in the same over, both caught behind off the off spin of De Silva. It was all down to Stokes, especially so when Archer hit Udana to long-on.

Wood arrived with 47 required off 38 balls. Stokes hit valiantly but Wood edged Pradeep behind with three overs remaining. It was a huge upset, and a huge setback for England.

PLAYER OF THE MATCH:
**_Lasith Malinga (Sri Lanka)_**

## WHAT THEY SAID

'You look at the basics of a run chase. Partnerships are very important; we struggled to get enough partnerships going. We had a couple of individual innings but that's not good enough to win a game.'

Eoin Morgan

'We lacked energy with the bat. That doesn't just mean hitting fours and sixes, that means showing intensity and trying to put pressure back on the bowlers.'

Jos Buttler

'It was a close one, we were under pressure but it was teamwork in the end – all the batters and bowlers did great work.'

Dimuth Karunaratne

## KEY NUMBERS

### 85
Angelo Mathews made his highest score in a World Cup match

### 50
Lasith Malinga's third wicket was his 50th at World Cups

THE TIMES

# sport

Saturday June 22 2019

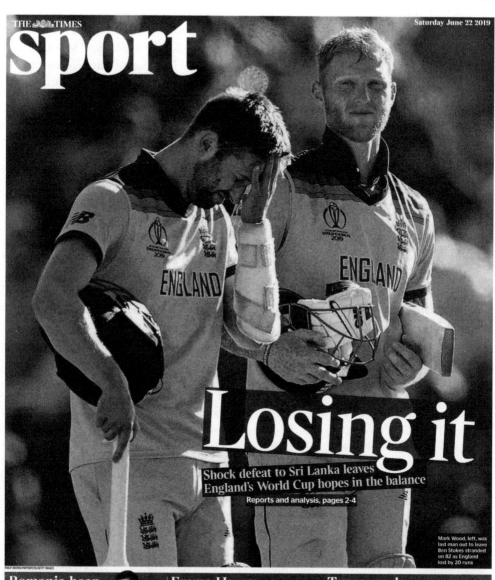

# Losing it

### Shock defeat to Sri Lanka leaves England's World Cup hopes in the balance

**Reports and analysis, pages 2-4**

Mark Wood, left, was last man out to leave Ben Stokes stranded on 82 as England lost by 20 runs

PHILIP BROWN/POPPERFOTO/GETTY IMAGES

## Romania heap more misery on misfiring under-21s

Page 5

## Emma Hayes: players being made VAR guinea pigs

Page 6

## Turner ends 32-year wait for women at Royal Ascot

Page 15

## ANALYSIS

MIKE ATHERTON

The World Cup, it was said, needed an upset. Try telling that to Eoin Morgan's team, who stumbled and stuttered and eventually stalled against little-fancied Sri Lanka, much as they had against Pakistan in Cardiff in the Champions Trophy semi-final two years ago. While defeat is not terminal as it was then, there was a common denominator: a dry, holding pitch on which England's batsmen struggled to play with the freedom and aggression that has defined them during their rise to the top of the world rankings.

The question about nerve and temperament in a run chase during a tournament where defeat carries consequences, as opposed to a run-of-the-mill bilateral series which carries none, would always need answering. Against South Africa recently, New Zealand's captain, Kane Williamson, showed that the way to win a tight World Cup encounter on a difficult surface is with intelligence, cool composure and good decision-making, qualities that eluded England's batsmen in the second half of the match against Sri Lanka.

How serious are the consequences? Not serious enough that they will likely fall short of the semi-finals, although it puts added scrutiny and pressure on their three remaining matches against the tournament's other strongest teams, Australia, New Zealand and India. But serious enough that they have shown their Achilles' heel to others watching on, who will surely look to bat first, put runs on the board and ask those questions of England's batsmen time and again. It may encourage Morgan, who would have batted first here, to set and defend rather than chase in future, which has been his preferred route.

When Sri Lanka crawled to 232 from their 50 overs, there were few who imagined that an upset was on the cards against a team that have passed 300 for fun. But maybe the clues were there in the way that the vastly experienced Angelo Mathews had struggled to break free from the shackles imposed by England's slower bowlers in the middle of the innings, and by the seamers when they bowled slower balls with increasing regularity – the kind of conditions, in other words, in which England's batsmen have sometimes come unstuck. Hitting through the ball, as the batsmen did so well against Afghanistan on Tuesday, is more difficult when the ball grips unhelpfully into the surface.

Mathews was one of three players who rose to the occasion as Sri Lanka fought tooth and nail to stay in the tournament in a manner most – including me – thought beyond them. The others were the veteran Lasith Malinga, who proved to be the battering ram with new ball and old by taking four wickets, and 21-year Avishka Fernando, who played a boisterous innings at the start of the day and showed the kind of audacious spirit that Sri Lanka had been lacking until now.

Mathews has been so horribly out of touch, scoring the grand total of nine runs before this game, that it was hard to know whether his difficulties were the result of his poor form or the conditions. Try as hard as he might, he struggled to find the boundary, hitting only five fours and a six in a stay that lasted the best part of 38 overs. Mathews once made a brilliant hundred here in a famous Test win, but will cherish this innings, with all the struggle that it entailed, just as much.

Malinga? He is on his last legs as an international bowler, but somehow wound back the clock, picking up Jonny Bairstow and James Vince with the new ball, the former leg-before first ball, the latter to one of those airy drives that sends his supporters into raptures when it goes well and his critics into a frenzy when it doesn't.

He was then brought back at the critical time by his captain, Dimuth Karunaratne, mid-innings and responded with the key wickets of Joe Root, tickling down the leg side, and Jos Buttler, leg-before in similar manner to Bairstow, too far across his stumps to a bowler who releases the ball from tight to the stumps. Malinga doesn't have many days left in him, but provided a lasting memory here.

Fernando's 39-ball assault was essential to give Sri Lanka some impetus after two wickets had fallen to the new ball in the opening three overs. His battle with Jofra Archer was a mini-classic, as he lashed the bowler for three fours and a pulled six in the sixth over of the game. Another six off Archer, that went clean over the electronic scoreboard and into the concourse behind, was the shot of the day and helped restore some belief to a sagging team. He played Archer with as much time as anyone has so far in the World Cup and has a bright future.

All this notwithstanding, and giving due credit, England should not have lost the match. There was some deeply unintelligent batting, as the wickets began to tumble and the tension rose. Ben Stokes, alone, made the right calls under pressure, shielding Mark Wood at the right time, playing big shots when necessary and scampering runs into the deep. He looked as though he might get England home almost single-handedly, although it was just beyond him in the end. It only needed one batsman to stay with him and the game was over.

When Root was dismissed, England needed only 86 in a little under 20 overs, with six wickets in hand, and a lower-middle order considered one of the strongest in the competition to come. Chris Woakes and Adil Rashid were dismissed in similar fashion, cutting Dhananjaya de Silva behind in a manner that Yorkshire folk of a certain age would have frowned upon.

Most culpable, though, were Moeen Ali and Archer, who both went hunting glory. Ali hoisted De Silva into the hands of long-off immediately after launching the off spinner for six, while Archer, too, was caught aiming for a six over long-on, when he simply needed to keep Stokes company. In the context of England's and Sri Lanka's recent history, it was a stunning upset, one that will give England tremors and will have been noted with interest by their closest challengers.

# AFGHANISTAN v INDIA

......................................................

*Saturday, June 22*

### Rose Bowl, Southampton

**India 224-8** (50 overs) (Kohli 67, Jadhav 52)
**Afghanistan 213 all out** (49.5 overs) (Mohammad Nabi 52; Shami 4-40)
*India (2pts) won by 11 runs*
*Toss India*

ELIZABETH AMMON

For a couple of hours yesterday afternoon, the sea of India fans in Southampton were very quiet. Afghanistan looked like they might, just might, pull off one of the all-time great World Cup shocks. They took India right to the wire and lost by just 11 runs.

Asked to bowl first, they made use of Southampton's unusually slow conditions to restrict India to 224 for eight – their lowest ODI total in 50 overs since 2011.

Afghanistan were impressive with the ball, quickly working out the lengths to bowl on a two-paced pitch. Mujeeb Ur-Rahman got the new ball to zip and move against India's powerful top order. He also got the first breakthrough in the fifth over, turning past the edge of Rohit Sharma's outside edge to hit the top of off stump. Lokesh Rahul and Virat Kohli put on a partnership of 57 in ten overs before Mohammad Nabi removed opener Rahul for 30.

The India captain looked to have conquered the conditions and the variations Afghanistan were using against him before Nabi picked up his second wicket.

MS Dhoni's innings of 28 from 52 was, at times, tortuous. For someone of his status, talent and experience, it was extraordinary to watch him struggle against spin, unable to time anything at all. It was something of a blessing when he was put out of his misery in being stumped for only the second time his career.

Rashid Khan bounced back from the mauling he took against England last week by bowling much better lengths and beating the bat on a number of occasions, ultimately finishing with one for 38 from his ten overs.

India stuttered to 224, hitting just 16 boundaries in the innings, four of which came from Kedar Jadhav, the only one of India's middle order to find any fluency. On that pitch against one of the strongest bowling attacks in the tournament, this was never going to be anything other than a difficult chase for Afghanistan.

It began steadily enough, reaching 106 for two by the 29th over before Jasprit Bumrah struck twice in three balls to remove Rahmat Shah for 36 and Hashmatullah Shahidi for 21 to end what was on course to become a threatening partnership.

Afghanistan's hopes were then pinned on Mohammad Nabi and Asghar Afghan, but with the run rate creeping up, the pressure was building and Asghar was bowled by Yuzvendra Chahal.

With ten overs remaining, Afghanistan needing 68 to win and having four wickets in hand, there was still hope. Those hopes faded when

Najbullah, who had timed the ball relatively well for his 21 from 23 balls, was caught at short midwicket off a slow cutter by Pandya, who romantically blew a kiss to the batsman as he was walking off. Given Rashid Khan was the last of the line-up with any recognised batting ability, the noise levels among the previously quiet crowd started to rise. Nabi tried to attack where he could but equally had to be mindful of the lack of batting ability in the tail, and the experience of India's death bowlers shone.

Having pulled off an audacious reverse sweep for four off Chahal, Rashid Khan was stumped for 14 on the next ball. Everything then rested with the experience of Nabi. He dispatched Bumrah over midwicket on the third ball of the 47th over for six, and smartly took a single from the final ball of the over. With 24 needed from the last three, he had to attempt something aggressive and tried to flick a length delivery by Mohammed Shami through the leg side, but missed. The LBW decision was overturned on referral as the replays showed the impact was outside off-stump and the match was still alive.

But India's death bowlers turned the screw, leaving Nabi needing 16 from the last over. Mohammed Shami was given the job of bowling the final over and made no mistake about finishing it, succeeding with a hat-trick. Nabi's impressive innings of 52 ended when he tried to loft Shami into the pavilion and miscued into the hands of long-on, and then two consecutive perfect yorkers removed Aftab and Mujeeb.

Victory takes Kohli's army towards the semi-finals with a perfect record from the matches they've played. They next move on to Manchester to take on the struggling West Indies on Thursday.

Afghanistan remain winless after six matches. While it will be little consolation to them as they languish at the bottom of the table, they were hugely spirited yesterday, giving the best account of themselves so far. They genuinely tested India and exposed some of their weaknesses. Ultimately the result went the way that was expected but there were some extremely uncomfortable passages of play for India until then.

After two weeks of miserable weather, the English summer hit the south coast and brought along with it some drama, entertainment and very nearly the most memorable of upsets.

PLAYER OF THE MATCH:
*Jasprit Bumrah (India)*

## WHAT THEY SAID

'Our shot selection could have been much better – a lot of horizontal bat shots costs us a lot of wickets.'

Virat Kohli

'The total was not that much but in the middle you need 80s or 100s – 30 or 25s are not enough. If you chase 250 then the middle-order batsmen should go longer and take responsibility.'

Gulbadin Naib

## KEY NUMBER

### I

Mohammed Shami took the first hat-trick of the tournament, the first by an India bowler since Chetan Sharma against New Zealand in 1987

## NEW ZEALAND v WEST INDIES

*Saturday, June 25*

*Old Trafford (day-night)*

**New Zealand 291-8** (50 overs)
(Williamson 148, Taylor 69;
Cottrell 4-56)
**West Indies 286 all out** (49 overs)
(Gayle 87, Hetmyer 54, Brathwaite
101; Boult 4-30, Ferguson 3-59)
*New Zealand (2pts) won by 5 runs*
**Toss** *West Indies*

SIMON WILDE, *SUNDAY TIMES*
CRICKET CORRESPONDENT
Carlos Brathwaite. Remember the name? The hero of the World Twenty20 final of 2016 has been a serial underachiever at international level since his astonishing assault on Ben Stokes' bowling in Kolkata, but at Old Trafford last night he rediscovered his magic in the most extraordinary fashion and it took West Indies agonisingly close to a victory over New Zealand that would have kept their World Cup hopes well and truly alive.

With his side needing six runs to win, and having two balls earlier reached a maiden international century off 80 balls, he could not resist attempting to clear the ropes for a sixth time – only to fall a metre short and be smartly caught by Trent Boult, who had to steady his feet to make sure he did not tumble over the rope. New Zealand had won by five runs to move top of the table.

West Indies' future in the tournament was left hanging by a thread, which was why, as he saw Boult had made good his catch, Brathwaite sank to his knees in despair. Several New Zealand players, including their captain Kane Williamson, who himself scored a brilliant century, consoled him.

Brathwaite, promoted to No. 6 because of an injury to Evin Lewis and only playing because Andrew Russell is unfit, soon found himself batting with the tail with West Indies sliding to 164 for seven, and still needing another 128. With the help of Kemar

Roach, Sheldon Cottrell and last man Oshane Thomas, the last three wickets would add 122. With time in hand, only towards the end did Brathwaite cut loose.

In 76 ODI and international Twenty20 appearances, he has never taken a man-of-the-match award. In Kolkata the award went to Marlon Samuels; yesterday Williamson.

It was West Indies' customary obsession with hitting sixes that got them into trouble. Chris Gayle hit six maximums in his 87 from 84 balls and was out attempting a seventh, while Shimron Hetmyer needlessly attempted to clear the ropes for a second time when he was bowled by a Lockie Ferguson slower ball. The two of them had added 122 from 97 balls and were controlling the game.

Ferguson, who again demonstrated his dangerous pace, followed up Hetmyer's wicket with that of Jason Holder next ball. Another West Indies collapse was under way: they shed five wickets for 22 in as many overs. New Zealand had given them every chance, dropping Gayle on 15, 58 and 59, the first chance put down by Boult, who otherwise did little wrong in his best performance of the World Cup. He finished with four wickets as well as the decisive catch.

To be fair, West Indies were unfortunate that Lewis damaged his hamstring in the field within moments of the start. He did bat, but only at No. 8 and was clearly struggling. He soon slogged a catch to deep square leg.

If Williamson was the saviour-in-chief of New Zealand's innings, he needed the help of Ross Taylor to ensure a competitive score was posted. When the irrepressible Cottrell struck twice in the opening over, removing openers Martin Guptill and Colin Munro for golden ducks with yorker-length deliveries, the third-wicket pair had little choice but to rebuild with care.

The first powerplay score of 30 for two was the lowest of the World Cup but by staying together until the 35th over in a stand of 160, Williamson and Taylor gave their side scope to push hard at the end and give themselves something decent to bowl at. Only one side at this World Cup has successfully chased down more than 250.

No one is better suited than Williamson to such meticulous reconstruction and as in the tight run-chase against South Africa he carried out his task to perfection. He spent 75 balls over his first 50 but only 49 over his second, and 30 balls over his final 45 runs. He lost Taylor on 92 when Gayle, rather improbably, induced a Taylor into unsuccessfully attempting to clear mid-off.

Williamson's innings of 148 was not only his highest in ODIs but also his longest at 154 balls. So often, he had judged well what constituted a good score. In a tournament in which the cream is rising, he is fit to live with the best.

PLAYER OF THE MATCH:
*Kane Williamson (New Zealand)*

## KEY NUMBER

# 148

Kane Williamson made his highest one-day international score

# PAKISTAN v SOUTH AFRICA

............................................

*Sunday, June 23*

*Lord's*

**Pakistan 308-7** (50 overs) (Babar Azam 69, Haris Sohail 89; Ngidi 3-64) **South Africa 259-9** (50 overs) (Du Plessis 63; Wahab Riaz 3-46, Shadab Khan 3-50) *Pakistan (2pts) won by 49 runs* *Toss Pakistan*

South Africa, who began the tournament as most people's bet for at least a semi-final place, crashed out of the World Cup after another comprehensive defeat. It was their fifth reverse in seven matches; their sole victory has come against bottom-of-the-table Afghanistan.

Pakistan, meanwhile, kept alive their hopes of sneaking into the top four, even if it was just their second victory. Their total was powered by Babar Azam's 69 and a brilliant 89 off 59 balls from the recalled Haris Sohail. Timing the ball wonderfully, he struck nine fours and three sixes and set the huge Pakistan contingent roaring.

Solid foundations were laid by Fakhar Zaman and Imam-ul-Haq who put on 81, but Fakhar survived a controversial moment when Imran Tahir claimed a low catch on the deep square-leg boundary. The umpires ruled he had not grabbed the ball before it touched the turf. Tahir had his revenge, though, when he dismissed both openers, Imam falling to a brilliant caught and bowled. Against a toothless attack, Pakistan had wickets in hand going into the final stages, adding 91 in the last ten overs.

Mohammad Amir snared the out-of-touch Hashim Amla with his first ball and Quinton de Kock survived a dropped catch by Wahab Riaz as South Africa got off to a shaky start. But De Kock and captain Faf du Plessis rebuilt with a second-wicket stand of 87.

Du Plessis went on to top score with 63, but no one went on to play the commanding innings that the situation demanded. This was in no small part down to the excellence of the Pakistan attack who posed a variety of challenges. Five South African batsmen went past 30, but they were crying out for at least one contribution of real substance and it did not materialise.

PLAYER OF THE MATCH:
*Haris Sohail (Pakistan)*

## WHAT THEY SAID

'It's becoming a little bit embarrassing, we're trying but it's not good enough. It's chipping away at me.'

Faf du Plessis

'Haris Sohail was hungry to play in the match and the way he batted was a turning point. You see Jos Buttler play that type of innings so the way he played was fantastic.'

Sarfaraz Ahmed

'One of the all-time brilliant innings that I've seen.'

Pakistan coach Mickey Arthur

# AFGHANISTAN v BANGLADESH

*Monday, June 24*

*Rose Bowl, Southampton*

**Bangladesh 262-7** (50 overs)
(Shakib Al Hasan 51, Mushfiqur Rahim 83; Mujeeb Ur Rahman 3-39)
**Afghanistan 200 all out** (47 overs)
(Shakib Al Hasan 5-29)
*Bangladesh (2pts) won by 62 runs*
Toss *Afghanistan*

JAMES GHEERBRANT
Bangladesh consolidated their position as the best placed of the outsiders to gatecrash the semi-finals with a thorough neutralising of Afghanistan, inspired by another magnificent performance from Shakib Al Hasan.

The all-rounder continued his stellar tournament with 51, five for 29 and a run-out to take his side to within a point of fourth-placed England in the standings. The 32-year-old, playing in his fourth World Cup, is the leading run-scorer in the tournament and, after his performance here, the owner of the best bowling figures.

'It's very satisfying,' he said. 'It was important from my perspective and the team's.' Asked if a poor Indian Premier League campaign – he scored only nine runs and took two wickets in the three matches he played for Sunrisers Hyderabad – had given him extra motivation, he added: 'I did prepare well, but I never felt I had a point to prove.'

Although England have a match in hand, defeat by Australia today would make being overtaken by Bangladesh a real possibility. 'It's difficult [for us] mathematically, but in cricket anything can happen,' Shakib said. 'We have to play two very important matches and get the result in our favour.' Bangladesh face India next Tuesday and Pakistan the following Friday.

Not for the first time in the tournament, the story of this match was a comfortably sub-300 total in the first innings proving a surprisingly formidable target. Bangladesh, who have passed 300 three times in the tournament, got nowhere close to that mark on this occasion. Their innings was underpinned by a solid partnership between Shakib and Mushfiqur Rahim, who made 83. But they lost wickets regularly and at one stage went 12 overs without hitting a boundary, resulting in a total that felt vulnerable.

However, Afghanistan, who narrowly failed to chase 225 against India at the same venue on Saturday, never really threatened to get close, in large part due to a masterful spell by Shakib. Bowling with control and subtle variation, his first seven overs cost ten runs and yielded four top-order wickets as the Afghan batsmen perished trying to escape his asphyxiating grip.

Having arrived at the tournament with some optimism of upsetting the established order and avoiding the wooden spoon, Afghanistan now have seven defeats from their seven games. Their captain, Gulbadin Naib, had issued a rallying cry on the eve of the match, telling Bangladesh: 'We're drowning and we'll take you with us.' As it turned out, Bangladesh kept their head above water while Afghanistan sank without trace. Gulbadin blamed a poor effort in the field. 'We missed a couple of catches and we didn't bowl in the right areas in the first ten overs,' he said.

The central figure in another disappointing bowling performance was Rashid Khan, the only one of Afghanistan's five frontline bowlers to go wicketless. He is on the opposite trajectory to Shakib, following an excellent IPL with Sunrisers, for whom he took 17 wickets, with a sub-par World Cup. He has only four wickets from his seven games and his underwhelming contribution continues to belie his status as the world's third-ranked ODI bowler. 'If you look for Rashid, where I want him, he's not [performing at that level],' Gulbadin said. 'He's trying hard, he's giving 100 per cent.'

For Bangladesh, attention now turns to trying to upset India. In Shakib, Mushfiqur and Tamim Iqbal, they have veterans of the side that stunned India at the 2007 World Cup. 'We have to play our best cricket to be able to beat India,' Shakib said.

....................................................

**PLAYER OF THE MATCH:**
*Shakib Al Hasan (Bangladesh)*

## WHAT THEY SAID

'Shakib is the world No. 1 all-rounder. He has a lot of experience, he took his time on the wicket when he batted, and he bowled really well.'

Gulbadin Naib

## KEY NUMBERS

### 2

Shakib Al Hasan became the second player to make a fifty and take five wickets in the same World Cup match. The other was Yuvraj Singh of India against Ireland in 2011

### 3

He also became only the third player to score a century and take a five-wicket haul in the same World Cup. The others were Kapil Dev of India in 1983 and Yuvraj in 2011

# ENGLAND v AUSTRALIA

................................................

*Tuesday, June 25*

*Lord's*

**Australia 285-7** (50 overs) (Finch 100, Warner 53)
**England 221 all out** (44.4 overs) (Stokes 89; Behrendorff 5-44, Starc 4-43)
*Australia (2pts) won by 64 runs*
**Toss** *England*

MIKE ATHERTON,
CHIEF CRICKET CORRESPONDENT
What could be more exhilarating for an Australian cricketer than producing a glorious heist at Lord's, in front of the panama hats, red trousers and egg-and-bacon-coloured blazers, just as the World Cup reaches its most ticklish stage? With two more points in the bag, courtesy of some top-class cricket with bat and ball at the start of both innings, they have gone to the top of the table and confirmed their place in the semi-finals, the first team to do so. What is more, they can have some fun watching England squirm over the next ten days trying to do the same.

If they can bear it, Eoin Morgan's team must now watch Pakistan attempt to beat New Zealand today because, should that happen, England would likely need to win their next two games against India and New Zealand. Given that England have stalled at precisely the wrong moment, that is not a straightforward proposition, especially since they must play India at Edgbaston, where Virat Kohli's team will be buoyed by heavy support and by the conditions, which, in the forecast warm weather, may help the spinners.

# Sport

**Matthew Syed**
VAR makes football part of the criminal-justice system
Page 63

TIMES PHOTOGRAPHER MARC ASPLAND

# England on the brink

● Morgan's side outplayed by Australia at Lord's
● Captain denies claim he was scared of Starc

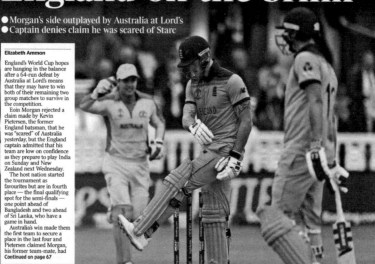

**Elizabeth Ammon**

England's World Cup hopes are hanging in the balance after a 64-run defeat by Australia at Lord's means that they may have to win both of their remaining two group matches to survive in the competition.

Eoin Morgan rejected a claim made by Kevin Pietersen, the former England batsman, that he was "scared" of Australia yesterday, but the England captain admitted that his team are low on confidence as they prepare to play India on Sunday and New Zealand next Wednesday.

The host nation started the tournament as favourites but are in fourth place — the final qualifying spot for the semi-finals — one point ahead of Bangladesh and two ahead of Sri Lanka, who have a game in hand.

Australia's win made them the first team to secure a place in the last four and Pietersen claimed Morgan, his former team-mate, had
Continued on page 67

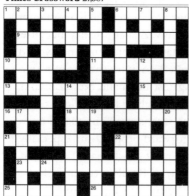

Ben Stokes kicks his bat away in frustration after Mitchell Starc's yorker bowled him out for 89, the only innings of substance from an England batsman yesterday

## FA exit for key strategy guru

**Matt Hughes** Sports News Correspondent

Dave Reddin, one of the key architects of England's recent resurgence, is to leave the Football Association after six years. The head of strategy and team performance has agreed a severance package, the governing body confirmed yesterday.

The FA did not comment on the reasons behind Reddin's departure but he is understood to have clashed with colleagues throughout his spell at St George's Park and developed a reputation as a demanding taskmaster.

The 49-year-old faced allegations of bullying two years ago. He was accused of presiding over a "climate of fear" but he was then cleared of any wrongdoing by the FA.

Reddin is understood to have experienced more difficulties in his relationships with key colleagues after those
Continued on page 61

## Nadal criticises seeding policy

**Stuart Fraser** Tennis Correspondent

Rafael Nadal has accused Wimbledon of disrespecting the world rankings by using a special mathematical formula to determine seedings for the men's singles — the only grand-slam tournament to do so.

The seedings list for the championships will be confirmed by the All England Club (AELTC) this morning. Nadal, the world No 2, will be seeded No 3 behind his arch-rival Roger Federer, who is ranked No 3 but will be seeded No 2 after winning the Halle Open on Sunday.

The Australian, French and US Opens simply replicate the latest world rankings, which are based on the previous 52 weeks of results across all surfaces, for their seedings. Wimbledon, however, uses a formula that gives
Continued on page 58

---

## Times Crossword 27,387

**ACROSS**

1 Critic opinion of the unenlightened? (1,3,4)
6 Tricky things to play in piano classes (6)
9 Fellow evidently about to drop off vital pump (7,6)
10 New Zealand port, one bringing in logs (6)
11 Misleading info put forward by a scoundrel (8)
13 Pants shed, liable to be in this state? (10)
15 Sandy area close to pool one loved previously? (4)
16 Led by boss, regularly put out flags (4)
18 Run round in Ireland collecting fresh stock (10)
21 To an extent, satirizing aristocratic amateur cricket club (1,7)
22 Macmillan's preference George, with wonderment, heard (3,3)
23 One ITV acquire to play a typical local? (5,8)
25 Come round on time before Easter (6)
26 Guy's initial dread, meeting leading female criminal (8)

**DOWN**

2 Comic hero's endless night in Hamlet? (3,4)
3 Fabulous sight, mind: a French star at twelve! (8,3)
4 Dearer pair relinquished? More reserved (5)
5 Other half of footballer's story recounted in flyer (7)
6 Paid and trained: at any time killings his speciality? (9)
7 Get a load of that missing heroin in old vessel (3)
8 Central theme in books grasped by reformist, mostly (7)
12 Instruction from ref: angry speech that can be ambiguous (4,2,5)
14 Stop publication on the web, attracting stick? (3,6)
17 One buzzing around organised quiz game (7)
19 Briefing is formal, stylish and grand (7)
20 ME airline, a casualty of America, turning bitter? (4,3)
22 Counter from judge upset me, for one (5)
24 Old prior to look for an audience (3)

9 771742 498639

Jofra Archer was fast tracked into the England team just weeks before the tournament, but his electrifying pace played a significant role in the team's success. *(Bradley Ormesher)*

Steve Smith made 69 in Australia's second match against India at the Oval, but the story was Virat Kohli's appeal to the Indian fans to stop booing him. *(Marc Aspland)*

Wherever India played their fanatical supporters provided a background of colour and noise. *(Marc Aspland)*

Australia's David Warner sweeps against India at the Oval. He made 56 but his runs came at an uncharacteristically slow pace. *(Marc Aspland)*

India captain Virat Kohli plays a studied forward defensive in his side's much-hyped meeting with Pakistan at Old Trafford. He made 76 off 65 balls. *(Bradley Ormesher)*

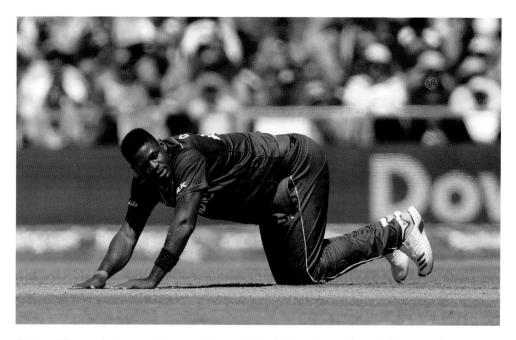

Oshane Thomas is down and out, and so are West Indies during their defeat by India at Old Trafford. *(Bradley Ormesher)*

Rohit Sharma, the India opener, was the best batsman in the competition with 648 runs and five centuries. Here he celebrates reaching three figures against Pakistan. *(Bradley Ormesher)*

Fakhar Zaman goes for a big hit on the leg side during his defiant innings of 62 against India at Old Trafford *(Bradley Ormesher)*

The vast temporary stand at Old Trafford was dominated by India fans for the eagerly awaited match against Pakistan. *(Bradley Ormesher)*

Joe Root was in quietly impressive form throughout the World Cup, and in the thrashing of Afghanistan at Old Trafford he made 88 off 82 balls. *(Bradley Ormesher)*

England captain Eoin Morgan shredded the record books in his innings against Afghanistan. His 148 included an ODI record 17 sixes. *(Bradley Ormesher)*

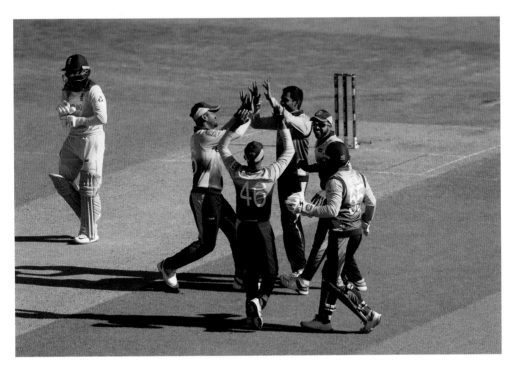

Adil Rashid is out and England are sliding towards an unexpected defeat against Sri Lanka at Headingley. *(Bradley Ormesher)*

Ben Stokes kicks his bat away in disappointment after being bowled by Mitchell Starc for 89 in England's group-stage defeat by Australia at Lord's. *(Marc Aspland)*

Jason Roy's return to the England team after a mid-tournament injury was crucial to their eventual victory. In the semi-final against Australia at Edgbaston he made a magnificent 85. *(Bradley Ormesher)*

Jofra Archer celebrates the wicket of Glenn Maxwell – caught by Eoin Morgan for 22 – in England's clinical demolition of Australia in the semi-final at Edgbaston. *(Bradley Ormesher)*

Jonny Bairstow and Chris Woakes try to catch up with Jos Buttler after he completed the run-out that won the World Cup at the end of the dramatic Super Over in the final at Lord's. *(Marc Aspland)*

For four years Eoin Morgan drove a revolution in England's approach to one-day cricket. His reward came at the end of an emotionally draining final at Lord's. *(Marc Aspland)*

Ben Stokes kicks out in frustration after failing to secure England's victory off the final ball of the match. The Super Over gave him a chance to make amends. *(Marc Aspland)*

MCC members in the Lord's pavilion abandon their habitual reserve after a lucky deflection off Ben Stokes's bat gives England four overthrows at a critical moment in the run-chase. *(Marc Aspland)*

What a time to lose a second consecutive one-day game – the first time at home for nearly four years. Having dominated Australia in one-day cricket since the previous World Cup, winning ten of the past eleven games against them and wrapping up a whitewash last summer, England lost the match that really counted, a galling state of affairs. They came up against a rejuvenated Australia team; well led, boosted by the return of big names who delivered on the day and by two key changes to their line-up, which gave their bowling attack a far sharper edge throughout.

Aaron Finch is proving to be an inspired choice as captain, having replaced Tim Paine with Australia's one-day cricket in the doldrums, and he led brilliantly here. In bowler-friendly conditions of the type that almost called for Test match-style application – an irony, given Finch's failure to cement a Test place – he scored his 15th ODI hundred and his seventh against England, more than anyone else. More than that, he was party to bringing in Jason Behrendorff, the lanky left-arm seamer, who took five wickets on his best day in international cricket.

Behrendorff may have taken one more wicket than Mitchell Starc, but Starc was the most dangerous bowler on show. His fast swingers accounted for Joe Root and Eoin Morgan with the new ball; the first leg-before beaten by pace and late swing, the latter bounced out by a deliberate short-ball ploy. Morgan has often looked uncomfortable against pace, but when he flapped at a bouncer and was caught at fine leg, memories were revived of the concussion that he suffered at the hands of Starc at Old Trafford in September 2015. Starc returned in his third spell to end England's hopes of a late revival, by producing the ball of the day – a fast, inswinging yorker to bowl Ben Stokes who, as at Headingley, was playing a lone hand as time ticked away.

The other big name to produce on the day was David Warner, the big, bad wolf of Australian cricket, who began the process of blowing England's house down with a precise half-century to go on to 500 runs for the tournament. His opening partnership with Finch, worth 123 in 22.4 overs, charted Australia's course to victory and if their final score of 285 for seven felt a little underwhelming, it was only because of the scale and nature of the start that they were given on a damp, muggy morning, when Morgan sent Australia in with high hopes that early wickets would lead to a comfortable day.

None of England's seamers responded to that expectation particularly well, although Chris Woakes was far less culpable than Jofra Archer and Mark Wood, who were too short in length, too often. There was lavish movement off the seam at times, and Finch needed some good fortune early on. His first scoring shot, off the edge, brushed Root's fingers at slip, as did a drive to backward point, where James Vince failed to hold on to a half chance, and a close leg-before shout went Finch's way, too. Vince, later on, became Behrendorff's first victim, bowled second ball, driving expansively. Jason Roy's credentials have never looked more impressive, and the scans of his hamstring will be never more heavily scrutinised than over the next few days.

If these were marginal chances at best, Jos Buttler's missed stumping off Usman Khawaja in the 28th over from an Adil Rashid googly was a straight-forward miss. By this stage, England's spinners had been called on to bring some order to proceedings, which they began to do when Warner cut Moeen Ali loosely to backward point. If England's out-cricket continued to stumble – there were fumbles and overthrows – the bowling improved in the second half of the innings, foiling the expected acceleration. Finch fell hooking, the ball after bringing up his hundred, and Wood's incisive second spell accounted for Glenn Maxwell, a key wicket given the intent Maxwell had signalled by launching Archer into the Mound Stand.

Steve Smith had been booed much more loudly to the crease than Warner, and might have felt the wrath of Marcus Stoinis, too, after a mix-up and a runout as the innings entered its final stage. It needed a flourish from Alex Carey to take the score to 285.

This seemed highly competitive in the circumstances, all the more so when England's first three wickets were accounted for within six overs, as Australia's bowlers located the danger areas that England's failed to. It was down to the middle order once Jonny

Bairstow became the fourth wicket to fall, pulling a short, wide ball from Behrendorff into the deep, the choice of shot ill-suited to the line of the ball.

Australia's catching and fielding was as sharp as anything we have seen so far and two excellent catches in the deep confirmed there would be no England victory. The first came from Khawaja on the square-leg boundary, as Buttler aimed to leg, a hard-running, well-judged catch, given the power behind the stroke. The second came at deep mid-wicket off Woakes, with Maxwell palming the ball to Finch, moments before he stepped from the field of play. Fielders working in combination is a common sight now, but no less remarkable for that.

Powering eight boundaries to the fence, mostly by charging at the seamers, Stokes was not lacking in self-belief, but he was hindered by cramp in his calf. When Starc returned in his third spell to produce a fiendish in-dipping yorker that Stokes was unable to keep out, England's challenge was done.

Used expertly by Finch, it was fitting that Starc took the final wicket, because it was a day when Australia's champions were better than England's. It is squeaky bum time now.

......................................................

**PLAYER OF THE MATCH:**
*Aaron Finch (Australia)*

## WHAT THEY SAID

'Australia outplayed us, showed us how strong their basics were and ours need to be better.'

Eoin Morgan

'It's something I'll treasure for sure. You don't play cricket for the accolades, but to play at Lord's and to take five today was really special.'

Jason Behrendorff

## KEY NUMBERS

# 41

Mitchell Starc took his 41st World Cup wicket (in his 15th match) to move to eighth on the all-time list

## ANALYSIS

STEVE JAMES

This was actually the least culpable of England's three defeats in this competition but it will undoubtedly provoke the most pressing and demanding of inquests.

Australia are a good side, much better than Pakistan and Sri Lanka, against whom England had previously lost, but they are the old enemy and suddenly England are in a right pickle over qualification for the knockout stage, looking as nervously at other results as much as they are eyeing their two remaining matches against India and New Zealand.

How has it come to this? Were we duped all along? Was that No.1 ranking, gleaned in less fraught bilateral series before the tournament, masking problems that have become glaring deficiencies under the cut-throat

pressure of the World Cup itself? What effect did the Alex Hales situation have upon the group and the preparations? There are a lot of questions to answer.

And there is little doubt that we are seeing the vital differences between those bilateral series, where often teams are not at full strength – especially among their fast bowlers – and there is another day to shine.

One-off games naturally bring unique pressures, especially when not played on the shirt-fronts on which most of England's home one-day internationals have taken place in recent years. England have simply been unable to deal with surfaces that have not allowed them to play their go-to explosive and aggressive game. For me, the defeat by Sri Lanka changed everything.

The Pakistan reverse was a blip that could be excused and explained.

The fielding was awful but England, with two century-makers in Joe Root and Jos Buttler, still scored 334 in pursuit of Pakistan's 348. It was no horror show.

Headingley last Friday was just that. It was truly horrible. A team with pretensions of winning the tournament should not lose a game like that.

It brought an unexpected tension to this game at Lord's, which England could not manage. They were jittery and sloppy from the start.

Eoin Morgan, the captain, had understandably asked Australia to bat yesterday, with dark clouds hovering above and, while the pitch had clearly been cut a number of times since Monday, it was still greenish.

The ball moved around lavishly and yet Australia's openers, Aaron Finch and David Warner, put on 123 in 22.4 overs. They had some luck – any batsman would have needed that in these circumstances – but, in such a big match, they played quite magnificently.

If Morgan was going to bowl, should he perhaps have considered playing the seamer Liam Plunkett, who has such a good ODI record at Lord's, instead of one of the spinners, probably Moeen Ali? Plunkett has been brilliant in the middle overs since the previous World Cup four years ago and yet he has missed all three defeats in this competition.

Morgan said afterwards that it would have been a 'horrific' decision to bat first and you could see what he was saying in these conditions, but from now on should he consider batting first? That is three losses chasing now.

Throughout the white-ball revolution since the 2015 World Cup,

England have maintained that they can chase anything. That has always been their preferred modus operandi. Well, that has been disproved. And then some. Runs on the board seem to be key.

Here, you could understand why Morgan might have lacked confidence in his batting unit, especially up top, against this strong Australia bowling attack. England really are missing the hamstrung Jason Roy.

How they could have done with an opening partnership like Finch and Warner here. England's first wicket lasted two balls before James Vince was bowled.

It was a beautiful inswinger from the left-armer Jason Behrendorff, and it would be harsh to heap too much blame on Vince, but it confirmed yet again how much England need Roy back. Even if it is considered a risk, he must surely play against India at Edgbaston on Sunday.

Granted, if you were wishing to enter into a batsman-versus-bowler debate (and many dressing rooms do easily descend into such arguments) and defend Vince, you could, from that point of view, observe that Australia's opening bowlers performed much better than England's.

Jofra Archer just did not appear himself in his opening stint and while Chris Woakes probed, there was far too much short stuff. It was a morning to hit an old-fashioned good length and England did not do that.

For Australia to reach the end of the opening powerplay without a wicket having fallen and 44 runs on the board was quite astounding.

At the same stage of their innings England had scored fewer runs – 39 – and they had lost three wickets. There was the game in a nutshell.

The brutal truth is that England are still waiting for Vince to make his mark in 50-over cricket, a batsman with one fifty and an average of 24.09 in 11 ODI innings, and they simply should not be doing that in a World Cup. This is no place for long shots.

It also emphasises what a fool Hales is. He could be here making a real name for himself. Instead he is in purdah and, without him and Roy, England are underpowered at the top of the order. You wonder how Sam Billings might have fared. The Kent batsman was here at Lord's doing some media work. Had he not dislocated a shoulder in an innocuous fielding accident at Cardiff in April, he might have been opening here. You had to feel considerable sympathy for him as he watched on.

Home World Cups do not come along too often. Hales had tossed his opportunity away, Billings' had been cruelly taken away from him.

Billings may be better known for his work in the middle order but he has opened in four ODIs and scored two fifties (yes, one more than Vince) in that time. His most recent innings for England was a stunning 87 from 47 balls in a Twenty20 international in the Caribbean three months ago.

The sight of Ben Stokes limping his way to a gutsy 89 will also cause considerable concern before Sunday. His character has been to the fore in both of the past two defeats.

The strong stand up in such circumstances, as Finch, Warner and Mitchell Starc did for Australia, with Behrendorff the surprise package.

For England Stokes stood up, but others did not. If England are to turn this around – and they have often used the sting of criticism to stir them memorably into action – then he is going to need a lot more assistance.

# NEW ZEALAND v PAKISTAN

......................................................

*Wednesday, June 26*

*Edgbaston*

**New Zealand 237-6** (50 overs) (Neesham 97 not out, De Grandhomme 64; Shaheen Afridi 3-28) **Pakistan 241-4** (49.1 overs) (Babar Azam 101 not out, Haris Sohail 68) *Pakistan (2pts) won by six wickets* **Toss** *New Zealand*

JOHN WESTERBY

To think there were fears that this World Cup was becoming predictable. Now Pakistan, seemingly dead and buried not so long ago, are on the charge and further threatening England's place in the semi-finals, propelled to victory yesterday with five balls to spare by Babar Azam's calculated, elegant century.

New Zealand, meanwhile, after scraping home in their previous two games, have now lost their unbeaten record, still one win short of confirming their semi-final place, with Australia and England as their final two qualifying games.

And Pakistan have continued their uncanny mirroring of the progress of Imran Khan's victorious team at the 1992 World Cup, starting the tournament with a splutter, then gradually gathering pace. Their final two opponents are Afghanistan and Bangladesh. With Haris Sohail joining Babar in a decisive fourth-wicket stand of 126, they were worthy winners yesterday, to the sheer, rowdy joy of a crowd completely dominated by the bottle green and white of Pakistan.

England can expect more of the same when they face India here on Sunday, the colours changing to the light blue shirts and flags of green, white and orange in support of Virat Kohli's side.

The new pitch that England will play on against India is expected to provide more pace than the stodgy strip being used for the second time yesterday. On its first outing, for New Zealand's game against South Africa a week earlier, this surface was sticky after preparations had been disrupted by several days of rain. Yesterday, it was scarred from that first game and turned sharply, albeit slowly, for the spin bowlers.

Mitchell Santner, New Zealand's left-arm spinner, bowled to two slips to right-handed batsmen and with a short leg to left-handers, rare sights in the modern white-ball game. Even Kane Williamson, an occasional off spinner, bowling in this tournament for the first time, found plenty of turn. It remains a moot point whether World Cup matches should be held on used pitches. New Zealand remain handily placed to qualify for the semi-finals, but they have been flattered by their early schedule. Their tally of 11 points includes a washout against India followed by skin-of-the-teeth victories over South Africa and West Indies.

Their fielding has been several notches below their usual high standards and they lack a spinner of the highest quality. Should Ish Sodhi, the leg spinner, have played yesterday? On such a helpful pitch, Santner was tidy but wicketless, although Babar was dropped off him by Tom Latham when he had made only 38.

Having elected to bat, New Zealand soon found themselves, yet again, looking to Williamson to hold their innings together. Having compiled masterful centuries in the previous two games, the captain entered the fray after Martin Guptill dragged Mohammad Amir's first ball on to his stumps and soon saw his side reduced to 46 for four by a fine spell from Shaheen Afridi, the 19-year-old left-arm seamer, who took three top-order wickets.

Williamson began a repair job, but when he edged a leg break from Shadab Khan, Pakistan were firmly on top. Jimmy Neesham (97 not out) and Colin de Grandhomme (64) combined in an excellent sixth-wicket stand of 132, but were never able to score at a rate that would seriously stretch Pakistan.

Once Babar had been reprieved by Latham, he played an innings of which Williamson would have been proud, seeing the task through to keep alive slim hopes of repeating the success of Imran's side 27 years ago.

PLAYER OF THE MATCH:
*Babar Azam (Pakistan)*

## WHAT THEY SAID

'We have seen in the last three games that the surfaces have assisted the bowlers and they have been mighty close games. We were outplayed on a tough surface by a great Pakistan side today.'

Kane Williamson

'When we started, the idea was to play out the fast bowlers, especially Ferguson. But when Santner came and got the ball to rip, we understood that it's important to keep him off. The idea was to just be careful against him.'

Babar Azam

## KEY NUMBER

# 3,000
On 29, Babar Azam passed 3,000 one-day international runs

# INDIA v WEST INDIES

*Thursday, June 27*

*Old Trafford*

**India 268-7** (50 overs) (Kohli 72, Dhoni 56 not out; Roach 3-36)
**West Indies 143 all out** (34.2 overs) (Shami 4-16)
*India (2pts) won by 125 runs*
Toss India

JOHN WESTERBY

If England are looking for signs of encouragement before their momentous meeting with India on Sunday, it can at least be said that Virat Kohli's team were some way below their best in maintaining their unbeaten record in this World Cup yesterday.

By a country mile, though, this substellar performance was enough to beat a West Indies team whose early departure from the tournament was confirmed by their failure to overhaul India's total of 268 for seven, a score built around a solid 72 from Kohli and burnished by late flurries from MS Dhoni and Hardik Pandya.

India need one win from three remaining matches to confirm their semi-final place, with Bangladesh and Sri Lanka to come after their clash with England on Sunday. They are as good as there and, with Edgbaston expected to be dominated by India fans, they will relish the chance to inflict another grievous blow on the host nation's World Cup hopes.

'If we play the kind of cricket we've been playing, we will most probably end up on the winning side,' KL Rahul, the opening batsman, said. 'It's a big game against England, hopefully the momentum we have we can carry to Birmingham.'

What a time it is to be an India cricket fan. Their team are now top of the world rankings in Tests and one-day internationals, after their elevation above England in 50-over cricket this week, and much of the game dances to an Indian tune.

In Kohli, they have a captain whose emotive presence mirrors that of his exuberant followers in the stands, their sky-blue shirts dominating a full house at Old Trafford yesterday. In the closing stages, as Jasprit Bumrah began to fillet West Indies' lower order, Kohli was the master conductor, leading the rhythmical hand-clapping of the fans even as Bumrah was running in to bowl. With successive balls, Bumrah dismissed Carlos Brathwaite and Fabian Allen, before Kemar Roach dug out a slower hat-trick ball.

If Kohli did not happen to be the best batsman in the world, stitching his side's innings together on a slow pitch here, he could easily be imagined in the stands.

As for West Indies, for all that they have provided some of the competition's most memorable moments – some thunderous fast bowling, Brathwaite's gallant century in vain against New Zealand, the bowling of Sheldon Cottrell (that catch, too) – but they have been a team of sparkles rather than substance.

With games still to come against Sri Lanka and Afghanistan, Brathwaite's heroic knock remains the only hundred by a West Indies batsman, putting those above him in the order to shame. From an inconsistent top five, only Shai Hope, against Bangladesh, and Chris Gayle, in that thrilling game against New Zealand, have made scores of more than 70.

They never looked likely to threaten India's total, once Gayle had scuffed a pull to mid-on and Hope was bowled by a ball from Mohammed Shami that nipped back through his drive. In the two matches since he came in for the injured Bhuvneshwar Kumar, Shami has taken eight wickets, a more than adequate replacement.

Whether they have shored up their batting quite as convincingly since the injury to Shikhar Dhawan is another matter.

Rahul's promotion to replace Dhawan at the top of the order has led to Vijay Shankar coming in at No. 4 and, in such a key position, he remains unproven.

Rohit Sharma was unfortunate to be adjudged caught behind on review and, with Kedar Jadhav coming in a place or two too high at No. 5, India briefly looked vulnerable when they slipped to 140 for four.

But there was still Kohli, looking assured until he pulled a slower short ball from Jason Holder to mid-wicket, then the late blows from Pandya and Dhoni gave India a cushion that they would not need.

If England can make early incisions into India's top order on Sunday, they will need to twist the knife in a way West Indies were unable to do.

PLAYER OF THE MATCH:
*Virat Kohli (India)*

## WHAT THEY SAID

'He knows exactly what he wants to do out in the middle. When he has an off day here and there, everyone gets up and starts talking.'

Virat Kohli defends MS Dhoni

'We let ourselves down significantly. I don't think we seized the crucial moments in this tournament as we should have. We missed crucial chances in the field.'

Jason Holder

## KEY NUMBER

# 20,000

Virat Kohli reached 20,000 runs in international cricket in fewer innings than anyone else

# SOUTH AFRICA v SRI LANKA

*Friday, June 28*

### The Riverside, Chester-le-Street

**Sri Lanka 203 all out** (49.3 overs) (Morris 3-46, Pretorius 3-25)
**South Africa 206-1** (37.2 overs) (Amla 80 not out, Du Plessis 96 not out)
*South Africa (2pts) won by nine wickets*
**Toss** *South Africa*

JOHN WESTERBY

The defining image of this game came in the closing stages of Sri Lanka's innings, when a swarm of bees entered the playing area. The two batsmen, 11 South Africa players and the umpires fell to the floor, taking cover until the invasion passed. They lay prone for a minute or more, wearing looks of mild embarrassment, like a group of adults being forced to play sleeping lions.

This was indeed a contest between two teams who are down and now, effectively, out of this World Cup. A second victory for South Africa, completed with 12.4 overs to spare, was consolation for Faf du Plessis, the captain, who scored an unbeaten 96.

Defeat for Sri Lanka, a third of the tournament to go with two washouts, prevented them from drawing level with England, most likely ending their chances of reaching the semi-finals, with games against West Indies and India to come.

At every World Cup since 1992, at least one of these teams has featured in the semi-finals but here, the two sides have found themselves in a rebuilding phase at the wrong time.

After dismissing Sri Lanka for 203 on another slow pitch, Du Plessis and Hashim Amla cantered home with few troubles during an unbroken stand of 175, having come together in the fifth over when a yorker from Lasith Malinga crashed into Quinton de Kock's leg stump. At 35, Malinga is past his formidable prime but his laser-guided yorker remains one of the best in the game.

Amla played with a fluency that had eluded him in recent weeks, leaning into his off drives and cutting Thisara Perera hard past point. Du Plessis, on the way to his third half-century of the competition, drove Suranga Lakmal straight for six and pulled him hard through mid-wicket next ball.

There was one alarm for Amla when, on 68, he swept at the leg spin of Jeevan Mendis and was given out leg-before. Amla reviewed but, on viewing the first replays on the big screen, set off for the pavilion. Ball-tracking technology revealed that the ball had pitched outside leg stump and, just as he reached the boundary, he turned to resume his innings.

Sri Lanka were never able to generate momentum from the moment Dimuth Karunaratne gloved the first ball of the match, from Kagiso Rabada, to slip. Too few batsmen showed the application necessary on a slow pitch. Amla and Du Plessis showed them the way but this was too little, too late for South Africa.

......................................................

### PLAYER OF THE MATCH:
***Dwaine Pretorius (South Africa)***

## WHAT THEY SAID

'It feels hollow. It's great winning, but it is very, very bittersweet because you know that we've let a lot of people down, and that was never the plan.'

Faf du Plessis

'I think all departments went wrong.'

Dimuth Karunaratne

## KEY NUMBER

### 175

The partnership between Hashim Amla and Faf du Plessis was the second highest for the second wicket by South Africa in a World Cup match

# AFGHANISTAN v PAKISTAN

*Saturday, June 29*

*Headingley*

**Afghanistan 227-9** (50 overs)
(Shaheen Afridi 4-47)
**Pakistan 230-7** (49.4 overs)
*Pakistan (2pts) won by three wickets*
**Toss** *Afghanistan*

IAN HAWKEY

Not so much cornered tigers, Pakistan are now in the proud role of the catch-us-if-you-can phoenix of World Cup 2019. A third win on the trot has barged England out of the top four and, for those inclined, as many seem to be, to see in this compelling storyline an exact mirror of the Pakistan comeback that propelled them to the title in 1992, well, the parallels with that adventure continue.

But if Pakistan's recovery, from apparently down and out after five games, is part of some eerie destiny, they certainly set that destiny some challenges at Headingley. They gained their points with two balls to spare and with seven wickets down in an attritional contest that left Afghanistan once again snatching at thoughts of what might have been. A week ago, the Afghans lost by 11 runs to India. After an even tighter finish, they remain frustrated, bottom of the table.

A baking hot day in Leeds ended edgily, Pakistan guided over the line in their run chase thanks to a courageous 49 not out from Imad Wasim, who had earlier taken two wickets and finished man of the match, cool and collected amid the frenzy. The day had began a little edgily, too, with confrontations between supporters around the perimeter of Headingley and then inside the stadium. A handful were evicted. After the winning runs had been struck, several spectators rushed onto the field, and, attempting to stop them, a security guard knocked over Afghanistan's Mohammad Nabi.

Nabi already had as much reason to feel wronged as any member of his losing team. He had bowled with almost impeccable discipline to make Pakistan's target, 228, look more and more improbable. He took two premium wickets, those of Imam-ul-Haq and Babar Azam, and he quite suffocated the run chase, conceding just 23 runs from his ten overs.

All of which contributed to Pakistan's gathering alarm. Neither Babar, attempting to sweep and losing his leg stump when well set, nor Imam, charging down the pitch, reacted with much sangfroid to their own cornered-tiger scenario and there were glimpses of a brittle Pakistan, not least Mohammad Hafeez's waft off Mujeeb Ur Rahman to Hashmatullah Shahidi. Nor will the captain, Sarfaraz Ahmed, be much inclined to look back at his dismissal, as he began to suspect, anxiously, that the control he had worked shrewdly to impose in the field was being taken away. He was run out, seeking to turn a single into an ill-advised two runs.

That put Pakistan's chase in real jeopardy, at 156 for six with 72 runs needed from 11 overs. With five overs left, they needed 46, at which point Afghanistan skipper Gulbadin Naib returned to the attack, and gave Imad pace on the ball to make use of. Poor Gulbadin almost instantly regretted the decision. Eighteen runs came from the over, all of them from the bat of Imad, who, opening his shoulders and

abetted by Wahab Riaz in the closing stages, guided Pakistan home.

They had cut it terribly fine, but can point out that a determined Afghanistan deserved credit for that. Having elected to take advantage of what looked benign batting conditions, Afghanistan had set their highest target of the tournament, in this, their fourth go at batting first. But they never truly escaped the control of the World Cup's most upwardly mobile team. At each moment the underdogs threatened to growl, their opponents seemed to tighten the leash.

The pattern set in early. Gulbadin, opening with Rahmat, had just begun to show a relish for Shaheen Afridi's wayward line, thumping the left-armer for two boundaries, when their duel was cut short, Gulbadin caught behind, following a Pakistan review, for 15.

Next ball, Shaheen, all strong-jawed, fresh-faced pugnacity and fresh from his three for 28 in the win over New Zealand, had his second wicket, Hashmatullah caught off a leading edge by Imad. Afghanistan struggled for momentum after that Shaheen blitz, and a burden fell on the young shoulders of Ikram Alikhil, the teenaged wicketkeeper-batsman. He took on the role of shock-absorber with stoicism but exaggerated patience. Although Ikram and Asghar Afghan stuck around for the fourth wicket, and Asghar, much the senior partner, played bold, stylish strokes, progress was never much more than steady. From the 20th over to the end of the 30th, Afghanistan added just 30 runs, none of them in boundaries.

For Pakistan, Shadab Khan and Imad both got some turn from the pitch, but the damaging performers with the ball were the trio of pacier left-armers. Wahab, as ever, bowled with a snarl and a ready bouncer, and might have sensed that this was Pakistan's day when he picked up the wicket of Nabi, caught by Amir at long leg. Amir has had his butterfingered moments at this tournament; here he made some amends as Pakistan had an ultimately sound day, mostly, in the field. That winning habit is refreshing all parts of their game.

PLAYER OF THE MATCH:
*Imad Wasim (Pakistan)*

## WHAT THEY SAID

'It was not an easy pitch to bat on but, credit should go to Imad for the way he batted till the end. We knew the chase was not easy and their bowlers used the conditions very well.'

Sarfaraz Ahmed

'In this tournament, you'll face these kinds of situations. You need to work slightly harder to win matches, so we need to improve.'

Gulbadin Naib

'When I went in, Rashid was bowling brilliantly. I couldn't pick him to be honest; I just hung in there.'

Imad Wasim

## KEY NUMBERS

# 19

The age of Shaheen Afridi, who became the youngest bowler to take four wickets in a World Cup match

# AUSTRALIA v NEW ZEALAND

......................................................

*Saturday, June 29*

*Lord's (day-night)*

**Australia 243-9** (50 overs)
(Khawaja 88, Carey 71; Boult 4-51)
**New Zealand 157 all out**
(43.4 overs) (Starc 5-26)
*Australia (2pts) won by 86 runs*
**Toss** *Australia*

SIMON WILDE, *SUNDAY TIMES*
CRICKET CORRESPONDENT
While Australia, the defending champions, serenely glide on, the wind has truly gone out of New Zealand's sails. A second defeat in four days for the World Cup's pace-setters means they are still waiting to secure a semi-final spot and may need points from their game against England on Wednesday to be sure of one.

Not only did they lose to the team they faced in the 2015 final, they were beaten by such a distance – thanks to a woeful middle-order collapse – that they suffered significant harm to their net run-rate, which could yet be relevant. However, if England lose to India today their qualification anxieties will be over.

On another good day for left-arm seamers, the match – only the second day-night ODI played at Lord's – featured a Trent Boult hat-trick as well as five wickets for Mitchell Starc and two for Jason Behrendorff, the destroyers of England in midweek. Starc's tournament tally now stands

at 24, two more than in 2015. The fast bowler is in a class of his own.

This was an old-fashioned game of attrition on a niggling pitch already used for the England-Australia match. On a day of baking heat in northwest London, it felt like the sort of occasion on which the crowd should have been entertained with a boundary-fest, but only two sixes were hit all day. Nobody really trusted their expansive shots, but Australia's batsmen were the more patient.

These were the sort of conditions in which part-time spinners could play a useful role, and there was one wicket for Kane Williamson and one for Steve Smith, his first in ODIs for five years.

It needed somebody to play a Test match-style innings if New Zealand were going to get to their target of 244. They lost both openers to Behrendorff by the time 42 was on the board, Henry Nicholls to a leg-side strangle and Martin Guptill leg-before, which brought the game to its tipping point: Williamson and Ross Taylor up against the best Australia could throw at them.

Williamson batted with his customary skill to reach 40 for the sixth time in six innings at this World Cup, only to give his wicket away in surprisingly careless fashion when, in the first over of Starc's second spell, he attempted another of his favourite glides to third man and feathered a catch to the keeper. Taylor and Tom Latham tried to regroup but with the asking rate climbing to around seven an over, Taylor lashed across the line at Pat Cummins and was caught by Alex Carey off an enormous skyer. The nature of the collapse that followed only confirmed suspicions that New Zealand's batting lacks depth against the best attacks, as Mitch Santner fell for 12 to close the game at 157 all out.

Australia had to battle hard to post a working total. So good in earlier matches at laying strong foundations, they found themselves in serious strife at 92 for five. Boult struck an early blow by nipping the ball into Aaron Finch's pads and Lockie Ferguson, sporting his trademark black bowling boots, weighed in with the wickets of David Warner and Smith with his first eight deliveries, Warner unsuccessfully trying to withdraw his bat from a bouncer. As Warner departed and Smith arrived, the crowd had the pleasure of booing two villains at once. Smith fell to a fine catch by Guptill at leg gully.

James Neesham also contributed a double-strike, having Marcus Stoinis caught behind, while the dangerous Glenn Maxwell was well held by Neesham as Maxwell toe-ended a pull wide to the bowler's left. Things could have been worse, too. Usman Khawaja would stay at the crease for 45 overs but he was missed by Guptill in the slips off his second ball. He survived to share the decisive partnership of the innings, worth 107 for the sixth wicket with Carey, of which his own share was a watchful 35 with no boundaries.

Carey, meanwhile, confirmed what an excellent first World Cup he is having with a career-best 71 from 72 balls with 11 fours. His previous best of 55 came in the match against West Indies in which he performed a similar rescue act. It had to be asked, though, why Williamson did not recall Boult, after a six-over spell up front, until the 40th over, or make more use of his front-line spinners. Boult fully played his part in the closing stages though as Australia were only able to muster 55 from the last ten. They might not have got that many, either, without the strong-arm tactics of Cummins, who hit an unbeaten 23 from 19.

Boult polished things off in style with a hat-trick in the 50th over that required no assistance from his fielders: Khawaja bowled for 88, Starc yorked by a tailing in-swinger reminiscent of the ball Starc had bowled to Ben Stokes from the same end and on the same strip four days earlier, and Behrendorff leg-before.

It was Boult's second ODI hat-trick in eight months and the eleventh at World Cups. After a quiet start to the tournament, Boult has now taken nine wickets in three games. England should note that he appears to be peaking at the right time.

.......................................................................

PLAYER OF THE MATCH:
*Alex Carey (Australia)*

## WHAT THEY SAID

'The turning point was probably that Indian game where we had a good chat as a bowling group and a batting group and we've just continued to improve as a whole group of players from that game, so it's been fantastic.'

Mitchell Starc

'I don't think we need to focus on recalibrating. Maybe there's a dent in momentum. But then at the end of the day, it is coming back to the cricket that we want to play.'

Kane Williamson

## KEY NUMBERS

### 6,000

On 32, Kane Williamson reached 6,000 runs in one-day internationals

### 3

Mitchell Starc became the first player to take three five-fors at World Cups

## ENGLAND v INDIA

*Sunday, June 30*

*Edgbaston*

**England 337-7** (50 overs) (Roy 66, Bairstow 111, Stokes 79; Shami 5-69)
**India 306-5** (50 overs) (Sharma 102, Kohli 66; Plunkett 3-55)
*England (2pts) won by 31 runs*
Toss *England*

MIKE ATHERTON,
CHIEF CRICKET CORRESPONDENT
In Lahore, Karachi and Faisalabad, in the villages, pastures and mountains, they would have been watching and listening and praying, remarkably, for an Indian victory. After the conclusion of a fine match, one in which the home team not only kept their hopes of qualification alive but once again exhibited their credentials, these supporters from Pakistan would have recognised, ruefully, in England's see-sawing performances something of their own unpredictable team.

After losing, abjectly, to Sri Lanka at Headingley and to the old enemy, Australia, at Lord's, Eoin Morgan's team showed their best face again to hand Virat Kohli's India their first defeat of the competition. More than that, it was the kind of performance – confident, assertive, aggressive with the bat – that will have restored their dented confidence and reminded others why they were so feared a few weeks ago. Most of all it was a performance full of courage.

The margin of victory was a comfortable one in the end, but it was a close-run thing for a long time, with the result never quite certain until the dismissal of the dangerous Hardik Pandya. When Rishabh Pant fell with 11 overs to go, India were still in the game, needing 112 to win, but MS Dhoni could never quite get going and when Pandya holed out at long-on, India never threatened again. It was a tame and baffling end to a pulsating match.

The veil of gloom drawing over England's World Cup campaign was lifted quickly in the morning by an opening partnership of real majesty between Jason Roy, fit again after hamstring trouble, and Jonny Bairstow, stung into action by a spot of internecine warfare and responding magnificently with his first World Cup hundred. They provided the groundwork for the victory, while Chris Woakes and a restored Liam Plunkett took five wickets between them to peg India back as their batsmen failed to keep up with a run rate that eventually ran out of control.

This match fits, then, into a pattern of sorts, with the pressure of the run chase proving to be too taxing even for India's dynamos, who were asked to make more than anyone had chased successfully in a World Cup match before. For that, England supporters can thank Roy and Bairstow, in particular, who, after a brief separation, were united again and embraced each other longingly with their ninth century partnership, and their most important. They whispered sweet nothings to each other for the best part of 23 overs, by which time any nerves were long forgotten and the threat of India's spinners had been dispatched.

It took Roy only two legitimate deliveries (the first ball of the innings was a wide) to show what England had been missing, when he cut Mohammed Shami to the fence with blistering intent. There was another boundary in the first over, too, a crisp cover drive. Bairstow is a better player with Roy around, but it took a little while for the good vibes to be transmitted, and he enjoyed some early moments of good fortune against Shami, with two inside edges just evading leg-stump.

The good fortune was not Bairstow's alone, as Roy, on 21 at the time, should have been given out caught down the leg side. The umpire, Aleem Dar, signalled a wide instead and India did not review.

Shami and Jasprit Bumrah have been the outstanding new-ball pair of the tournament, conceding a run per over fewer than their competitors in the opening powerplay period. So, while the 50 posted by the openers was their slowest together in ODI cricket, it was not slow in the context of what had come before against India. When the next ten overs brought 98 runs, it was clear a challenging score was in the offing.

The leg spinner Yuzvendra Chahal was pitched into the fray early in the sixth over, but retreated, tail between his legs, having conceded 16 runs. Each time, he and Kuldeep Yadav, the left-arm wrist spinner, were introduced Bairstow and Roy attacked with gusto, so that the threat on a dry surface that offered minimal spin was quickly nulli-fied. All told, India's spinners conceded 160 runs from their 20 overs, with Chahal enduring his most expensive day in ODI cricket.

Although Roy fell eventually to Kuldeep – the only wicket to fall to India's spinners on the day – the enve-lope had been sealed and the message to the dressing room sent by then that the threat lay elsewhere. A bonus for England was the blow that Roy took to his forearm off Bumrah, which allowed England to remove him from fielding duties and so protecting his hamstring injury. He really is that important to the cause, now.

It was Bairstow's turn to take centre stage, then, which is just where he likes to be. He is a remarkable cricketer, one who uses any and every slight, real or imagined, to tap into the places where his most competitive instincts lie. Where his teammates sounded relaxed before the match, Bairstow found him-self drawn into a spat after questioning whether supporters and, or, media commentators wanted England to fail. After that, it was nailed on certainty that he would respond with a hundred, as he did in Colombo last winter, after being left out of England's Test team.

He really found his stride when, in the 13th over, he hit a glorious drive back over Pandya's head and some of the tension seemed to disappear from his game. He accelerated rapidly after that, with his half-century coming in 56 balls – seven fours and two sixes – and his hundred in only 34 balls more, four more sixes coming in his second fifty.

England hit 13 sixes in all while India, even with one short square boundary, failed to clear the ropes until the final over. Bairstow was one of Shami's five wickets, which also included Eoin Morgan, caught hook-ing. England's captain will be peppered from here on in.

Bumrah had been given five of the final ten overs, and responded magnificently by conceding only one boundary and 26 runs, while 92 came in all for England in that time, with Ben Stokes continuing his fine batting form.

As if taking his cue from Bumrah, Woakes began with three consecu-tive maidens – each as rare in modern ODI cricket as a pearl in an oyster – including the wicket of KL Rahul, well caught and bowled in tumbling fashion on the follow-through.

It was always likely, then, that the match would be settled by the length and strength of the partnership between India's best players, Rohit Sharma and Kohli. Sharma had been badly missed by Joe Root at slip fourth ball, in Jofra Archer's first over, and he made Root wait nervously, by making his 25th ODI hundred, and his third in this World Cup.

If Sharma was not quite wearing his most elegant finery at the start, Kohli made up for it, and their partnership of 138 in 26 overs was threatening, especially since Adil Rashid was again below his best in the middle overs.

Kohli averages more than 60 when India chase a total of 300 or more, and he has scored – staggeringly – nine hundreds when doing so, seven in a winning cause. His wicket was the vital one, then, and it fell to Plunkett, restored to the team in place of Moeen Ali and completing ten overs for the first time in a World Cup match.

Driving loosely, Kohli was taken at backward point and when Sharma aimed a heave to leg and edged a slower ball from Woakes, India's challenge began to falter. Woakes took a marvellous running catch in the deep to see off the dangerous Pant and enjoyed a fine day on his home ground. England are back on track.

...................................................

PLAYER OF THE MATCH:
*Jonny Bairstow (England)*

## WHAT THEY SAID

'Jonny does tend to get fired up a lot, and that suits him. He likes a bit of fire in his belly, and I don't mind that when he comes out and plays like that.'

Eoin Morgan

'The toss was vital, especially since the boundary was that short, the shortest you can have. It is bizarre on a flat pitch. If batsmen are able to reverse-sweep you for six on a 59-metre boundary there is not much you can do as a spinner.'

Virat Kohli

## KEY NUMBER

# 9

Jason Roy and Jonny Bairstow shared their ninth century opening stand for England. The next most successful pair are Marcus Trescothick and Nick Knight with four

# Sport

**WIMBLEDON**

**Wimbledon 16-page guide**
Murray's return and how Konta can win as tournament starts today
Inside T2

# England restore fear factor

Fired-up Bairstow hits century to set up win over India and put hosts back on course for semi-finals

**Elizabeth Ammon**

The England captain Eoin Morgan said his side had "an outstanding day" after they kept their World Cup hopes alive with a 31-run victory that ended India's unbeaten run.

England bounced back from successive losses to Sri Lanka and Australia, and yesterday's win means that they are guaranteed a semi-final spot if they beat New Zealand on Wednesday at Chester-le-Street.

An exceptional 111 from the opener Jonny Bairstow, who had reacted to criticism after England's defeat by Australia by accusing people of wanting the team to fail, proved crucial in settling any nerves from the under-pressure hosts at Edgbaston.

"He [Jonny] does tend to get fired up a lot, and that suits him," Morgan said. "He likes a bit of fire in his belly, and I don't mind that when he comes out and plays like that. It's outstanding. It was
Continued on page 59

Bairstow takes the acclaim on reaching his 90-ball hundred in England's victory over India at Edgbaston, which boosted their World Cup semi-final hopes Pages 56-59

## US accused in World Cup spying row

**Molly Hudson** Lyons

England and the United States have become embroiled in a spying row before their women's World Cup semi-final after two plain-clothed members of American staff were spotted in a private area of the Lionesses' team hotel in Lyons yesterday.

The FA is believed to be furious at the unwelcome intrusion from the US, who were scoping out the Fourvière Hotel as a potential base for Sunday's final. England face the US at Parc Olympique Lyonnais tomorrow and the final will also be played there.

England were training at a different location 30 minutes from the hotel while the two Americans were being shown around by staff at their hotel. The FA is said to be concerned that the Americans went into rooms where England have held team meetings.

They were not wearing any US-branded kit and did not show their team credentials to security on their way in. Eventually the pair were spotted by a member of the FA team.

The US coach Jill Ellis dismissed the idea that it was arrogant to be scouting a base for a final her team may not even reach, and to do it when their semi-final opponents were staying there. "I would assume everybody is doing that — you have to plan ahead," Ellis, 52, said. "The only two people who are thinking of planning ahead is my administrator, because she has to book all the flights and do all of that stuff, and her boss. Everybody else, we don't worry about that, so that is probably who the two people [at the hotel] were.

"So, in terms of arrogance, that has nothing to do with us, that is planning and preparation for our staff."

Phil Neville, the England head coach, said that it was poor etiquette and insisted his staff would not have done the same. "It'll have no bearing on the game — I found it funny," he said. "I
Continued on page 55

---

## Times Crossword 27,391

**ACROSS**

1 What Man Ray was, having a platform in outskirts of Detroit (7)
5 A theatre award in New Mexico? It means the opposite (7)
9 Self-denying sailors can finally purchase books (9)
10 All the players make nearly half the ice cream (5)
11 Daggers produced by old boy and priest (5)
12 At that time a group of nations invested in American club (9)
13 Jurassic creature's talons oddly displayed in a house (13)
17 Affected elegance of melodies with decorations (4,3,6)
21 Attractive English teacher dips into trifle half-heartedly (9)
24 US city entertaining male climber (5)
25 Stuff oneself with something close to Cheddar (5)
26 When swimming, lady dives with due consideration (9)
27 Fate sailors reversed, avoiding area by island (7)
28 Faker cops finally decisively overcome (7)

**DOWN**

1 Racing yacht — something a female impersonator might have? (6)
2 Go with detectives, finding ruin (9)
3 First letter, one I penned in ancient language going north (7)
4 Bored agent with woman in Thailand's borders (9)
5 Letter revealing a union problem after seven years? (5)
6 Giant, one meeting a fairy queen (7)
7 In action it resembles saltpetre (5)
8 Part of sailing vessel popular in mother's time (8)
14 Old, old city's little people — us, emphatically (9)
15 Scallywags generally in right order crossing a burn? (9)
16 Eccentric leader leaving NW town for a Welsh one (8)
18 Stuffy, like follicularly challenged Cockneys? (7)
19 Church cheers fellow visiting, one giving out notes (7)
20 Hungarian publication unknown artist set up (6)
22 Originally such a strange Wiltshire diocese (5)
23 The cheek of some musicians! (5)

**Prize solution 27,384**

9 771742 498615

## ANALYSIS

**STEVE JAMES**

Ben Stokes is having some tournament. England's opening match against South Africa at the Oval seems an awfully long time ago now and it is easy to forget the stunning entrance that Stokes made into this competition on that day, making 89, taking two wickets and, of course, snaring a catch for the ages.

Much has happened since, not least England's three unexpected dalliances with defeat, but amid it all, Stokes has simply grown and grown in presence.

While others stumbled and faltered in the most recent losses against Sri Lanka and Australia, Stokes stood tall, displaying immense character in the two run chases, running out of partners in the first of them (82 not out) against Sri Lanka at Headingley and receiving little support in the second (89), at Lord's against Australia.

Here was a different scenario, with England batting first and, with Jason Roy restored to the side, the openers having provided a fine start. But Stokes still played an important innings, making 79 from 54 balls – and at last his efforts received their due reward with victory.

Lone defiance was not on the menu upon his arrival at this Birmingham bistro but Stokes still chose his order shrewdly.

It was not the time to stuff one's face immediately. After the freewheeling batting of Roy and Jonny Bairstow, the manner in which Joe Root was batting – nowhere near his usual tempo of a run a ball – told a story.

This was a good pitch but it was not necessarily, as they say in the game, a road – certainly not in the same category of highway as many of the surfaces upon which England rose to No. 1 in the world in the past four years. It was slightly two-paced. A bowler could take his dues, too.

Mind you, that Root's final score of 44 was achieved at a strike rate of 81.48, which was not a million miles behind Virat Kohli's 86.84 for his 66 later on, also tells a tale. Root is usually quite brilliant at the role assigned to him.

England's middle-innings stickiness – remarkably, they did not hit a boundary for ten overs and two balls, from the moment Bairstow reverse-swept just after his century to Stokes' first four – begged the question, of course, of whether Jos Buttler should have been promoted to No. 4 in place of captain Eoin Morgan, who is acting like a magnet to a barrage of short balls at the moment. Continuing to be out hooking will not change that.

Hindsight is always the sharpest selector but Buttler really should have been used earlier here. When belatedly summoned, he made 20 from eight balls. It was a glimpse, but England needed a fuller viewing.

Yes, England toyed with a similar dilemma against Afghanistan earlier in the tournament, going with Morgan then and resulting in his blizzard of sixes, but this felt different.

Anyway, Stokes arrived at No. 5 – before Buttler – in the 34th over and took his customary amount of time to settle in. That is just his method.

His wrists appear to be made of steel rather than rubber, so manoeuvring the ball into the gaps is not his forte.

When you can catch up with the pace later on, it is not necessarily a problem. The way that Stokes sets about his innings confirms that it is not only as a person that he has matured since standing trial last summer for his actions outside a Bristol nightclub in September 2017. His batting is so much smarter. He has always possessed the technique of a batsman rather than that of a mere hitter, but now he has attached a calmer, more discerning mind.

While England know that they have Root at the top of the order to stick some glue around the stroke-makers if needs be, they know that they have Stokes to perform a similar role later on, as well as being able to smite the ball out of the park.

In every innings he has played in this World Cup, it is almost as if he is attempting to make up for the time he missed – an Ashes tour, no less – and all the concomitant negative publicity and turmoil.

After a poor Indian Premier League, his English summer did not begin especially positively, but it was towards the end of the one-day international series against Pakistan – aided by some clever repositioning of him up the order at No. 4 by the England management – that he started to show some excellent form with the bat.

That he now has four fifties in this tournament, and is incredibly unfortunate not to have added to England's six centuries, is evidence of his reaping the benefits of the hard work that he put in. He has peaked at precisely the right time.

Stokes did not hit that first boundary until his 14th ball here, reverse-sweeping the leg spin of Yuzvendra Chahal for four, but once he began to find his range, the ball-striking was quite exceptional.

In Chahal's next over there was an outrageous reverse-hit for six and in his following over – the poor bowler eventually returned his worst ODI figures, conceding 88 runs in his ten overs with no reward – there was another six, this time clipped high over deep midwicket. His fifty occupied 38 balls.

Jasprit Bumrah proved difficult to collar, with Stokes finally scooping him to fine leg in the last over, but three consecutive boundaries – four, six and four – from the 49th over of the innings, bowled by Mohammed Shami, ensured that England had a total that was mightily competitive and beyond. It always looked well above par.

Stokes could not make an impact with the ball, his four overs going for 34 runs as Kohli and Rohit Sharma looked to accelerate, and he even made an uncharacteristic misfield at the death, but without his batting, England could easily have wasted the start given to them.

Stokes, clearly chastened, is obviously determined not to waste anything now in this tournament or in the rest of his career.

# SRI LANKA v WEST INDIES

*Monday, July 1*

*The Riverside, Chester-le-Street*

**Sri Lanka 338-6** (50 overs)
(Kusal Perera 64, Fernando 104)
**West Indies 315-9** (50 overs)
(Pooran 118, Allen 51; Malinga 3-55)
*Sri Lanka (2pts) won by 23 runs*
**Toss** *West Indies*

It may have been a dead rubber, but it did not stop the teams producing a richly entertaining encounter featuring two impressive performances from players who may be stars of the next World Cup. Sri Lanka's Avishka Fernando, 21, hit 104 off 103 balls to set up a daunting challenge for West Indies. That they almost got there owed much to Nicholas Pooran, 23, who hammered a brilliant 188 off 103 balls.

But it took one of the old guard to settle the outcome in Sri Lanka's favour. With three overs left and West Indies needing 31, Dimuth Karunaratne brought on former captain Angelo Mathews for his first bowl of the tournament. Remarkably, the gamble paid off. Pooran slashed wildly at his first ball and was caught behind by Kusal Perera. Lasith Malinga returned to take his third wicket and finish things off in the next over.

Until Mathews' intervention, West Indies had looked poised to complete the highest run chase in World Cup history. They had seemed out of it at 145 for five in the 29th over, but Pooran launched a counter-attack, first in partnership with Carlos Brathwaite – content to play the anchor role this time – and then with Fabian Allen, who enhanced his growing reputation by racing to 51 in 32 balls before he was run out after a mix-up with Pooran.

Sri Lanka started impressively and just kept going. In compiling his first international century, Fernando shared stands of 85 with Kusal Mendis, 58 with Mathews and 67 with the unbeaten Lahiru Thirimanne. Sri Lanka's pre-match work on dealing with the short ball paid dividends. But perhaps the most eye-catching moment of their innings came when Allen produced one of the best catches of the tournament, leaping sideways to complete a stunning caught and bowled to remove Mendis.

Barbadian pop superstar Rihanna, a keen West Indies follower, was at the game, but was unable to inspire her team to arrest their dismal run of results.

PLAYER OF THE MATCH:
*Avishka Fernando (Sri Lanka)*

## WHAT THEY SAID

'I knew once myself and Fabian was batting, we were in control. Actually the bowlers didn't know where to bowl and it got easy. Unfortunately then Fabian got run-out there and I felt a bit responsible for that, but we were in total control of the game and it just slipped.'

Nicholas Pooran

'Now we have to wait for other results. We're not a side who should be in this position. We have talent, and skill to compete with anyone. But we only performed in certain games.'

Dimuth Karunaratne

## KEY NUMBER

# I

The first time two batsmen under 25 scored centuries in the same World Cup match

# BANGLADESH v INDIA

*Tuesday, July 2*

*Edgbaston*

**India 314-9** (50 overs) (Rahul 77, Sharma 104; Mustafizur Rahman 5-59)
**Bangladesh 286 all out** (48 overs) (Shakib Al Hasan 66, Mohammad Saifuddin 51 not out; Bumrah 4-55, Pandya 3-60)
*India (2pts) won by 28 runs*
Toss *India*

Rohit Sharma enhanced his player-of-the-tournament credentials with his fourth century as India eased in to the semi-finals alongside Australia. But for Bangladesh, defeat meant the end of their slim hopes of reaching the last four.

Rohit, badly dropped by Tamim Iqbal on nine, put on 180 for the first wicket with KL Rahul (77), the best opening partnership of the competition and the seventh highest in World Cup history. But the Indian middle order failed to drive home that advantage; after being 162 for no wicket at the halfway point, a final total of 314 for nine was disappointing.

Credit for that was due to the Bangladesh bowlers who shrewdly tried to ensure that India could not target the short boundary which had attracted criticism from Virat Kohli after his team had lost to England on Sunday. Shakib Al Hasan was again superb, and Soumya Sarkar bowled six cheap overs as well as claiming the wicket of Rohit. But the man who really prevented India cutting loose was Mustafizur Rahman, who took his first World Cup five-for. India managed just 63 in their last ten overs.

Remembering their brilliantly paced chase against West Indies at Taunton, Bangladesh set off in confident mood. But only two of their batsmen – Shakib and Mohammad Saifuddin at No. 8 – passed 50 while others failed to build on promising starts. Several seemed unable to read the pace of an increasingly sluggish surface.

Jasprit Bumrah capped another highly impressive performance by taking the final two wickets with superbly executed yorkers.

PLAYER OF THE MATCH:
**Rohit Sharma (India)**

## WHAT THEY SAID

'I am very proud with the way we played against the big teams. Maybe we will be the people's team for the amount of fight we have shown.'

Bangladesh coach Steve Rhodes

'My mantra is whatever has happened in the past, keep it in the past. It is a new day, present day and I don't try to think about what has happened.'

Rohit Sharma

## KEY NUMBERS

### 3

Rohit Sharma's third man-of-the-match award matched the achievement of Sachin Tendulkar at the 2003 tournament

### 6

India reached their sixth successive semi-final in ICC tournaments (World Cup, World T20 and Champions Trophy)

# ENGLAND v NEW ZEALAND

............................................

*Wednesday, July 3*

*The Riverside, Chester-le-Street*

**England 305–8** (50 overs)
(Roy 60, Bairstow 106)
**New Zealand 186 all out** (45 overs)
(Latham 57; Wood 3–34)
*England (2pts) won by 119 runs*
**Toss** *England*

MIKE ATHERTON,
CHIEF CRICKET CORRESPONDENT
Hallelujah. For the first time in more than a quarter of a century, England have made the semi-finals of the World Cup.

They did not make life easy for themselves, and have not always played at their swaggering best in the qualification stages, but they were good enough when it mattered, handing India a first defeat and now beating a short-of-confidence New Zealand team in what were effectively knock-out games to book a date at Edgbaston next Thursday. What was billed as a potentially fraught encounter ended as a gentle stroll in the evening sunshine to the strains of *Sweet Caroline*.

Whether Eoin Morgan's team will be good enough to beat their probable opponents, India, again remains to be seen, but playing under this kind of pressure in consecutive games cannot have done them any harm. With elimination on the line, some key performers produced somewhere near their best when it mattered and

confidence, that precious and fragile commodity in sport, is high again. If they ever doubted that they could win it, that doubt has evaporated. The swagger is back.

It is a swagger best encapsulated by the opening combination of Jonny Bairstow and Jason Roy, whose partnership has been the principal reason for England emerging from a mid-tournament slump. They added 123 in 18.4 overs, in the same manner as they put India's bowlers to the sword, Bairstow hitting a second consecutive World Cup hundred and Roy continuing his fine form since his recovery from injury with another half-century. It has been as much the manner with which they have carried themselves as the runs they have scored – confident, bristling, aggressive – that has rubbed off on the rest.

The cards fell nicely for Morgan throughout the day. He won a good toss, on a gorgeous Durham morning, and enjoyed early use of the pitch when it was at its best. It was much easier for England's batsmen to try to play their natural game without the added weight of a run chase, and Kane Williamson would have been well aware that England's three defeats have come batting second. At one stage, they were going so well that a final score of 305 for eight felt underwhelming, but the story of this World Cup is that such a total is usually sufficient, especially on a surface, like yesterday's, that slowed appreciably as the game wore on.

New Zealand were without their strike bowler, Lockie Ferguson, who suffered a hamstring strain the day before the game and who was badly missed, after Bairstow and Roy cut loose against the new ball. To cap it off, their champion batsman, Williamson, was run out in terribly unfortunate circumstances, stranded at the non-striker's end after a firm drive from Ross Taylor brushed the tip of Mark Wood's bowling hand before hitting the stumps.

Williamson walked off head bowed, looking like a man with the weight of the world on his shoulders, and having scored about a third of his team's runs in the tournament before this game, he is carrying the heaviest burden of any World Cup captain.

He was one of two key run-outs that scuppered New Zealand's chase. Taylor is the only other Kiwi batsman who has shown flashes of his best form and he was run out by Adil Rashid, of all people, going for a chancy second to fine leg. A rising tide floats all boats and Rashid was lifted, no doubt, by Jos Buttler's brilliance with the gloves 11 overs earlier when Martin Guptill was caught one-handed down the leg side, the catch being a high watermark of Buttler's wicketkeeping career.

Guptill was one of two wickets to fall to the new ball, the other being Henry Nicholls, who baulked at calling for a review for a leg-before decision that looked questionable in real time. The guts of New Zealand's batting line-up had been ripped out before the halfway mark, then, and the game quietly meandered, uncompetitive for the most part, except for when a male streaker gave the stewards the run-around and the players stood bemused and a little embarrassed until he was

removed. With Williamson and Taylor gone, New Zealand never threatened.

Once again, as against India, the new ball was vital in both innings. After Bairstow and Roy's rollicking start, Jofra Archer and Chris Woakes pegged New Zealand back with incisive new-ball spells, each taking a wicket – Archer's courtesy of Buttler's stunning catch. In the past three matches, Woakes has been impressive with the new ball, helping to put opponents behind the rate at the start with nagging accuracy and the odd vital wicket. Outstanding in the field, too, he is an indispensable, if unheralded, part of England's set-up.

It was a curate's egg of a performance from England's batsmen, though, whose initial swagger dissipated as the pitch slowed and New Zealand bowled their cutters cleverly into the surface. The crowd, boisterous and relaxed at the start of the day as Bairstow and Roy ran amok, sat silent and concerned for the final 20 overs after the dismissal of Joe Root, as the expected acceleration never quite came.

To negate the openers' threat, Williamson had given the left-arm spinner, Mitchell Santner, the first over, a ploy that almost worked when an arm ball nearly shaved Roy's leg stump first ball. Instead, four byes were followed three balls later by a full toss that was hammered to the boundary, and England were off and running again. Given width, Bairstow was especially fluent through the off side and off the front foot, while Roy punished anything short.

They marched side by side to their half-centuries, Roy reaching the milestone three balls before Bairstow, even though he had faced nine more. While they were together, thoughts turned towards scores of 350 and more and when Roy hit a flat-footed drive to cover, after taking Jimmy Neesham for consecutive boundaries through the leg side, a perfect platform had been set.

Once Root edged a bouncer down the leg side and Bairstow dragged on to his stumps, England's charge faltered. Buttler, promoted to bring chaos to proceedings, was undone by a clever knuckle ball from Trent Boult and Ben Stokes laboured for 11 runs off 27 balls, a clear sign that batting was becoming more difficult. The final 20 overs brought only 111 runs and seven wickets. Given the way the middle order struggled to hit the ball to the boundary, the total always felt enough.

PLAYER OF THE MATCH:
*Jonny Bairstow (England)*

## WHAT THEY SAID

'Williamson doesn't know how unlucky he is because I've got the smallest hands for a bloke you've ever seen.'

Mark Wood

'It has been the theme of the tournament, that the wicket will get slower over the course of the game. If that continues, we will continue to bat first.'

Eoin Morgan

'If we are allowed the opportunity, anything can happen in the semi-finals and we haven't played our best cricket yet.'

Kane Williamson

## KEY NUMBERS

### 3
New Zealand lost three consecutive World Cup matches for the first time

### 3
Jason Roy and Jonny Bairstow recorded their third successive three-figure opening partnership – no other pair has managed that at a World Cup

# THE TIMES

Thursday July 4 2019 | thetimes.co.uk | No 72890

£1.80 Only £1.10 to subscribers

## The name's Elba, Idris Elba Exclusive interview

INSIDE TIMES2

### Deborah Ross
How I'd like to punish the Brexit MEPs

# Osborne prepares bid to become first British head of the IMF

**Francis Elliott** Political Editor
**Philip Aldrick** Economics Editor

George Osborne is preparing a campaign to become the next head of the International Monetary Fund.

The former chancellor has told friends that he is considering a bid to replace Christine Lagarde and become the fund's first British managing director in Washington. The IMF, jointly governed by 189 countries, was set up to co-ordinate global financial policy after the Second World War. It provides bailouts and policy advice to member states and acts as a global financial policeman.

Alongside the World Bank it is home to the "Washington consensus", an attempt to spread liberal market doctrines. Mr Osborne will need the nomination of Britain's next prime minister to succeed. The Evening Standard, which he edits, recently endorsed Boris Johnson in the Conservative leadership race.

Although Mark Carney, the governor of the Bank of England could also be a candidate, Mr Osborne's allies believe that Mario Draghi, the outgoing head of the European Central Bank (ECB), may become his main rival because the governor is more closely focused on Canadian politics.

Supporters of Mr Osborne say that the former chancellor could win backing from both President Trump and President Xi. Mediating between the United States and China requires a politician rather than a technocrat, they claim. They concede, though, that Brexit has made the appointment of a British candidate less likely.

The role of IMF chairman and managing director became available after Ms Lagarde was appointed to replace Mr Draghi as head of the ECB in the latest round of European Union appointments. The new head must be Continued on page 2, col 3

# Labour poll support at record low

### 18% back Corbyn as he equals joint worst result

**Henry Zeffman** Political Correspondent
**Matt Chorley** Red Box Editor

Jeremy Corbyn has taken Labour to its lowest level of support in polling history, with fewer than one in five voters planning to back him at the next election, according to a new survey.

Labour are fourth for the first time, with 18 per cent saying that they would vote for the party if an election were held today, the Times/YouGov poll shows.

The only previous occasion when Labour has scored 18 per cent since polling began in the 1940s came in May 2009 as Gordon Brown's government grappled with the financial crisis.

Labour has fallen two points since last week, a drop in support that will intensify doubts among the party's MPs about Mr Corbyn's leadership. It bolsters claims that his Brexit strategy and failure to quell the antisemitism row are harming the party with the general public.

Twenty-five per cent of Remain voters say that they will back Labour, compared with 40 per cent at the end of April and 48 per cent at the start of the year. The party has also been abandoned by Leavers, with 8 per cent backing them, down from 21 per cent in January.

As the Conservatives enter the final three weeks of their leadership election campaign they have reclaimed the sole lead. They are six points ahead of Labour on 24 per cent, two points higher than last week.

The Brexit Party, which last week was tied with the Conservatives, is second on 23 per cent, while the Liberal Democrats, who were one point behind Labour last week, have overtaken them and are on 20 per cent. The results again indicate that British politics is in a period of four-party competition, with the seat distribution difficult to predict under the system of first past the post.

Mr Corbyn, 70, and Sir Mark Sedwill, the cabinet secretary, yesterday had a "frank" meeting over the Times report last week that some senior civil servants fear the Labour leader is not up to the job "physically or mentally" and has become "too frail and is losing his memory".

Mr Corbyn, accompanied by Jon Trickett, the shadow Cabinet Office minister, met Sir Mark for 45 minutes in the Labour leader's office.

The meeting was "frank and detailed, with a full exchange of views", a Labour spokesman said. "The seriousness of the civil service breach and the evident malicious intent behind it was acknowledged by all participants in the meeting."

"Jeremy Corbyn and Jon Trickett pressed the case for a fully independent investigation to restore trust and confidence in the civil service. They were promised an independent element to the civil service investigation, that they will receive regular updates on its progress and that it would report as soon as possible. They made clear that the credibility of the investigation will be assessed on the basis of its results."

A Cabinet Office spokeswoman agreed that the discussion had been "open and constructive". The investigation will be conducted by civil servants unrelated to the events, and the findings will be shared with the first civil service commissioner, she said.

The Times reported at the weekend that the future of Mr Corbyn was Continued on page 2, col 3

High hopes Jonny Bairstow celebrates his century as England beat New Zealand by 119 runs in Durham yesterday to reach the World Cup semi-finals. Pages 69-72

# Not your call: bosses take smartphones from workers

**Jack Malvern**

Posting updates on social media and texting your friends at work could soon become a thing of the past as bosses confiscate smartphones to keep noses to the grindstone.

Unions are warning that "a new front for friction" between workers and organisations is opening as managers feel that they cannot trust people to resist the temptation to post updates.

While it is normal for retailers such as Tesco to make their employees put their phones in lockers, the practice is spreading to office workers.

A director of a marketing company in West Yorkshire recently ruled out recruiting candidates who would not hand over their mobile devices. Gerard O'Shaughnessy, of Business Marketing Services in Cleckheaton, said that he felt so aggrieved by people using phones during working hours that he confiscated them until lunchtime.

Café staff at the British Library must surrender their phones to their supervisor in case they are tempted to look at them between serving customers.

Mr O'Shaughnessy, 48, said that his company began confiscating its workers' mobile phones two months ago. "We've had girls have meltdowns when they've been told they need to put their phone in a box. Others have said it's almost like a separation anxiety," he said. "When we didn't have this policy in place people would be checking social media updates during staff meetings. Every customer I deal with tells me the same happens in their organisation with younger staff."

Strict phone policies have alarmed organisations such as Prospect, the union for clerical workers that represents some staff at the British Library. Mike Clancy, its general secretary, said: "Rigid controls over phone use, where no clear security and safety issues are involved, risks being rigid worker control, reflecting a culture that lacks trust." A British Library spokesman said that it was talking to its catering contractor Graysons about the matter.

## ANALYSIS

STEVE JAMES

This must rank as one of Jonny Bairstow's finest innings, even better than the very fine century he scored against India on Sunday. To score a second hundred in a match of such magnitude and importance on a pitch that was much trickier than he made it appear was a quite stunning effort.

Given how he timed the ball, he looked a class above every other batsman on show in the match. Only his opening partner, Jason Roy, came close. While those two were batting, it appeared that the pitch was a belter. But it was not.

Yes, the England openers batted when the conditions were at their freshest but Bairstow in particular made a mockery of the slowness and stickiness of the surface.

In doing so he demonstrated his enormous value to the side after a week in which he has been seemingly determined not to lurk quietly in the shadows. All that business after some comments he made about criticism of the team last week was duly followed by that century at Edgbaston, and now this.

It was almost predictable really that he would respond in that manner against India last weekend. Bairstow likes the fuel of persecution, whether perceived or not and whether he will admit it or not.

Neither is a crime. Bairstow can be complicated and sensitive, but he also possesses bucketfuls of character and resolve. He is a serious international cricketer, who truly relishes the battle.

He also likes the fuel of form, of making the most of a hot streak. Last year he scored three consecutive one-day international centuries; indeed he went on to make four hundreds in six innings. And he likes playing against New Zealand. In striking his second successive century in this tournament, he also made his third consecutive ODI century against the Kiwis.

To put this into perspective, this was England's seventh century of this tournament; England had scored only 11 centuries in the previous 11 World Cup tournaments. In fact, Bairstow has made as many World Cup centuries in four days as England did in five tournaments from 1987 to 2003 (the two were made by Graham Gooch against India in 1987 and Graeme Hick against Netherlands in 1996). The game has changed, but so have England.

To think that it took Bairstow so long to secure his place in this side. He now has nine ODI hundreds, putting him level with Roy, Jos Buttler and Kevin Pietersen. For England, only Joe Root (16), Marcus Trescothick and Eoin Morgan (both 12) have more.

Bairstow played quite magnificently here. The return of Roy to the side has transformed England in this competition and has undoubtedly helped Bairstow, who clearly feels more comfortable with him for company, but here Bairstow, 29, was obviously the man in the sharper and more assured touch.

At Edgbaston against India, when the opening partnership had been 160 (Roy made 66 and Bairstow 111),

Bairstow had been the one to rely more on Lady Luck early on, especially when inside-edging a couple of fours perilously close to his leg stump.

Here it was Roy who flirted with the good Lady, and he could so easily have been dismissed from the first ball of the innings.

New Zealand had surprisingly opened with the left-arm spin of Mitchell Santner (that tactic seemed to have disappeared after the first part of the tournament) and the first delivery was an arm ball that swung into Roy as the right-hander attempted an ambitious cut shot. The ball went between Roy and his leg stump and past the wicketkeeper for four byes.

Roy went on to score 60 from 61 balls, playing some powerful shots, most notably a violent pulled four off the left-arm pace of Trent Boult, but even in his innings, as he battled with his timing, there were signs that the pitch was not quite as flat as it first appeared.

There were rarely any such concerns for Bairstow. In the fifth over he took Tim Southee for three consecutive boundaries, driving through and over the off side with wonderful freedom and aggression.

By the end of the opening powerplay England were 67 without loss – New Zealand were 37 for two at the same point – equalling their best start in this competition, against Bangladesh in Cardiff.

The openers had set a superb tone yet again. One on-driven four from Bairstow off Matt Henry simply drew gasps of astonishment, such was the purity of its strike and execution.

There was some deftness from Bairstow too, twice guiding Colin de Grandhomme's medium pace down to the untenanted third-man boundary, and the overriding impressions coming from the ginger Yorkshireman were those of absolute balance and command at the crease.

It is doubtful that his technique has ever been in better shape. In the Pakistan ODI series that preceded this tournament, he played well but he clearly favoured the leg side. At the moment he appears able to play all around the wicket with equal ease and precision.

The century partnership, the tenth between Bairstow and Roy and their third in succession, was almost a formality. Both players reached their fifties in the same over from Jimmy Neesham, Roy getting there first but having taken more balls (55) than Bairstow (46).

Roy went, driving to cover in a harbinger of what was to come as the pitch slowed, having slapped Neesham for two consecutive leg-side fours.

The partnership had ended at 123 in 18.4 overs but Bairstow raced on. He hit the only six of the match, straight down the ground off Southee to take himself into the nineties, before taking two boundaries from three balls off the same bowler – first a pull, then a leg-side clip from a full toss – to reach his hundred off 95 balls.

He celebrated with a lot more excitement than he had at Edgbaston, and why not? He had played some innings, indeed the innings of the day, to usher England into the semi-finals.

# AFGHANISTAN v WEST INDIES

.....................................................

*Thursday, July 4*

*Headingley*

**West Indies 311-6** (50 overs)
(Lewis 58, Hope 77, Pooran 58)
**Afghanistan 288 all out** (50 overs)
(Rahmat Shah 62, Ikram Alikhil 86;
Roach 3-37, Brathwaite 4-63)
*West Indies (2pts) won by 23 runs*
**Toss** *West Indies*

ELGAN ALDERMAN

The thankful crowd rose to show their appreciation. One of the greats walked towards them in his final World Cup match, his wicket taken, his helmet removed, all that he had achieved before this day lodged firmly in the memory bank. Chris Gayle had scored seven off 18 balls.

The self-styled Universe Boss, 39, was at Headingley for a World Cup goodbye. Each member of the West Indies squad had given him a congratulatory catch and handshake in the warm-ups. There was no rousing farewell, though – with the bat, at least. Gayle played a hand in the dismissals of Afghanistan's top-scorers, catching Rahmat Shah at cover and dismissing 18-year-old Ikram Alikhil leg-before, in a 23-run victory against their winless opponents.

West Indies' solitary group-stage win before yesterday was in May. Gayle teeing off would have improved results – he scored 242 runs at 30.25, the red-hot form he showed against England earlier in the year evading

him – but he is not to blame for the lack of victories.

There was one boundary, off his 12th ball, before Universe Boss tried to flail the ball out of his jurisdiction, succeeding only in feathering an edge behind.

The fireworks came elsewhere. Evin Lewis, assistant to the intergalactic honcho, lifted huge sixes over mid-wicket and fine leg. Shimron Hetmyer was typically watchable in his sun hat, Nicholas Pooran continued to enhance his reputation, Shai Hope the glue around whom the others swashed with varying results.

We thought this would be Gayle's international goodbye but he has said he is open to playing in the ODI series against India, which starts next month, and maybe even a first Test in five years.

Franchise cricket's archetypal travelling salesman is playing international cricket. Is this not what we want? Yes. Yet with Gayle, it feels as if this has been a greatest-hits farewell with none of the best songs and all of the distracting rigmarole.

The fun and games are maverick foibles when Gayle comes off. Out of form nearing 40, they can resemble a joke too far.

All of this takes nothing away from the legacy of the man, he of two Test triple hundreds – only three others have done that – and 21 T20 centuries, 14 more than anyone else. We may see him next year in the Hundred to help, in his own words, 'explode the tournament'.

If he scores big runs for his country, everyone's a winner. Call him whatever you like then. Boss of the universe. Chief executive of the cosmos. The centre-stage sideshow rolls on.

PLAYER OF THE MATCH:
*Shai Hope (West Indies)*

## WHAT THEY SAID

'The World Cup wasn't the ideal one from my point of view, but there's nothing much we can do about it. But it is definitely my last World Cup … I would have loved to lift the trophy, but it didn't happen. It was fun … life goes on.'

Chris Gayle

'It's good to get over the line, we've had some close encounters where we didn't.'

Jason Holder

'I have learnt a lot at this tournament. Fitness is a big issue – the boys are struggling. Also, we can work more on our skills under pressure.'

Gulbadin Naib

## KEY NUMBER

## 12

Successive defeats for Afghanistan. They are third on that list –
Zimbabwe are at the top with 18

# BANGLADESH v PAKISTAN

......................................................

*Friday, July 5*

*Lord's*

**Pakistan 315-9** (50 overs)
(Imam-ul-Haq 100, Babar Azam 96;
Mohammad Saifuddin 3-77,
Mustafizur Rahman 5-75)
**Bangladesh 221 all out** (44.1 overs)
(Shakib Al Hasan 64; Shaheen Afridi 6-35)
*Pakistan (2pts) won by 94 runs*
**Toss** *Pakistan*

Pakistan's stars of the future shone brightly in their final game, but even with a decisive victory they were nowhere near the mathematical miracle they needed to reach the last four. They became the first team to go out of a World Cup after winning four successive games.

Batting first – their minimum requirement to stay in the competition – Pakistan went just beyond the minimum total they needed, 308, but that meant they had to bowl Bangladesh out for eight. Even Shanheen could not manage that.

Lord's was packed with different shades of green and the crowd were treated to a thoroughly entertaining match. Pakistan needed a flying start but off-spinner Mehidy Hasan was given the new ball and they were unable to get going until Imam-ul-Haq and Babar Azam put on a sparkling 157 off 151 balls for the second wicket.

Babar was out four runs short of his century, but became Pakistan's most prolific batsman at a single World Cup by surpassing the 437 runs scored by Javed Miandad in 1992. Imam did reach three figures, but was out hit wicket next ball and from that point Pakistan lost impetus. Mustafizur Rahman continued to make a good impression with five for 75.

Bangladesh yet against pinned their hopes on the slender shoulders of Shakib Al Hasan. He did not disappoint, going past 50 for the sixth time in this World Cup and becoming only the third player to score more than 600 runs at a single tournament. He lacked support, however, and a Bangladesh campaign that got off to such a promising start ended meekly.

......................................................

### PLAYER OF THE MATCH:
***Shaheen Afridi***

## WHAT THEY SAID

'We played very good cricket in the last four matches, but unfortunately we couldn't qualify. Only the one match against West Indies cost us the whole tournament, but the way the boys responded after the India match was honestly commendable.'

Sarfaraz Ahmed

'We are extremely sorry that we couldn't lend a helping hand to Shakib who batted, bowled and fielded very well in every match in this tournament.'

Mashrafe Mortaza

## KEY NUMBER

# 6-35

Shaheen Afridi's figures were the best by a Pakistan bowler in a World Cup match

# JOS BUTTLER PROFILE

JOHN WESTERBY

Now that they are safely into the World Cup semi-finals, there are comforts that can be drawn from the wobbles England encountered on their uncertain progress through the group stage. One is that they now have momentum – the victories over India and New Zealand carrying them into the last four with the wind in their sails – another is that they have been sorely tested as a team, staring down the barrel of an early exit, and come through the other side, the sort of experience that can bind a squad together more tightly.

A third is that they have reached this point without a defining innings from their most potent match-winner. Perhaps this is a little unfair on Jos Buttler, who hit a 75-ball hundred in the defeat by Pakistan, then 64 from 44 balls in the victory over Bangladesh, before embarking on a run of lower scores.

Yet Buttler still goes into the semi-finals as the batsman with the highest strike rate among those who have made more than 200 runs, he remains the player opposing bowlers fear the most, poised to enter in the middle stages of an innings and take the game away with the intelligence and calculated brutality of his strokeplay.

No player has embodied England's spectacular revival since the 2015 World Cup more than Buttler. As the 2019 tournament moves into its knockout phase, there is a sense that this will be Buttler's time, a moment for which he has long seemed destined.

## *THE POWER*

It was not that Buttler was particularly large or physically advanced as a teenager, but, when he was wielding a bat, he had the ability to make it look that way. 'To see someone strike the ball so cleanly, with so much power, you think at first that he must be a big lad,' Mark Garaway, his coach at Somerset's academy, said. 'But when he came off, you could see that he was quite slight, no more than average build. He just happened to have a huge talent for striking a ball.'

The knack can be particularly useful, either in the animal kingdom or the sporting arena, to persuade a potential foe that your physical threat exceeds your actual size. In Buttler's case, the illusion was created by the speed with which the ball left his bat and the distance it travelled.

At King's College, Taunton, where Buttler went to school, there are some pastel-pink buildings behind trees beyond the longest straight boundary on the first-team pitch. 'Those houses can't be far off 120 metres away and Jos would not be far off reaching with his straight hits,' Alex Barrow, the former Somerset batsman and a school-mate of Buttler's, said. 'The rest of us were happy just to reach the boundary.'

# THE STAND

Word of Buttler's burgeoning reputation as an all-round sportsman of considerable promise was already spreading around Somerset when a partnership in a school game in his lower sixth year generated much wider attention. It was the first game of the 2008 season at home to King's Bruton. A daunting challenge was in prospect, as Buttler opened the batting with Barrow, who was a year younger than his partner.

To make matters worse for the visiting bowlers, Buttler had recently suffered a setback when one of his peers in the academy, Adam Dibble, had been offered a senior contract by Somerset. Buttler had hoped to be the first of his cohort to make the step up. And it just so happened that two of the Somerset coaches, Jason Kerr and Greg Kennis, had popped down to watch that April afternoon. 'I don't think I'd ever seen Jos so determined,' Barrow said.

Buttler began dismantling the bowling, this time with added feeling, with Barrow contentedly playing second fiddle. Barrow's father, Guy, and Buttler's father, John, sat together, as they often did, and would not budge until their sons were parted. 'We were in a while, so they had people bringing them food and cups of tea as the day went on,' Barrow said.

It was 49.3 overs before Barrow was dismissed, their opening stand worth 340, leaving Buttler to finish on 227 not out, a strident message to the watching Somerset coaches. 'When he'd reached his double hundred, I remember him muttering a few quiet words to me,' Barrow said.

'Something like, "I hope that's shown them what I'm all about."' To this day, the Buttler-Barrow Trophy is awarded to the highest partnership of the season at their old school.

# THE CHALLENGE

Those destructive qualities are now familiar all over the cricketing world, with Buttler the scorer of England's two quickest centuries in one-day internationals, from 46 and 50 balls.

Despite his frustrations when Dibble was awarded a contract before him, there was never doubt among the Somerset coaches about his ability. At an earlier stage, their concern was that such a gifted player might not have been challenged enough.

'The first time I saw him he was 12 and we weren't supposed to include players on academy programmes until they were 14, but I rang Hugh Morris [the managing director of England cricket at the time] and asked if we could make an exception,' Garaway said. 'Hugh asked why and I said, "Because this lad will play for England." You don't get that sort of thing right all the time, but I was pretty sure on this one.'

As the extent of Buttler's talent was evident, the academy coaches wanted to test his mettle. In particular, they had noticed his unconventional grip, his bottom hand further round the handle, and wondered whether more could be gained from an orthodox grip.

'We felt he might be able to keep the bat face on the ball a bit better,' Garaway said. 'That was a painful process for Jos and reduced him to tears on quite a few occasions.

'It didn't feel comfortable for him and was compromising his strengths. But the thing I remember the most is that his mum, Patricia, knew that we were challenging him. When Jos was feeling teary, he'd look over towards his mum for comfort and she would avert her eyes. She was a tennis coach herself and understood the process. That's a big thing for a parent to do.'

Eventually, after a few weeks, the decision was made to revert to Buttler's preferences. 'He uses the same grip now as when he was 12 or 13,' Garaway said. 'It suits his game perfectly. He's a very right-sided player, he lines the ball up with his right eye and takes aim with his right shoulder. The MCC coaching manual would rather you line up with both eyes and, as a right-hander, lead with your left shoulder. But fair to say it hasn't turned out too badly for Jos.'

# THE EDGE

The resilience that Somerset were seeking was building nicely. Having grown up in Wedmore and started his cricket at Cheddar with his older brother, James, Buttler moved to play for Glastonbury and was playing senior cricket in the West of England Premier League from the age of 15, alongside first-class cricketers such as Wes Durston and Gareth Andrew. 'He was very quiet and polite,' Durston said. 'But what struck me was how composed he was at the crease, how confident he was in his ability.'

When a young player takes the plunge in such circumstances, and survives to tell the tale, he grows a few inches on returning to face his peers. The harder edge he had acquired was soon evident.

'Jos is very softly spoken and people get surprised when they see him getting angry, but there's a ruthless competitor in him,' Barrow said. 'I saw it when I was 15 and playing against Canford. When I was batting with Jos, I nicked off and didn't walk, and for the rest of the innings their keeper really got stuck into me.

When he then came out to bat, [the keeper] nicked one and didn't walk either. I didn't say anything but Jos got really angry with me, saying I should have been giving him plenty back. When Jos is there in the heat of battle, there's a really hard competitive edge.'

# THE STUDENT

From an early stage, Buttler seemed to have a clear sense of where he was heading. One of the toughest aspects for young cricketers is balancing the requirements of schoolwork with the demands of a time-consuming summer sport.

'We noticed when he was coming through that he was a very capable organiser,' Andy Hurry, the Somerset director of cricket, said. 'He would manage his workloads at school and still commit to every training session at the academy. The players all had diaries for their cricket and there would be more written in Jos' diary than most of the others.'

When school and cricket permitted, he also availed himself to a wide range of other sports. He had been a good tennis player from a young age, played for the school at hockey and and there was further evidence of that hard edge in the fearlessness of his tackling at full back for the rugby team.

'We played against Truro College one day, we'd heard a lot about these big Cornish lads and when they turned up, they were massive,' Barrow said. 'The thing that everyone remembers from that game is one of their lads running towards the line and Jos smashing him in the tackle.'

As a natural ball-player, now accomplished with the gloves for England's one-day team, it might be assumed that Buttler was always destined to be a wicketkeeper too. Not so. 'He quite liked his medium pacers, but I could see they weren't up to much, and he loved his fielding,' Garaway, a former Hampshire wicketkeeper, said. 'He was 13 or 14 before he started keeping and I had to bully him into it. Like most things, he picked it up pretty quickly.'

# THE SHOTS

Once Buttler had played his way into Somerset's first team, he quickly became known for the innovative variety of his shots, including the reverse-sweep as a frontline stroke, rather than a risky alternative. There was also the ramp and the scoop, which had been seen before, but Buttler was the first in English cricket to master them.

At a time when Twenty20 batting was dispensing with old orthodoxies, he had been experimenting with new possibilities for some time.

'Most of his shots were orthodox when we were at school, but I do remember the first time I saw the reverse-sweep come out,' Barrow said. 'We were batting in a Twenty20 match at Millfield and he was getting frustrated. He came down the wicket and said, "I'm going to reverse sweep this bloke for six." I watched the next two balls disappear over cover for six.

'I'd been told he had a pair of left-handed batting gloves in his bag and had been practising batting left-handed. But that was amazing. Nobody was playing shots like that back then.'

In the academy at Somerset, he began to look for other ways that he could develop his game. Garaway was combining academy duties with overseeing the second XI and on Wednesdays he would open the equipment store and leave the young players to their own devices. 'We called it "Open Cupboard Wednesdays", giving them the space to create their own drills,' Garaway said. 'I noticed Jos had set up the bowling machine to send down a load of yorkers and he was trying to clip them over fine leg. I thought that was pretty impressive. This was back in the mid 2000s, when Twenty20 was just getting going.'

The time soon came for Buttler's innovations to be tested against more competitive bowling. 'I put him in a net with a couple of our first-teamers, Keith Parsons was bowling at him and Rob Turner was standing up keeping wicket,' Garaway said. 'When Jos started flipping these balls over his shoulder, Rob wasn't at all impressed. He stormed out and said, "I'm not staying in there if he's doing that." They hadn't seen anything like it.'

## THE LEADER

Buttler made his first-team debut for Somerset shortly after turning 19 in September 2009, only a season after making that record stand with Barrow. A month later he would be playing in the Champions League Twenty20 tournament in India against New South Wales and coping admirably with the pace of Brett Lee.

'He's always had the ability to think his way through a new situation and adapt his game,' Hurry said. 'When Arsène Wenger was asked what was the right time to blood a young player in the first team, he said it was when the senior players were passing to him in training. With Jos, I remember watching a group of senior players clustering round the back of a net to watch when he was batting. Every level he's gone up to, he's picked the brains of players who were there, like Justin Langer at Somerset, and seen what there was to learn.'

It was only two years from his county debut before Buttler's burgeoning Twenty20 skills saw him called up to play for England in the shortest form. He has since become an indispensable leader, vice-captain to Eoin Morgan in white-ball cricket and to Joe Root in Tests.

He first captained the 50-over team in Bangladesh three years ago, when Morgan had opted not to travel over security fears. 'That ODI team was very much Morgan's side, but Jos stepped into his shoes brilliantly,' Hurry, a member of the

England coaching staff in Bangladesh, said. 'He has so much respect from the other players now and in white-ball cricket he's just grown with the game.'

Like many of the best leaders, Buttler has often appeared one step ahead. He has grown into the player that he promised to become when punching above his weight against Somerset schoolboys more than a decade ago. Now he is poised to prove his worth in the World Cup when it really matters.

# INDIA v SRI LANKA

*Saturday, July 6*

*Headingley*

**Sri Lanka 264-7** (50 overs) (Mathews 113, Thirimanne 53; Bumrah 3-37)
**India 265-3** (43.3 overs) (Rahul 111, Sharma 103)
*India (2pts) won by seven wickets*
**Toss** *Sri Lanka*

IAN HAWKEY

Several ominous messages from Leeds, to India's semi-final opponents. Mainly, that India will be more exhilarated than weary after completing their meander through the group stage. They cantered to a seven-wicket victory, with 39 balls to spare, over Sri Lanka; a win featuring more muscle-flexing from their in-form men at both ends of the order. Rohit Sharma made a record-breaking fifth hundred in this World Cup alone, after Jasprit Bumrah had applied his padlocks to Sri Lanka's effort to set a challenging target.

There were welcome reminders of India's strength in depth, too, of their options ahead of next week. Ravindra Jadeja, until yesterday a very active 12th man at this tournament, yesterday made the XI, with Mohammed Shami rested, and he was an important contributor in establishing India's early command. There was a century for KL Rahul — one of three hundreds in the match — runs that help soothe any lingering concerns that India may not be quite the top-order juggernaut they looked before Shikhar Darwan left the

World Cup with injury. In the end, their seventh World Cup win was comprehensive and morale-boosting, its flaws one or two instances of straggly fielding — two dropped catches — and some unflattering bowling figures for Bhuvneshwar Kumar. Were it not for Angelo Mathews, who, with a mature and resourceful century rescued the Sri Lankan innings, the day might not even have given India their extended chance to get a good workout ahead of the pressured, intense few days ahead.

Mathews' 113 pushed Sri Lanka to a total of 264 for seven. But Rohit and Rahul had already shrunk the target considerably by the end of the opening powerplay of the chase. Unsentimentally, they punished Lasith Malinga, in this the veteran's likely World Cup swansong. They savaged Dhananjaya de Silva when Sri Lanka brought spin to the attack. De Silva was immediately launched for two Rohit sixes off his first three balls. The first of them, thumped over extra cover, took Rohit past 50.

Rohit reached his hundred from 92 balls, via 14 fours and the two sixes off Dhananjaya, and when he was first man for India, they were within 76 runs of victory with 20 overs left. That gave captain Virat Kohli a chance to spend some unstressed time in the middle and to directly congratulate Rahul on his first World Cup century. By the time Rahul was out, for 111 off 118 balls, with 11 fours and a six, India were home and dry. They reached their target with only the further loss of Rishabh Pant.

As for Sri Lanka, they go home having lost four out of seven games, and regretting both the games that suffered from bad weather and above all their disastrous opener, a thrashing by New Zealand.

After Dimuth Karunaratne had chosen to bat, they started badly. The skipper was first to yield to Bumrah, edging a delivery wide enough to tempt him to cut. That gave MS Dhoni the first of three catches – plus a stumping – before the day was 12 overs old.

Then with a ball that appeared to straighten, Bumrah found the inside edge of Kusal Perera's bat, Dhoni making an agile catch. The wicketkeeper, who turns 38 today, would then move nimbly again to bring an end to the resistance of Avishka Fernando. Fernando overreached, misjudging one of the impressive Hardik Pandya's slower, shorter balls. Jadeja had by then collected his significant memento from this World Cup. Four balls into his first over, he found turn, and bamboozled an impatient Kusal Mendis. Dhoni, as nifty close up as he had been at distance to the quicker bowlers, stumped him.

Sri Lanka were 55 for four. Enter Mathews, whose World Cup has been as lopsided as Sri Lanka's: two ducks to start off with, then his 85 not out in the win over England. Judiciously picking the gaps, with the odd reverse-sweep, he took the lead in a partnership with Lahiru Thirimanne worth 124, and though neither of them mastered Bumrah, they remembered the pre-match plan to target Bhuvneshwar, whose ten overs went for 73.

Thirimanne struck 53, from 68 balls; De Silva then supported Mathews with a diligent 29. Mathews had been dropped, attempting to clear the ropes off Jadeja, by Kuldeep Yadav, but until he spooned the canny Bumrah to Rohit at extra cover with ten balls of the Sri Lanka innings remaining, he had negotiated difficult circumstances very capably. He was out on 113, having struck ten fours and two sixes in his 128-ball stay.

It seemed the foundation for a robust total, although Mathews did warn, at the halfway stage: 'We have to try and get Rohit and Kohli.' Alas, they only got Rohit after he had broken a World Cup record – five centuries in one tournament – and by the time Kohli came in, a swaggering India hardly needed their skipper.

........................................................

PLAYER OF THE MATCH:
*Rohit Sharma (India)*

## WHAT THEY SAID

'When the tournament started, a lot of people told me "Angelo isn't performing." But he knows no matter how much he fails, how to get into that rhythm. He has that experience. He showed the whole team how to bat on this wicket.'

Dimuth Karunaratne

'We didn't expect to do this well heading into the semis. That's what hard work gets you. I am really proud of this team as a captain, they are amazing people.'

Virat Kohli

## KEY NUMBERS

### 5

Rohit Sharma became the first player to score five centuries at one World Cup

### 56

Lasith Malinga's wicket in his final World Cup match took him to 56 and into third place in the all-time list

## AUSTRALIA v SOUTH AFRICA

*Saturday, July 6*

*Old Trafford (day-night)*

**South Africa 325-6** (50 overs)
(De Kock 52, Du Plessis 100,
Van der Dussen 95)
**Australia 315 all out** (49.5 overs)
(Warner 122, Carey 85; Rabada 3-56)
*South Africa (2pts) won by 10 runs*
**Toss** *South Africa*

SIMON WILDE, *SUNDAY TIMES*
CRICKET CORRESPONDENT
In a drama-laden conclusion to the World Cup's group stage at Old Trafford last night, Australia, the tournament pace-setters, sank to an unexpected ten-run defeat by South Africa to set up a blockbuster of a semi-final with England at Edgbaston on Thursday. Had they won, the defending champions would have finished top of the group and guaranteed themselves a match with the eminently beatable New Zealand at this same venue on Tuesday.

Australia's lack of intensity in the first half of the game was baffling considering the prize at stake. Perhaps it was the result of a six-day break since their previous game, during which they had two days off, played golf and netted. But they were trying like mad by the end, desperation etched on every face.

The South Africans, by contrast, were from the outset well up for the contest, the first involving David Warner and Steve Smith since 'sandpapergate'. It was a cracking game.

Now, Australia must head to Birmingham, where they have yet to play in this tournament and where England's support is often rabid, and with only two days rather than four to prepare for the final, should they get there. Their head coach, Justin Langer, will be livid. Even before England had extricated themselves from their difficulties in qualifying for the last four, he insisted Australia remained wary of England. 'They are a very, very good team,' he said.

Led by a bristling third century of the campaign from Warner, who might have been run out third ball, Australia battled hard to chase down a target of 326, but after he fell to an excellent catch by Chris Morris – South Africa's catching under pressure was exemplary – it proved just too stiff a task on a dry pitch which justified South Africa's decision to field two frontline spinners. Australia nonetheless pushed to the end.

An England-Australia semi-final is mouthwatering. Although Australia have not lost any of their previous seven World Cup semi-final matches, and won the group game between the sides, they have lost 12 of their past 15 ODIs against England. The teams have not met in a World Cup knockout match since the final in Kolkata in 1987, which Australia won by seven runs.

Against that, England have won all three meetings in global one-day tournaments in Birmingham, all in the Champions Trophy. In the most recent, in 2017, England won with plenty to spare thanks to 87 from Eoin Morgan and an unbeaten century from Ben Stokes. The 2013 match-up resulted in the Warner-Joe Root confrontation in the Walkabout Bar.

To add to Australia's problems, Usman Khawaja, their No. 3 batsman, retired hurt in the fifth over of the chase with a hamstring problem that makes him a doubt for the semi-final, although he came back out at the fall of the seventh wicket. He played on tricking to flick the ball fine. Australia have already lost Shaun Marsh to a broken arm. He is in the process of being replaced in the squad by Peter Handscomb.

Marcus Stoinis was also in trouble with what appeared to be a recurrence of the side strain that forced him out of two earlier games. He took tablets early in his innings and later had treatment from the physio before being brilliantly run out by Quinton de Kock's back-flick.

When De Kock later accounted for Glenn Maxwell with a breathtaking leap to snare a top-edged hook, Australia's hopes appeared to have all but perished. However, Warner found a gutsy partner in Alex Carey and together they put on 108 in 90 balls. Warner began to find the gaps with unerring precision and Carey was scarcely less adroit.

When Warner was out, 99 runs were needed off 65 balls, but Carey, in his highest one-day score of 85, kept going with Pat Cummins. They fell in the 45th and 46th overs as South Africa held their nerve superbly.

South Africa had flown out of the blocks and they appeared powerless to stop the assault as Aiden Markram and De Kock struck 11 boundaries during the first power-play, the most for any side at this World Cup. Nathan Lyon removed both but Faf du Plessis and Rassie van der Dussen forged on in a stand worth 151 in 25.2 overs.

This was a different-looking South Africa from the one that had laboured through the group. Where had they been?

Du Plessis came in on the back of two half-centuries and struck the ball imperiously to complete South Africa's only century of the tournament, off 93 balls. Van Der Dussen was struck on the head by Cummins when he had scored only two but grew in confidence and scored his last 45 in just 26 balls before holing out while attempting to reach his hundred off the last ball of the innings. South Africa plundered 49 from the last five overs.

There were also suspicions that Mitchell Starc was feeling his knee but he got through nine overs without complaint. Two late wickets took his tournament haul to 26, equalling the record for a World Cup set by his compatriot Glenn McGrath in 2007.

Australia's chase faltered from the start, Aaron Finch driving Imran Tahir – playing his last ODI – to cover in the third over. After Khawaja retired, Smith was leg-before to Dwaine Pretorius for his third single-figure score in four innings.

PLAYER OF THE MATCH:
**Faf du Plessis (South Africa)**

## WHAT THEY SAID

'It is going to be a blockbuster. It doesn't get much bigger than England v Australia in a World Cup semi-final.'

Aaron Finch

'I think India will be happy we won today – I think it'll be an England v India final.'

Faf du Plessis

## KEY NUMBERS

### 26
Mitchell Starc took his 26th wicket to equal the record set by Glenn McGrath in 2007

### 17
David Warner's third hundred of the tournament took him to 17 overall and into third place in Australia's all-time list

# FINAL TABLE

|             | P | W | T | L | NR | Pts | RR |
|-------------|---|---|---|---|----|-----|------|
| INDIA       | 9 | 7 | 0 | 1 | 1  | **15** | 0.809 |
| AUSTRALIA   | 9 | 7 | 0 | 2 | 0  | **14** | 0.868 |
| ENGLAND     | 9 | 6 | 0 | 3 | 0  | **12** | 1.152 |
| NEW ZEALAND | 9 | 5 | 0 | 3 | 1  | **11** | 0.175 |
| PAKISTAN    | 9 | 5 | 0 | 3 | 1  | **11** | −0.430 |
| SRI LANKA   | 9 | 3 | 0 | 4 | 2  | **8**  | −0.919 |
| SOUTH AFRICA| 9 | 3 | 0 | 5 | 1  | **7**  | −0.030 |
| BANGLADESH  | 9 | 3 | 0 | 5 | 1  | **7**  | −0.410 |
| WEST INDIES | 9 | 2 | 0 | 6 | 1  | **5**  | −0.225 |
| AFGHANISTAN | 9 | 0 | 0 | 9 | 0  | **0**  | −1.332 |

£1.80 Only £1.10 to subs

**Deborah Ross**
How I'd like to
punish the
Brexit MEPs

INSIDE
TIMES2

's Elba,
Exclusive
interview
a

# become first British head of the IMF

doctrines. Mr Osborne will need the nomination of Britain's next prime minister to succeed. The Evening Standard, which he edits, recently endorsed Boris Johnson in the Conservative leadership race.

Although Mark Carney, the governor of the Bank of England could also be a candidate, Mr Osborne's allies believe that Mario Draghi, the out-

going head of the European Central Bank (ECB), may become his main rival because the governor is more closely focused on Canadian politics.

Supporters of Mr Osborne say that the former chancellor could win backing from both President Trump and President Xi. Mediating between the United States and China requires a politician rather than a technocrat.

they claim. They concede, though, that Brexit has made the appointment of a British candidate less likely.

The role of IMF chairman and managing director became available after Ms Lagarde was appointed to replace Mr Draghi as head of the ECB in the latest round of European Union appointments. The new head must be
Continued on page 2, col 3

## Not your call: bosses take smartphones from workers

**Jack Malvern**

Posting updates on social media and texting your friends at work could soon become a thing of the past as bosses confiscate smartphones to keep noses to the grindstone.

Unions are warning that "a new front for friction" between workers and organisations is opening as managers feel that they cannot trust people to resist the temptation to post updates.

While it is normal for retailers such as Tesco to make their employees put their phones in lockers, the practice is spreading to office workers.

A director of a marketing company in West Yorkshire recently ruled out recruiting candidates who would not hand over their mobile devices. Gerard O'Shaughnessy, of Business Marketing Services in Cleckheaton, said that he felt so aggrieved by people using phones during working hours that he confiscated them until lunchtime.

Café staff at the British Library must surrender their phones to their supervisor in case they are tempted to look at them between serving customers.

Mr O'Shaughnessy, 48, said that his company began confiscating its workers' mobile phones two months ago. "We've had girls have meltdowns when they've been told they need to put their phone in a box. Others have said it's almost breaching their human rights. It's almost like a separation anxiety," he said. "When we didn't have this policy in place people would be checking social media updates during staff meetings. Every customer I deal with tells me the same happens in their organisation with younger staff."

Strict phone policies have alarmed organisations such as Prospect, the union for clerical workers that represents some staff at the British Library. Mike Clancy, its general secretary, said: "Rigid controls over phone use, where no clear security and safety issues are involved, risks being rigid worker control, reflecting a culture that lacks trust." A British Library spokesman said that it was talking to its catering contractor Graysons about the matter.

High hopes Jonny Bairstow celebrates his century as England beat New Zealand by 119 runs in Durham yesterday to reach the World Cup semi-finals. Pages 69–72

in association with
sky sports cricket

## result

he results olitics is in ompetition, ifficult to f first past

ark Sedwill, erday had a Times report or civil servies set up to ally" and has is losing his

nied by Jon abinet Office 45 minutes in

nk and detailed, ews", a Labour seriousness of and the evident it was acknowling in the meeting, d Jon Trickett ully independent re trust and confiervice. They were ndent element to igation, that they updates on its y made clear that e investigation will asis of its results." ffice spokeswoman discussion in the active." The investiducted by civil serthe events, and the shared with the first mmisioner, she said. orted at the weekend of Mr Corbyn was
2, col 3

# England on the bri

- Morgan's side outplayed by Australia at Lord's
- Captain denies claim he was scared of Starc

**Elizabeth Ammon**

England's World Cup hopes are hanging in the balance after a 64-run defeat by Australia at Lord's means that they may have to win both of their remaining two group matches to survive in the competition.

Eoin Morgan rejected a claim made by Kevin Pietersen, the former England batsman, that he "feared" of Australia yesterday, but the England team admitted that his drop low on confidence as they prepare to play India today and New Zealand next Wednesday.

The nation started the tournament as favourites but are in fourth place in the final qualifying spots for semi-finals — two points ahead of ... and two ahead ... who have a a

... in made them ... to secure a ... four and ... of Morgan, mate, had ... 67

in frustration after Mitchell Starc's yorker bowled him out for 89, the only innings of substance from an England batsma

THE TIMES

# Sport

# England restore fear factor

Fired-up Bairstow hits century to set up win India and put hosts back on course for semi-

**Elizabeth Ammon**

The England captain Eoin Morgan said his side had "an outstanding day" after they kept their World Cup hopes alive with a 31-run victory that ended India's unbeaten run.

England bounced back from successive losses to Sri Lanka and Australia, and yesterday's win means that they are guaranteed a semi-final spot if they beat New Zealand on Wednesday at Chester-le-Street.

An exceptional 111 from the opener Jonny Bairstow, who had reacted to criticism after England's defeat by Australia by accusing people of wanting the team to fail, proved crucial in settling more nerves from the under-pressure hosts at Edgbaston.

"He [Jonny] does tend to get fired up a lot, and that suits him," Morgan said. "He likes a bit of fire in his belly, and I don't mind that when he comes out and plays like that. It's outstanding. It was
Continued on page 99

Bairstow takes the acclaim on reaching his 90-ball hundred in England's

**Times Crossword** 27,391

# THE
# SEMI-FINALS

Wednesday June 26 2019 | THE TIMES

ew Syed

akes football part of
nal-justice system

## FA exit for key strategy guru

Matt Hughes Sports News Correspondent

Dave Reddin, one of the key architects of England's recent resurgence, is to leave the Football Association after six years. The head of strategy and team performance has agreed a severance package, the governing body confirmed yesterday.

The FA did not comment on the reasons behind Reddin's departure but he is understood to have clashed with colleagues throughout his spell at St George's Park and developed a reputation as a demanding taskmaster.

The 49-year-old faced allegations of bullying two years ago. He was accused of presiding over a "climate of fear" but he was then cleared of any wrongdoing by the FA.

Reddin is understood to have experienced more difficulties in his relationships with key colleagues after those

Continued on page 61

## Nadal criticises seeding policy

tuart Fraser Tennis Correspondent

afael Nadal has accused Wimbledon disrespecting the world rankings by ng a special mathematical formula determine seedings for the men's gles — the only grand-slam nament to do so.

he seedings list for the champion-s will be confirmed by the All and Club (AELTC) this morning. d, the world No 2, will be seeded behind his arch-rival Roger er, who is ranked No 3 but will be No 2 after winning the Halle on Sunday.

Australian, French and US simply replicate the latest world which are based on the 52 weeks of results across all gles, for their seedings. Wimble-ever, uses a formula that gives

on page 58

---

Monday July 1 2019 | THE TIMES

## Wimbledon 16-page guide

Murray's return and how Konta can win as tournament starts today

Inside T2

## US accused in World Cup spying row

Molly Hudson Lyons

England and the United States have become embroiled in a spying row before their women's World Cup semi-final after two plain-clothed members of American staff were spotted in a private area of the Lionesses' team hotel in Lyons yesterday.

The FA is believed to be furious at the unwelcome intrusion from the US, who were scoping out the Fourvière Hotel as a potential base for Sunday's final. England face the US at Parc Olympique Lyonnais tomorrow and the final will also be played there.

England were training at a different location 30 minutes from the hotel while the two Americans were being shown around by staff at their hotel. The FA is said to be concerned that the Americans went into rooms where England have held team meetings.

They were not wearing any US-branded kit and did not show their team credentials to security on their way in. Eventually the pair were spotted by a member of the FA team.

The US coach Jill Ellis dismissed the idea that it was arrogant to be scouting a base for a final that her team may not even reach, and to do it when their semi-final opponents were staying there. "I would assume everybody is doing that — you have to plan ahead," Ellis, 52, said. "The only two people who are thinking of planning ahead is my administrator, because she has to book all the flights and do all of that stuff, and her boss. Everybody else, we don't worry about that, so that is probably who the two people [at the hotel] were.

"So, in terms of arrogance, that has nothing to do with us, that is planning and preparation for our staff."

Phil Neville, the England head coach, said that it was poor etiquette and insisted his staff would not have done the same. "It'll have no bearing on the game — I found it funny," he said. "I

Continued on page 55

---

THE TIMES

Sport

### Now Wimbledon ge

● Where Federer-Nadal
● Serena storms into fin

Pages 64-67

# One match from g

### England dominate Australia for shot at making history

Elizabeth Ammon

England have the chance to win their first World Cup after hammering Australia by eight wickets in their semi-final at Edgbaston.

They will play New Zealand at Lord's on Sunday, the first time that they have reached the final for 27 years, in a match that will be broadcast on Channel 4 as well as Sky. The pay-TV broadcaster agreed to allow the match to be shown free-to-air in a move that they hope will allow the widest possible audience to be inspired by Eoin Morgan's team, should they make history by winning at Lord's.

Morgan, 32, said "It's the game I love so it's great news that it's on free-to-air." Reflecting on his side's dominant performance with ball and then bat, he said "Everybody out there on the field and even in the changing room loved every ball. There was no lack of commitment, application and we had a bit of a day out which is cool when it happens like that, particularly when the bowlers bowl like that, it is awesome."

The only blemish on England's day came when Jason Roy was sanctioned by the ICC for showing ssent to the umpires after being

ontinued on page 69

### World Cup final

New Zealand

---

THE TIMES

DIEU ET MON DROIT

ONLY £1.10 TO SUBSCRI

MONDAY JULY 15 2019 | THETIMES.CO.UK | NO 72899

---

ton, which boosted their World Cup semi-final hopes Pages 56-59

## DOWN

1 Racing yacht — something a female impersonator might have? (6)
2 Go with detectives, finding ruin (9)
3 First letter, one I penned in ancient language going north (7)
4 Bored agent with woman in Thailand's borders (9)
5 Letter revealing a union problem after seven years? (5)
6 Giant, one meeting a fairy queen (7)
7 In action it resembles saltpetre (5)
8 Part of sailing vessel popular in mother's time (8)
14 Old, old city's little people — us, emphatically (9)
15 Scallywags generally in right order crossing a burn? (9)
16 Eccentric leader leaving NW town for a Welsh one (8)
18 Stuffy, like follicularly challenged Cockneys? (7)
19 Church cheers fellow visiting, one giving out notes (7)
20 Hungarian publication unknown artist set up (6)
22 Originally such a strange Wiltshire diocese (5)

Prize crossword 27,384

Check today's answers by ringing 0906 757189 by midnight. Calls cost 80p per minute plus your telephone company's network access charge. SP: Spoke 0333 202 3390.

The winners of Prize Crossword No 27,384 are
Denis Desmond, Kidderminster;
Julian Leach, London SW18;
Robin Parker, Holt, Norfolk;
Rachel Baker, Little Eaton, Derbyshire;
Alex Conner, Birmingham

Buying The Times: Austria £3.00; Belgium €4.50; Cyprus €3.50; North Cyprus 11.35; Denmark DKR35; France €4.50; Gibraltar £2.70; Greece €3.50; Italy €4.50; Luxembourg €4.50; Malta €4.50; Netherlands €4.50; Portugal €3.50; Spain €4.50; Switzerland CHF6.00; Turkey TL 25

---

ay was, having a
outskirts of Detroit (7)
ward in New Mexico? It
opposite (7)
g sailors can finally
ooks (9)
ers make nearly half the
5)
duced by old boy and

a group of nations
American club (9)
eature's talons oddly
in a house (13)
egance of melodies with
s (4,3,6)
English teacher dips into
heartedly (9)
ntertaining male climber

elf with something close
ar? (5)
imming, lady dives with
deration (9)
ars reversed, avoiding area
(7)
finally decisively

# SEMI-FINAL PREVIEW

MIKE ATHERTON

Cricket's Fab Four – Virat, Joe, Kane and Steve – are, by common consent, among the most accomplished of the multi-format batsmen playing today, similar in age and importance to their teams. For those who would compare and contrast, the cards have fallen well: the four maestros find themselves on opposing sides in the forthcoming semi-finals of the World Cup and it would be surprising if one of them does not play a defining innings to determine the trophy's destination.

Kohli, Root and Williamson have had fine tournaments, without enjoying complete dominance, while Smith has been more anonymous. Each knows that the next week will shape permanent perceptions of the tournament and that a defining innings will leave a more lasting impression than anything achieved in the group stage. Which of them will do what Clive Lloyd managed in 1975, or Viv Richards in 1979, or Adam Gilchrist in 2007, for example? Which of them will imprint their name indelibly on the 2019 World Cup?

Boos have followed Smith around as inevitably as night follows day and it would be easy to draw the conclusion that they have not driven him to greater heights, as they have David Warner; Smith being a more sensitive soul than his left-handed colleague. The explanation for Smith's relatively lacklustre returns – although he has hit three half-centuries – may be a little more prosaic: Australia are wasting one of their key assets by batting him at No. 4 (for the most part) instead of at No. 3, the position from where his contemporaries like to set the scene.

Opening or No. 3 are the best positions to bat in 50-over cricket, given the time that they have to set the agenda and the added advantages of field restrictions, good pitches and a white Kookaburra ball that rarely swings. It stands to reason that the top ten run-scorers in the competition bat in the top three and that the 11th, Ben Stokes, would probably not have had the opportunity to score so many runs had Jason Roy not missed three matches through a torn hamstring.

Australia, though, continue to hamstring Smith by batting him at No. 4, where he has less time to influence the game. In nine outings, Smith has batted at No. 4 six times (although he was effectively No. 3 against South Africa on Saturday because of Usman Khawaja's injury), once at No. 6 and only twice at No. 3, because Khawaja has to bat high in the order and Smith is a little more adaptable and a better player of spin than some. As with his three contemporaries, Smith's greatest strength is not as a power-hitter, rather as a player of touch and class and it would be to his benefit if he were given maximum time to show it. The hamstring strain that has ruled Khawaja out of the tournament may be a blessing in disguise for Australia.

Smith has ceded ground in the run-scoring stakes to Aaron Finch and Warner, whereas Williamson's problem has been the absence of colleagues to share the load. You will notice whenever New Zealand play, a gathering of supporters each wearing a naval captain's cap and a 'Steady the Ship' T-shirt, in homage to the skipper, who invariably finds himself coming in after the loss of an early wicket with a rescue job in hand, having to steer the ship away from the rocks.

Early in the tournament, his responses were stunning, with scores of 79 not out (Afghanistan), 106 not out (South Africa) and 148 (West Indies) but more lately the burden has started to tell. He has failed to reach fifty in his past three innings, the latest against England, when he was run out in unfortunate fashion at the non-striker's end after the ball clipped the bowler's finger.

Some may think of Williamson as the least eye-catching of the four, but to my mind he has played the shot of the tournament. Amid an infatuation for sixes, Williamson's delicate glide to the third-man boundary, with the fielder inside the inner circle, during the heat of a run-chase against South Africa said so much about his calm, poise and skill. Few others would have considered that option at that point; fewer would have been able to place the ball with such accuracy.

Perhaps there is no greater contrast between the characters of all four than between Williamson and Kohli. Williamson's straggly, surfer's beard looks as though it is designed to act as a screen against the outside world, while Kohli's is a sculpted, look-at-me adornment.

If Williamson wants to melt into the background and let his bat do the talking, then Kohli is the Sun King of the cricketing arena, the point from which dazzling rays emanate. From instructing India fans not to boo Smith and Warner, to giving batsmen out when taking a catch, to getting into trouble with umpires for excessive appealing, Kohli's ball of fire shows no sign of burning itself out.

The India captain has been consistent with the bat, without quite dominating. He scored five consecutive half-centuries, without turning any into a hundred which, for a man who has scored an incredible 41 hundreds in this format at a conversion rate of 43 per cent, is a frustrating return. His highest score in this tournament is 82 against Australia. Teams are trying to thwart him by holding a wide line outside off stump, which has had some success because, unlike most great players, Kohli rarely plays the cut shot. He has plenty enough arrows in his quiver to make up for that limitation and in this format at least he remains, to my eye, pre-eminent – especially when chasing a target.

So far, though, Kohli has been outshone by Rohit Sharma, who has hit a record five hundreds, just as Root has had to share the limelight with England's openers, Jonny Bairstow and Roy, who have been the principal reason for the host nation emerging from their mid-tournament slump. Indeed, the key to Root's one-day game has been to make peace with the fact that he may not dominate in one-day cricket as he does in Tests, and that it would be to his detriment to try to take on the likes of Bairstow and the middle-order dynamos, Jos Buttler and Stokes, in the hitting stakes.

Instead, he must be content to be the glue that holds the innings together, one that allows others free rein to play their natural games. Mostly, it has looked as though he has been content to play that role, hitting fine hundreds against Pakistan – albeit in a losing cause – and West Indies, with three more half-centuries to boot. Of the four, Root has scored most runs. It is often the case in big series, though, that he starts well and his form drops away, and he must be careful that this World Cup does not fit a similar pattern. He has not passed fifty in his past three matches.

Kohli v Williamson and Root v Smith it is, then. Root has never played in a World Cup semi-final. Kohli has played in two, and one final, and his top score is only 35.

Smith has played in one of each, scoring an unbeaten hundred and a fifty (both at No. 3) and Williamson had two low scores in the semi-final and final four years ago.

All are in their prime now. One of them, surely, is set to play a tournament-winning innings in the week to come.

# INDIA v NEW ZEALAND

*Tuesday, July 9– Wednesday, July 10*

## *Old Trafford*

**New Zealand 239-8** (50 overs) (Williamson 67, Taylor 74; Bhuvneshwar Kumar 3-43) **India 221 all out** (49.3 overs) (Dhoni 50, Jadeja 77; Henry 3-37) *New Zealand won by 18 runs* **Toss** *New Zealand*

MIKE ATHERTON, CHIEF CRICKET CORRESPONDENT The game has a way of confounding the strongest hopes and expectations. This was not the result that the vast majority inside Old Trafford wanted, nor the all-powerful Indian television networks with a commercial interest, but it will be New Zealand's humble hard workers who will contest a second consecutive World Cup final on Sunday, having edged past Virat Kohli's team in a tense, taut thriller that encapsulated much that is great about knockout cricket.

The scores were low. There were only six sixes in all. The pitch, dry and cracked, was tricky for batting. The tension, though, was undeniable, rising all the while as the day ebbed and flowed, and the prospect of a final receded, agonisingly, for some. It was a marvellous, nuanced game that asked questions of players' intelligence, skill and nerve, for which New Zealand were not found wanting.

The atmosphere at Old Trafford – Tuesday's play was washed out after 46.1 overs, with New Zealand 211 for five – was like a morgue after play, with India supporters wandering around in a daze, unable to comprehend their fate and shocked at what was an undeniable upset, given New Zealand's three consecutive defeats before this game. It was a cruel letdown, too, given the way that Ravindra Jadeja and MS Dhoni had raised hopes with a record seventh-wicket partnership in a World Cup of 116.

New Zealand? They celebrated with partners, wives and children on the outfield and will enjoy a rest before Sunday, when their experience of four years ago – where they lost in the final to Australia – should stand them in good stead.

It was only a half-day's cricket, but it offered so much that it is difficult to know where to begin. Maybe, then, it is best to start with two superlative pieces of fielding that went a long way to lifting New Zealand's players; encouraging and enabling them to hold their nerve and defend a small target. The first was a startling one-handed catch at backward point by Jimmy Neesham – the catch of the tournament in my estimation – that brought New Zealand their fourth wicket at the close of the opening powerplay, a remarkable piece of anticipation and skill.

The second, which was even more important in the context of the game, came in the penultimate over, just as Dhoni looked as though he would produce another miracle and get his team over the line. Running in from square leg to save two, Martin Guptill swooped, took aim at the one stump in his line of vision and hit it direct, with Dhoni millimetres short of his line, and Tom Latham, the New Zealand wicketkeeper,

nowhere to be seen, having set off earlier in pursuit of the ball.

India had needed 31 runs from the final two overs and Dhoni, 38, had smote his first six over point two balls before, but from that point on, there was no coming back. Dhoni's final World Cup match would produce no miracle finish.

This is a very different New Zealand team from four years ago, conforming more to type than Brendon McCullum's swashbucklers, and so a low-scoring game on a tired pitch suited them just fine. If Kane Williamson and Ross Taylor were key men on Tuesday, wisely limiting their ambitions, it was the new-ball bowlers, Trent Boult and Matt Henry, who were vital yesterday, taking a wrecking ball to India's top order, before Mitchell Santner squeezed the life out of the middle order with some suffocating left-arm spin. The first tremor for India came as early as the second over, when Henry produced a gorgeous leg-cutter to dismiss the run-machine that is Rohit Sharma.

The tremors became a full-blown earthquake when Virat Kohli fell leg-before sixth ball to Boult. India are not as reliant on these two as New Zealand, say, are on Williamson and Taylor, but they have dominated to a significant degree and suddenly India were looking to their lesser lights to carry them home.

Kohli was the victim of a marvellous piece of bowling from Boult, getting dragged across his crease with two wide balls, before missing a sharp inswinger when having to play around his front pad, a classic left-armer's dismissal. Boult also required the co-operation of Richard Illingworth, the on-field umpire, because replays suggested that the ball, having hit Kohli above the knee roll, would have only grazed the top of the stumps, and the inevitable review would have gone the batsman's way had Illingworth demurred.

The India captain, as is his way, looked supremely relaxed before the day's play – playing football and rolling his arm over in the middle. Maybe appearances are deceptive as this great player has failed to produce his best in World Cup semi-finals, this latest failure bringing his total to 11 runs in three innings. When KL Rahul nibbled at another leg-cutter from Henry, the top three had each been dispatched with a sorry single to their names and India were five for three.

New Zealand's opening powerplay was not yet done and, with Boult and Henry tightening the screw, the best moment was to come. Dinesh Karthik had taken 21 balls to get off the mark – all told there were a remarkable 49 dot balls in the opening ten overs – and having done so with one drive to the boundary, he attempted another off Henry, only to see Neesham, advancing with intent to swoop low to his left.

Neesham had almost given up the game 18 months before and was quickly reminded of its vagaries, of the cruelty that can so often follow the glory, when he dropped Rishabh Pant at mid-wicket off Lockie Ferguson's first ball shortly afterwards.

The recovery began through Pant, initially, and then Hardik Pandya, and it needed Santner to continue what the new-ball bowlers had started. The left-arm spinner's first eight overs went for 15 runs, and included the key wickets of Pant and Pandya, and then it was just a case of whether Jadeja and Dhoni, the last hopes, could get India over the line.

Jadeja, the left-arm spinner, had already excelled in the morning, with a smart catch and run-out, and his innings of 77 from 59 balls was the most fluent of the match. Brought into the team for the final group match against Sri Lanka on Saturday, he was criticised in one quarter for being a 'bits and pieces' cricketer, but the pieces fitted together almost perfectly in this match.

His injection of pace allowed Dhoni some breathing space and with 37 runs required from three overs, the outcome was by no means certain, especially given Williamson still had one over to find from his fifth bowler.

Having been criticised in the group-stage match against England for batting too slowly, it would be hard to level that same criticism at Dhoni here, given where India found themselves at 24 for four. He and his younger, more energetic, colleagues gave them a chance.

It was not to be, though. Jadeja aimed a massive blow with 13 balls to go and sent a mighty skier into the air, only to see Williamson hold a nerve-shredding catch.

Like so much of New Zealand's out-cricket, it summed up his team's greatest strength: while they are not the best team in the competition, who will say they cannot win it? Character goes a long way in this game.

......................................................

PLAYER OF THE MATCH:
*Matt Henry (New Zealand)*

## WHAT THEY SAID

'I woke up at 3 o'clock this morning, wondering how I was going to bat these last 23 balls. I texted my wife at about five saying I still can't go to bed. She said, "Oh dear." So I just turned my phone off because there were a lot of messages from back home. So in terms of my sleep, I had terrible sleep.'

Ross Taylor

'To just go out on the basis of 45 minutes of bad cricket is saddening and it breaks your heart because you have worked so hard throughout the tournament to build momentum.'

Virat Kohli

## KEY NUMBER

# 3

Number of attempts it took for New Zealand win a
World Cup semi-final in Manchester

# LIAM PLUNKETT PROFILE

JOHN WESTERBY

For a measure of the character that has sustained Liam Plunkett through the course of a career of wildly fluctuating fortunes, it is worth going back to April 2012 and a second XI County Championship game between Durham and Yorkshire at Marton, on the outskirts of Middlesbrough. To say the least, this was a point at which the pace bowler's career was stalling. At 27, it was five years since his most recent Test appearance, more than a year since an isolated one-day international recall, and now he was straining to play his way into Durham's first team.

The rain was falling and Paul Farbrace, then the Yorkshire second XI coach, was saddened to see a player he had first encountered as a rising star with England Under-19 languishing in his county's second team at an age when he should have been in his prime. 'But I went round the back of the pavilion while it was raining and there was Liam, practising his bowling drills on his own,' Farbrace said. 'You might expect someone who has played international cricket to be sulking on a day like that. I thought, "This lad's going to be OK." When a player has got Liam's physical capabilities, combined with a resilience and a work ethic like that to go with it, he's probably going to end up back where he belongs.'

Seven years on, to those who have followed his progress, Plunkett's response to being dropped after England's opening game of the World Cup came as little surprise. He went away, bided his time and trained his socks off. And when the selectorial pendulum swung his way again, he was ready to seize his chance, reasserting himself so convincingly that he has come to be seen as a lucky charm for Eoin Morgan's side. England have won every game Plunkett has played at the World Cup, while he was absent from each of the three defeats they suffered during the group stage.

Survival was eventually achieved with wins over India and New Zealand, earning a place in the semi-final against Australia tomorrow, helped in no small way by the bowling of Plunkett, himself one of the game's great survivors. His longevity can be measured in any number of ways. On his County Championship debut for Durham in 2003, one of his victims in a five-wicket first-innings haul was Darren Gough. His Test debut came on a tour to Pakistan two years later, when he replaced an injured Simon Jones, who had triumphed in the fabled 2005 Ashes series a few months earlier. Plunkett is playing in his second World Cup, but his first was in 2007 in the Caribbean, pedalos and all. Another time.

So it is quite some achievement, at 34, still to be playing at the top level, particularly as a fast bowler, in a game that has made ever greater athletic demands of its players in recent years.

Cricket has undergone seismic changes and Plunkett, blessed with pace, a 6ft 4in frame and a burning determination, has managed to change with it, reviving his career with a move from Durham to Yorkshire in 2013, then earning an international recall a year later, before joining Surrey this season. 'He's had a complete metamorphosis,' Geoff Cook, the former Durham director of cricket, said 'Anybody you speak to will be delighted for him because he's one of those lads that everybody would want in their team.'

His ability to survive the physical demands of the modern one-day game are the result of a career-long commitment to keeping himself in optimum condition. 'That athleticism has always been there,' Martyn Moxon, the Yorkshire director of cricket, who worked with Plunkett at both Durham and Yorkshire, said.

'If anything, we often wondered if there was a danger he would overtrain. But that's something he's always been passionate about.'

Perhaps a greater factor is that resilience when things have not been going his way. After such a bright start to his career, cutting a swathe through county batting line-ups and making his Test debut at 20, he suffered a steep decline, the result of attempts to remodel his action when injuries began to creep in. 'He was probably picked by England prematurely,' Cook said. 'And it was his misfortune to come through at a time when the science was suggesting that everybody's action conform to a certain type.'

Plunkett's action was a mix of front-on and side-on and ECB coaches attempted to make him fully front-on. 'It was a bit of a fetish at the time and Liam was a real victim of that,' Cook said. 'It wasn't anybody's fault, that was just the current thinking. But it took him a while to recover properly from that.'

There were tough times away the cricket, too.

His mother, Marie, had two separate forms of cancer and his father, Alan, a fast bowler in local club cricket in Middlesbrough, had a rare kidney condition. Plunkett offered his father one of his kidneys, but he refused, fearing for his son's career, and embarked on a successful course of dialysis. 'The family went through a lot, but they're a good bunch and all stuck together,' Cook said.

The complications with Plunkett's action forced him to overthink his bowling and his form suffered badly. 'It had got to the point where, when I was going to sleep at night, I was thinking about bowling four wides first ball,' Plunkett said later. Salvation came in a fresh start with Yorkshire. Jason Gillespie, the former Australia fast bowler, was first-team coach and he told Plunkett simply to run in and bowl fast. 'When Yorkshire signed him, he was unsure what sort of bowler he was,' Gillespie said. 'Our thinking was, "You can bowl 90mph, your job is to run in, hit the track hard on a good length and use your bouncer."'

The results were not long in coming. Word began to spread of Plunkett's rediscovered pace and in 2014 he played his first Tests for seven years. When England were then looking – after a disastrous 2015 World Cup – for a bowler to shake up batsmen in the middle stages of a 50-over innings, Plunkett's time had come and Farbrace was again involved, this time as assistant coach.

'His pace was just what we wanted,' Farbrace said. 'We could attack in those middle overs, with Adil Rashid bowling leg spin at the other end. If we could get the opposition seven or eight down in the first 40 overs, we knew they wouldn't be able to smash 100 off the last ten.'

But still there would be changes that Plunkett needed to make. Trevor Bayliss, the head coach, recognised that pace in itself would not be enough and Plunkett did not play in the winter Test series against Pakistan and South Africa in 2015–16. 'He didn't moan once, he just went to Trevor and said, "What do I need to do?"' Farbrace said. 'Trevor told him he needed more variations, so he developed the slower bouncer, the cutters and the cross-seam balls to add to the yorker and bouncer. Against India [last week] he was the first to start bowling cross-seam balls and, against fantastic batsmen, you could see how good he was.'

There have been countless diversions and byways on Plunkett's path to this World Cup, but his ability to adapt and survive make him a rare asset to England. 'He's an incredibly professional professional and a great man to have in your team,' Farbrace said. 'The fact that he's come back from second-team county cricket to a World Cup semi-final is a great lesson for anyone.'

# ENGLAND v AUSTRALIA

*Thursday, July 11*

*Edgbaston*

**Australia 223 all out** (49 overs)
(Smith 85; Woakes 3-20, Rashid 3-54)
**England 226-2** (32.1 overs) (Roy 85)
*England won by eight wickets*
**Toss** *Australia*

MIKE ATHERTON,
CHIEF CRICKET CORRESPONDENT
The World Cup will have a new owner. Neither England nor New Zealand have ever won it, but they will now play each other at Lord's on Sunday after Eoin Morgan's players bared their teeth on the biggest cricketing day of their lives and mauled Australia with what Kane Williamson's side may see as alarming ease. Semi-finals can be fraught, nervy affairs but this was a thrashing – a glorious thrashing – England winning by eight wickets with almost 18 overs to spare.

At England's most fervently patriotic and boisterous ground, the game ended joyously to the strains of *It's Coming Home* and *Sweet Caroline* as the crowd relished the lack of drama or tension that was involved. England supporters once cheered an Ashes win at the Oval, 14 years ago, after bad light stopped play, and this had a similar feel. No one was bothered about the quality of the match, or the closeness of the finish. They simply wanted England to win. Playing Australia has that effect on supporters.

The manner of the victory was important, though, since it conformed to the type of victory that had become commonplace in their rise to the top of the rankings, before a mid-tournament blip caused one or two to question their credentials. There was more than a touch of arrogance here as well as supreme confidence in the way that they approached chasing what was a relatively small target.

These mundane totals can, sometimes, stymie the aggressive instincts of batsmen, who know that such games can be won by playing the percentages. Jonny Bairstow and Jason Roy were having none of that and they set off like a train, another century opening partnership, their fourth of the competition, coming in the 16th over, by which time the game was effectively over. They are a remarkable combination. The numbers indicate they are among the best ever in one-day cricket, but the transformative effect they have had on this team in the past two weeks goes beyond that.

Yesterday, Roy targeted not Australia's weakest link, but their most potent threats. Mitchell Starc was dispatched for 70 runs from his nine overs, with only one wicket to show for his endeavours, one flick from Roy over the fine-leg fence for six being both dismissive and remarkable at the same time.

When Nathan Lyon, the king of spin, was introduced, Roy smashed his first ball over long on for six, despite there being a fielder protecting that very boundary. The message, and intent, was clear. Lyon's five overs cost 49 runs.

# Sport

**Now Wimbledon gets serious**
● Where Federer-Nadal will be decided
● Serena storms into final against Halep
Pages 64-67

TIMES PHOTOGRAPHER BRADLEY ORMESHER

# One match from glory

## England dominate Australia for shot at making history

**Elizabeth Ammon**

England have the chance to win their first World Cup after hammering Australia by eight wickets in their semi-final at Edgbaston.

They will play New Zealand at Lord's on Sunday, the first time that they have reached the final for 27 years, in a match that will be broadcast on Channel 4 as well as Sky. The pay-TV broadcaster agreed to allow the match to be shown free-to-air in a move that they hope will allow the widest possible audience to be inspired by Eoin Morgan's team, should they make history by winning at Lord's.

Morgan, 32, said: "It's the game I love so it's great news that it's on free-to-air." Reflecting on his side's dominant performance with ball and then bat, he said: "Everybody out there on the field and even in the changing room loved every ball. There was no lack of commitment, application and we had a bit of a day out which is cool when it happens like that, particularly when the bowlers bowl like that, it is awesome."

The only blemish on England's day came when Jason Roy was sanctioned by the ICC for showing dissent to the umpires after being Continued on page 69

### World Cup final

New Zealand v England

Lord's, Sunday, 10.30am

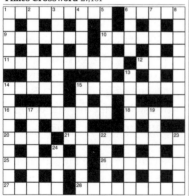

Jofra Archer celebrates the wicket of Glenn Maxwell, with Ben Stokes, left and Eoin Morgan. It reduced Australia to 157 for six at Edgbaston as England powered into the final against New Zealand on Sunday

---

## Times Crossword 27,401

9 771742 498653

Only Bairstow, of the four batsmen needed, scored at less than a run a ball (will that suffice as media criticism and spark him into life for the final?) while the rest played with the kind of carefree abandon that many said was beyond them in the knockout stages of a World Cup. Australia's premier bowlers dismantled, Aaron Finch was forced to turn to Steve Smith's part-time leg spin to try to break the deadlock and Roy promptly smashed him for three consecutive sixes, the third landing on the fourth tier of the giant new stand, before rebounding to an Australia fielder below.

In a tournament where teams have chased targets with all the wariness of a big-game hunter approaching a pride of lions in the bush, this confidence was refreshing and will remind them (and New Zealand) that it is possible to chase and win. Once Bairstow and Roy had been separated, the first leg-before, using up a review that the second would have dearly wanted to use after being adjudged caught behind despite there being daylight between bat and ball, Joe Root and Morgan continued in much the same vein, so that there could be no doubt about the result.

It was always likely that the start of both innings would determine the outcome of the match. England won both periods, convincingly. The new-ball bowlers, so poor against Australia in the group stage, were superb here, taking three wickets in the opening ten overs, a position from which Australia struggled to recover. Chris Woakes and Jofra Archer were the big-game hunters

on this occasion, two of the big five, Finch and David Warner, who have been so pivotal to Australia's success in this tournament, failing to reach double figures.

If there were any nerves in the England team, they lasted precisely the one ball it took Warner to get off the mark, when he drove the opening ball of the game from Woakes for four. Certainly, there were no nerves apparent in Archer's first ball, which was perfectly pitched on a full length and nipping back to Finch, who became the first Australia batsman to record a golden duck in a World Cup match. He used up Australia's review for good measure.

Finch has an exceptional record against England and was at the heart of Australia's victory in the group match at Lord's, and so this represented the most significant dividend from Archer since his elevation to England colours. Archer then looked threatening throughout a rapid opening five-over spell, and although there were no further wickets for him in it, he did hit Alex Carey on the jaw fifth ball, which necessitated a standing count and serious bandaging for Australia's wicketkeeper. Later, a perfect knuckle ball completely deceived the dangerous Glenn Maxwell, so that there was real guile added to the mix.

At No. 5, Carey found himself at the crease as early as the seventh over, because at the other end from Archer, Woakes was soon at his metronomic best. After a second thunderous drive from Warner, Woakes brought back his length and duly found the left-hander's outside edge, Bairstow taking the catch at first slip to general glee. Peter Handscomb's dozen-ball stay reflected that of a man who had played precious little cricket of late and he looked totally out of touch, before being gated in Woakes' fourth over.

For this new-ball spell, and a third wicket towards the end of the innings, Woakes was given the man-of-the-match award, and it was fitting that this unassuming man should receive it at what he subsequently called 'the greatest ground in the world'. It is his home ground, of course, and he was cheered to the rafters, but he has become the Mr Reliable of Morgan's team, rarely missing a beat with the new ball, and temperamentally sound should he need to bowl the 'death' overs. He has caught two of the outstanding catches in the competition as well and is enjoying a fine tournament.

Having been hit, the side of Carey's face started to swell badly. Initially, the medical staff stemmed the bleeding from his jaw with simple sticking plaster, but then the swelling required more extensive bandaging, so that, underneath his helmet, he began to resemble Rick McCosker, the Australia batsman who had his jaw broken by Bob Willis in the 1977 Centenary Test, but who continued to bat with so much bandaging wrapped around his head that he was almost mummified. Carey had the helmet that McCosker did not, but his bravery was not in question.

His partnership with Smith was the only significant one of the Australian innings, and ended when he chipped Adil Rashid into the deep. Rashid has not been at his best, but three wickets, with Marcus Stoinis and Pat Cummins following Carey, will have done his confidence no end of good before the final. This was a fine all-round display by England's bowling pack.

It was left to Smith, then, to try to shepherd Australia to something competitive and his innings of 85 gave their supporters some cheer. It was ended by a marvellous piece of fielding from Jos Buttler, who collected a mishit pull shot and threw down the stumps at the non-striker's end. Smith, alone of Australia's big guns, had fired when it mattered. The rest were put well and truly in the shade by a team that will be very hard to beat in two days' time.

........................................

PLAYER OF THE MATCH:
*Chris Woakes (England)*

## WHAT THEY SAID

'Sunday's not a day to shy away from – it's a day to look forward to, much like today. It will be a matter of the same again, trying to produce everything we can performance-wise, but enjoy the day.'

Eoin Morgan

'It's disappointing how it ended, especially to put up one of our worst performances of the tournament.'

Aaron Finch

'Eoin is as cool as ice with everything he does. He is great to have as a captain – he just keeps everything simple and doesn't change his emotions too much, which in the heat of the battle helps to keep your mind clear.'

Chris Woakes

## KEY NUMBERS

### 27

Number of years since England played in a World Cup final

### I

Australia's first defeat in a World Cup semi-final

## ANALYSIS

**STEVE JAMES**

One ball was all that it took. One ball from Jofra Archer, the seventh of the day, and the Australia captain Aaron Finch was gone.

It was some statement, and Australia never really recovered. Archer had dismissed Finch in the recent group match at Lord's but the problem then was that the opener already had a century. It was Finch's seventh one-day international hundred against England; he usually scores runs against England for fun.

At Lord's Archer's first ball to him had been a gentle half-volley that was dispatched to the cover boundary. This was different. This was pitched on a good length. It may not have been ferociously fast, but 85mph is not too bad for an opening salvo, and, crucially, the ball hit the seam and nipped back at Finch.

Finch's body shape and shot were aiming at extra cover. The ball was dancing to another tune and thudded into his front pad. The appeal was plaintive. The decision was in the affirmative. Finch reviewed but it was in vain. The disappointment of losing the toss had dissipated for England in one moment. A golden moment for England, a golden duck for Finch.

The analysts CricViz reckoned that it was the first time in the tournament that the 24-year-old's first ball would have gone on to hit the stumps. Some timing. Some ball.

It set the tone. Archer and Chris Woakes then bowled an opening spell that was as probing as any visit to the dentist. They bowled quite magnificently, as they used every ounce of assistance from the surface to reduce

Australia to 14 for three in the seventh over, as Woakes took two wickets.

By the end of the initial power-play Australia were 27 for three, their lowest score at that stage in the tournament. It was a long road back from there. Too long.

Steve Smith is fidgety at the best of times, but Archer, beginning with a fizzing first-ball bouncer, rendered him even more restless than usual. There was much playing and missing. The speedometer spent time above 90mph. But it was Alex Carey who was most discomforted by Archer. The Australian left-handed batsman/wicketkeeper was on four in the eighth over when Archer hit him with a horrible blow to the helmet.

It was a wicked bouncer, which Carey could not avoid. One of Archer's many outstanding attributes is that he bowls so close to the stumps that, when he does bowl a short ball, there is no angle with which the batsman can work.

That wicket-to-wicket quality, of course, is a problem for batsmen with all of Archer's deliveries, but the others do not carry this sort of physical threat. Swaying one way or the other is almost impossible. There also does not appear to be any obvious clue when Archer's bouncer is coming. With most bowlers there is an inkling, however small.

With Archer it is just that same languid approach of a man about to bowl at 80mph. Except he bowls much faster than that with so little apparent effort; his shoulder speed is astonishing.

Carey was hit so hard on the chin that his helmet flew off. He did brilliantly to

catch it before it fell on to the stumps, bringing to mind an incident involving an old Glamorgan colleague of mine, Matthew Maynard, way back in 1988, when, in a Benson & Hedges Cup semi-final against Derbyshire, his helmet was dislodged by the great Michael Holding for him to be out hit wicket.

Carey needed lengthy treatment, the medical staff returning later to put strapping around his head, making him look much like Rick McCosker once had in the Ashes Centenary Test in Melbourne in 1977 as he bravely batted with a broken jaw.

Archer had served notice again of his pace and hostility – he had hit South Africa's Hashim Amla on the opening day of the tournament – a message that will doubtless continue ringing out as the Ashes approaches, a series in which Archer is now certain to make his Test debut.

It has been remarkable how easily he has taken to international cricket. To think that there were some who were a little hesitant about his inclusion for this tournament. He has 19 wickets, more than any England bowler in a World Cup, and only Australia's Mitchell Starc and Bangladesh's Mustafizur Rahman have taken more in this competition.

It will be a huge surprise if Archer does not have a similar effect upon that Ashes series. He is a special talent.

Having seen him for just four overs in a rain-ruined ODI against Pakistan at the Oval in May, my judgment may have tended a little towards hyperbole, saying later that I had never been more certain of a cricketer enjoying a long and prosperous international career since a young batsman called Alastair Cook appeared in Nagpur in 2006.

But, after all the talk about him, Archer has walked the walk. To talent we can now add big-match temperament. It is a heady mix.

There is already huge respect for Archer within the game. It was evidenced here by Smith, and not just because they know each other from their time at the Indian Premier League with Rajasthan Royals. That respect is becoming universal.

Smith was on 63 at the time and having put aside his early troubles when he inside-edged Archer down to fine leg for a single. He knew little about the ball. He admitted as much almost immediately by apologising to Archer, tapping the bowler on the backside a couple of times as he ambled his single.

It is not just Archer's pace and sang-froid that set him apart. It is his skill too, and that was manifested in his second wicket here.

The England captain Eoin Morgan had shrewdly called Archer back into the attack (and continued with him to bowl out, rather than keeping him, as usual, for the death) upon the arrival of Glenn Maxwell at No. 7. Maxwell had been troubled by the short ball in this tournament, and Archer did not spare him further practice in that respect, but it was actually with a wonderfully disguised knuckle ball that he eventually dismissed him, persuading Maxwell to chip to cover.

Maxwell looked accusingly at the pitch, but he had been deceived by Archer rather than by the surface, with the bowler changing his grip in his action and the batsman certain it was a normal seamer, when in fact it was a ball gripped not by the knuckles, as the name suggests, but by the fingertips.

It summed up the day. England were always one step ahead of Australia, from the moment Archer dismissed the skipper.

# e's Elba,
## Exclusive interview

**INSIDE TIMES2**

**Deborah Ross**
How I'd like to punish the Brexit MEPs

## o become first British head of the IMF

doctrines. Mr Osborne will need the nomination of Britain's next prime minister to succeed. The Evening Standard, which he edits, recently endorsed Boris Johnson in the Conservative leadership race.

Although Mark Carney, the governor of the Bank of England could also be a candidate, Mr Osborne's allies believe that Mario Draghi, the outgoing head of the European Central Bank (ECB), may become his main rival because the governor is more closely focused on Canadian politics.

Supporters of Mr Osborne say that the former chancellor could win backing from both President Trump and President Xi. Mediating between the United States and China requires a politician rather than a technocrat,

they claim. They concede, though, that Brexit has made the appointment of a British candidate less likely.

The role of IMF chairman and managing director became available after Ms Lagarde was appointed to replace Mr Draghi as head of the ECB in the latest round of European Union appointments. The new head must be
Continued on page 2, col 3

---

result

The results politics is in competition. difficult to of first past

Mark Sedwill, yesterday had a Times report nior civil service is not up to ntally" and 1 is losing his

panied by Jon Cabinet Office for 45 minutes in ice.

ank and detailed, views", a Labour e seriousness of and the evident at it was acknowledged nts in the meeting, and Jon Trickett a fully independent ore trust and confiservice. They were endent element to estigation, that they it would report as They made clear the investigation will e loss of its results."

Office spokeswoman discussion had been ructive." The investiconducted by civil serto the events, and the shared with the first nmissioner, she said. reported at the weekend re of Mr Corbyn was
page 2, col 3

---

## Not your call: bosses take smartphones from workers

Jack Malvern

Posting updates on social media and texting your friends at work could soon become a thing of the past as bosses confiscate smartphones to keep noses to the grindstone.

Unions are warning that "a new front for friction" between workers and organisations is opening as managers feel that they cannot trust people to resist the temptation to post updates.

While it is normal for retailers such as Tesco to make their employees put their phones in lockers, the practice is spreading to office workers.

A director of a marketing company in West Yorkshire recently ruled out recruiting candidates who would not hand over their mobile devices. Gerard O'Shaughnessy, of Business Marketing Services in Cleckheaton, said that he felt so aggrieved by people using phones during working hours that he confiscated them until lunchtime.

Café staff at the British Library must surrender their phones to their supervisor in case they are tempted to look at them between serving customers.

Mr O'Shaughnessy, 48, said that his company began confiscating its workers' mobile phones two months ago. "We've had girls have meltdowns when they've been told they need to put their phone in a box. Others have said it's almost breaching their human rights. It's almost like a separation anxiety," he said. "When we didn't have this policy in place people would be checking social media updates during staff meetings. Every customer I deal with tells me the same happens in their organisation with younger staff."

Strict phone policies have alarmed organisations such as Prospect, the union for clerical workers that represents some staff at the British Library. Mike Clancy, its general secretary, said "Rigid controls over phone use, where no clear security and safety issues are involved, risks being rigid worker control, reflecting a broader culture that lacks trust." A British Library spokesman said that it was talking to its catering contractor Graysons about the matter.

High hopes **Jonny Bairstow celebrates his century as England beat New Zealand by 119 runs in Durham yesterday to reach the World Cup semi-finals. Pages 69-72**

in association with
sky sports cricket

---

# England on the br

● Morgan's side outplayed by Australia at Lord's
● Captain denies claim he was scared of Starc

Elizabeth Ammon

England's World Cup hopes are hanging in the balance after a 64-run defeat by Australia at Lord's means that they may have to win both of their remaining two group matches to survive in the competition.

Eoin Morgan rejected a claim made by Kevin Pietersen, the former England batsman, that he was scared of Australia today, but the England captain admitted that his side were low on confidence as they prepare to play India and New Zealand next Wednesday.

...nation started ...ement as ...but are in fourth ...e final qualifying ...semi-finals — ...ead and two ahead ...who have a

...in made them ...o secure a ...four and ...f Morgan, ...ate, had ...or 67

...y in frustration after Mitchell Starc's yorker bowled him out for 89, the only innings of substance from an England batsm

---

THE TIMES

# Sport

# England restore fear factor

Fired-up Bairstow hits century to set up win
India and put hosts back on course for semi

Elizabeth Ammon

The England captain Eoin Morgan said his side had "an outstanding day" after they kept their World Cup hopes alive with a 31-run victory that ended England's unbeaten run.

England bounced back from successive losses to Sri Lanka and Australia, and yesterday's win means that they are guaranteed a semi-final spot if they beat New Zealand on Wednesday at Chester-le-Street.

An exceptional 111 from the opener Jonny Bairstow, who had reacted to criticism after England's defeat by Australia by accusing people of wanting the team to fail, proved crucial in settling any nerves from the under-pressure hosts at Edgbaston.

"He [Jonny] does tend to get fired up a lot, and that suits him," Morgan said. "He likes a bit of fire in his belly, and I don't mind that when he comes out and plays like that. It's outstanding. It was
Continued on page 99

Bairstow takes the acclaim on reaching his 90-ball hundred in England

## Times Crossword 27,391

## w Syed

es football part of
al-justice system

### FA exit for key strategy guru

**Matt Hughes Sports News Correspondent**

Dave Reddin, one of the key architects
of England's recent resurgence, is to
leave the Football Association after six
years. The head of strategy and team
performance has agreed a severance
package, the governing body confirmed yesterday.

The FA did not comment on the
reasons behind Reddin's departure but
he is understood to have clashed with
colleagues throughout his spell at St
George's Park and developed a
reputation as a demanding taskmaster.

The 49-year-old faced allegations of
bullying two years ago. He was accused
of presiding over a "climate of fear" but
he was then cleared of any wrongdoing
by the FA.

Reddin is understood to have experienced more difficulties in his relationships with key colleagues after those

Continued on page 61

## Nadal criticises seeding policy

**art Fraser Tennis Correspondent**

ael Nadal has accused Wimbledon
isrespecting the world rankings by
g a special mathematical formula
etermine seedings for the men's
es — the only grand-slam
ament to do so.

e seedings list for the champion-
will be confirmed by the All
nd Club (AELTC) this morning,
the world No 2, will be seeded
n his arch-rival Roger
behind his arch-rival Roger
r, who is ranked No 3 but will be
No 2 after winning the Halle
on Sunday.

Australian, French and US
imply replicate the latest world
s, which are based on the
52 weeks of results across all
for their seedings. Wimble-
ever, uses a formula that gives

on page 58

---

### Wimbledon 16-page guide

Murray's return and how Konta can
win as tournament starts today

inside T2

### US accused in World Cup spying row

**Molly Hudson Lyons**

England and the United States have
become embroiled in a spying row
before their women's World Cup semi-
final after two plain-clothed members
of American staff were spotted in a
private area of the Lionesses' team
hotel in Lyons yesterday.

The FA is believed to be furious at the
unwelcome intrusion from the US, who
were scoping out the Fourvière Hotel
as a potential base for Sunday's final.
England face the US at Parc Olympique
Lyonnais tomorrow and the final will
also be played there.

England were training at a different
location 30 minutes from the hotel
while the two Americans were being
shown around by staff at their hotel.
The FA is said to be concerned that
the Americans went into rooms where
England have held team meetings.

They were not wearing any US-
branded kit and did not show their team
credentials to security on their way in.
Eventually the pair were spotted by a
member of the FA team.

The US coach Jill Ellis dismissed the
idea that it was arrogant to be scouting
a base for a final that her team may not
even reach, and to do it when their
semi-final opponents were staying
there. "I would assume everybody is
doing that — you have to plan ahead."
Ellis, 52, said. "The only two people who
are thinking of planning ahead is my
administrator, because she has to book
all the flights and do all of that stuff, and
her boss. Everybody else, we don't
worry about that, so that is probably
who the two people [at the hotel] were.

"So, in terms of arrogance, that has
nothing to do with us, that is planning
and preparation for our staff."

Phil Neville, the England head coach,
said that it was poor etiquette and
insisted his staff would not have done
the same. "It'll have no bearing on the
game — I found it funny," he said. "I

Continued on page 95

ston, which boosted their World Cup semi-final hopes Pages 56-59

---

# Sport

**Now Wimbledon get**
● Where Federer-Nadal w
● Serena storms into fina

Pages 64-67

# One match from g

**England dominate Australia for shot at making history**

**Elizabeth Ammon**

England have the chance to win
their first World Cup after
hammering Australia by eight
wickets in their semi-final at
Edgbaston.

They will play New Zealand at
Lord's on Sunday, the first time
that they have reached the final
for 27 years, in a match that will be
broadcast on Channel 4 as well as
Sky. The pay-TV broadcaster
agreed to allow the match to be
shown free-to-air in a move that
they hope will allow the widest
possible audience to be inspired by
Eoin Morgan's team, should they
make history by winning at Lord's.

Morgan, 32, said: "It's the game I
love so it's great news that it's on
free-to-air." Reflecting on his side's
dominant performance with ball
and then bat, he said: "Everybody
out there on the field and even in
the changing room loved every
ball. There was no lack of
commitment, application and we
had a bit of a day out which is cool
when it happens like that,
particularly when the bowlers
bowl like that, it is awesome."

The only blemish on England's
day came when Jason Roy was
sanctioned by the ICC for showing
dissent to the umpires after being

Continued on page 69

**World Cup final**
New Zealand

---

ONLY £1.80 TO SUBSCRI

## DOWN

Ray was, having a
outskirts of Detroit (7)
ward in New Mexico? It
opposite (7)
g sailors can finally
ooks (7)
yers make nearly half the
5)
roduced by old boy and

e a group of nations
American club (9)
eature's talons oddly
n a house (13)
elegance of melodies with
s (4,3,6)
English teacher dips into
heartedly (9)
entertaining male climber

self with something close
ar? (5)
mming, lady dives with
ideration (9)
s reversed, avoiding area
(5)
ys finally decisively

1 Racing yacht — something a
female impersonator might have?
(6)
2 Go with detectives, finding ruin (9)
3 First letter, one I penned in ancient
language going north (7)
4 Bored agent with woman in
Thailand's borders (9)
5 Letter revealing a union problem
after seven years? (5)
6 Giant, one meeting a fairy queen
(7)
7 In action it resembles saltpetre (5)
8 Part of sailing vessel popular in
mother's time (8)
14 Old, old city's little people — us,
emphatically (9)
15 Scallywags generally in right order
crossing a burn? (9)
16 Eccentric leader leaving NW town
for a Welsh one (8)
18 Stuffy, like follicularly challenged
Cockneys? (7)
19 Church cheers fellow visiting, one
giving out notes (7)
20 Hungarian publication unknown
artist set up (5)
22 Originally such a strange Wiltshire

**Prize solution 27,384**

Check today's answers by ringing 0906
757789 by midnight. Calls cost 80p per minute plus your telephone company's network
access charge. SP. Spoke 0333 202 3390.

The winners of Prize Crossword No 27,384 are
Denis Desmond, Kidderminster;
Julian Leach, London SW18;
Robin Parker, Holt, Norfolk;
Rachel Baker, Little Eaton, Derbyshire;
Alex Connor, Birmingham.

Buying The Times: Austria €4.40; Belgium €4.50;
Cyprus €4.50; Denmark DKK35; Denmark DKK35;
France €4.50; Gibraltar £2.70; Greece €4.50; Italy €4.50;
Luxembourg €4.50; Malta €4.50; Netherlands €4.50;
Portugal €4.50; Spain €4.50; Switzerland CHF6.80;
Turkey TL25

# FINAL PREVIEW

MIKE ATHERTON,
CHIEF CRICKET CORRESPONDENT

To get to this point, to the eve of a World Cup final with a favourite's chance of winning, an entire cricketing culture had to be overhauled. For years, England had treated the one-day game casually, almost amateurishly, which was fine until the realisation came that the rest of the world had moved on.

Analogue England were struggling in a digital age.

From the moment that Andrew Strauss was made director of cricket in 2015, shortly after another early exit from the World Cup, he was determined to bring England up to speed. The entire contract system was overhauled to favour one-day cricket. Players were encouraged to seek out franchised opportunities. Resources were redirected away from Test cricket into the one-day game. Winning the World Cup became an obsession.

Regardless of what happens tomorrow, this reordering of priorities has already borne fruit. Reaching the top of the rankings, which England did, is arguably a tougher achievement than winning the World Cup, it being a reflection on performances over time, in a variety of conditions, against all-comers. This England team have played the most thrilling one-day cricket the country has seen, they have raised the bar for the rest of the world as Australia's captain, Aaron Finch, admitted after his team were brushed aside in the semi-final

on Thursday. Defeat tomorrow would not invalidate these achievements.

But it would be unsatisfactory. The rankings provide no climax, no single moment of acknowledgement and, let's be honest, nobody really remembers who was No. 1, given the arcane points system that determines these things. In Test cricket, we remember Ashes winners. The World Cup is one-day cricket's equivalent. Tomorrow's final, then, represents a chance for these players to put a gloss on their achievements of the past four years and it is their one shot at sporting immortality.

There is a broader context here, as it comes at a time when English cricket has gone through, is going through, one of its common periods of existential angst. Next summer represents the start of a profound shift away from the county-based system that has anchored the English game to its historic foundations, towards a city-based format that, the authorities hope, will engage a newer, younger, more diverse audience.

The World Cup followed by five Ashes Tests was seen as the perfect route into this new landscape, a summer when it was hoped that cricket might dominate the agenda. The success of the women's football World Cup, with the remarkable audience it generated, stymied that hope to some degree and it provided further pressure to find a way to put tomorrow's match on free-to-air television. Sky's generosity and its relationship with Channel 4 allowed that to happen and so live cricket will be back on terrestrial TV for the first time in 14 years.

That Ashes series of 2005 inspired a generation of supporters, not simply because of its widespread availability but because of the epic drama that ebbed and flowed over five remarkable Test matches, qualities that a one-off match will struggle to emulate, no matter how good it is. The growth of the game is a complex issue and is best left for another day, but a personal opinion is that cricket will never be as popular as football in this country and fundamentally altering the game to the point where it loses what makes it unique and special is a fool's gold. Nevertheless, the match provides a platform and a wonderful opportunity to show the qualities of the greatest game and this fine one-day side.

England's team, after all, is an alluring mix, rich and diverse of background and character. There is Eoin Morgan, the Irishman who leads it, who was five years old when England previously played in a World Cup final. He cannot have imagined, in his wildest dreams growing up on the outskirts of Dublin, that he would one day have a chance of winning a World Cup at Lord's. It would be the culmination of a remarkable stint in charge.

There is Jofra Archer, quick and deadly, whose mix of heat-seeking missiles and knuckleballs have confounded batsmen, who was born and brought up in Barbados but now finds himself in England blue. Mark Wood, Durham born and bred, and a little bit mad, is pushing Archer all the way for the title

of the fastest bowler at the World Cup. These pace aces could not be more different in character and style.

There are the spin twins, Adil Rashid and Moeen Ali, two peas in a pod, rarely seen apart, except during a match now that Ali has been relegated to the bench. For all English cricket's desire to engage with its South Asian audience – and this World Cup has been fuelled by the passion among it – nothing beats a role model or two, and in Rashid, with his whirring leg breaks, and Ali, with his thoughtful reflections on modern British life, England have two fine examples to look up to.

There are the yeoman types too. Liam Plunkett first played in a World Cup a dozen years ago, which is a significant achievement for a fast bowler. He has endured some ups and downs in the game, especially in the early days when coaches saw fit to tinker with his action to the extent that he lost what was natural and instinctive. This would represent a career high point, as it would for Chris Woakes, another unassuming, honest-to-goodness, English-style seamer, whose cricket has peaked just at the right time. When Morgan looks around the changing room tomorrow morning, he will be happy to have sight of these two.

Then there are the pretty boys, the superstars, a group of players so outrageously talented as to be the envy of every other team. Which, among them, would not like a combination of Jonny Bairstow, Jason Roy, Joe Root, Jos Buttler and Ben Stokes? What an opportunity tomorrow represents for these players to show off their skills and their talent. All of them would get into any all-time England one-day team, and have been at the heart of the resurgence under Morgan.

Standing between them and ultimate glory are New Zealand. It feels like a win–win final. I would imagine that most supporters would applaud a New Zealand victory should England fail to win. Hard-working, humble, delightful company and led by one of the giants of the modern game – not that you'd know it, speaking to him – Kane Williamson, they are a hard bunch to dislike. A generalisation, maybe, but there are a lot of similarities in character between the English and New Zealanders: a sense of humour, a willingness to embrace the absurd and a desire not to take ourselves too seriously.

There is another similarity: neither of these teams have won a World Cup before. This is England's fourth appearance in the final, a first for 27 years, and New Zealand's second, after defeat by Australia four years ago. More than half of New Zealand's team experienced that loss, and the lessons learnt may be one of their few advantages tomorrow. Four years ago, having crossed the Tasman Sea for the first time in the competition, they were too nervous, excitable and overeager. They may be better for that run now.

Famously, Australia's wicketkeeper, Brad Haddin, unloaded a stream of invective at a couple of New Zealand batsmen in that final. When asked why, he said that New Zealand had been too nice during the group stages and that had made him, and his Australian colleagues, uncomfortable. 'I'm not playing cricket like this,' Haddin said. 'If we get another crack at these guys, I'm letting everything out.' He did and Australia won, although the one did not necessarily lead to the other.

It is unlikely that any England player will feel the same way as Haddin. Morgan learnt the leadership ropes from Brendon McCullum, New Zealand's captain four years ago. They remain the closest of friends. There is a high degree of mutual respect between both sets of players and while the rivalry will be fierce, it is likely that we will witness the best of what the game has to offer.

A personal view is that England will be too strong and New Zealand may have already played their final, when they beat India in a pulsating game at Old Trafford. They are a fine bowling outfit, resourceful and canny, and are superb in the field, but they have too many batsmen who are out of form. There is only so much Williamson and, to a lesser extent, Ross Taylor can do. England have peaked at the right time. They have come through a mid-tournament slump and are playing the kind of cricket, confident and dominant, that has characterised their one-day side for four years. Like many, I felt strongly that England would win the World Cup before it started and have seen nothing yet to make me change my mind.

# ENGLAND v
# NEW ZEALAND

*Sunday, July 14*

*Lord's*

**New Zealand 241-8** (50 overs)
(Nicholls 55; Woakes 3-37, Plunkett 3-42)
**England 241 all out** (50 overs)
(Stokes 84 not out, Buttler 59;
Ferguson 3-50, Neesham 3-43)
*Tie*
*Toss New Zealand*
**Super over**
**England 15-0**
**New Zealand 15-1**
*England won on boundary countback*

MIKE ATHERTON,
CHIEF CRICKET CORRESPONDENT
It was a little after 8pm on a glorious
summer's evening, with the old ground
scarcely able to believe what it had
just witnessed, when Eoin Morgan,
the 32-year-old Irishman from Rush
in County Dublin, did what no other
England men's cricket captain had done
before. He lifted the World Cup, made
of silver gilt but far more precious than
that, high above his head in celebration
and by so doing he placed himself and
his team at the apex of England's sporting pyramid, alongside the other glory
boys of 1966 and 2003.

If there is any merit in mentioning
this victory in the same sentence as
the greatest moment in English sporting history in 1966, it is because of the
drama of extra time that concluded
what was surely the finest one-day
match of all time. After 50 overs, the

game had ended in a pulsating tie
and therefore was decided by a Super
Over, which was also eventually tied,
England winning on a countback of
26 boundaries to 17. These things are
not supposed to happen in cricket, at
Lord's, that most traditional of grounds.

The Super Over involved two of
the players, Ben Stokes and Jos Buttler,
who had played such a role in getting
England to that point by hitting nerve-
less half-centuries in a tense run chase,
and Jofra Archer, who a little over ten
weeks ago had never played an international match. Stokes, who had ended
the match unbeaten on 84, out on his
feet and exhausted, came out again
with Buttler and set New Zealand 16
to win, and Archer did the rest – just.

It came down to the final ball of the
extra over, with two required for victory, and ended with Martin Guptill
diving agonisingly for the line and
landing short after a throw from the
boundary from Jason Roy.

Both teams knew that a second tie
was in England's favour according to
the rules of the competition, and the
reaction told the story. England's players set off, jubilant, with the reserve
players dashing on to the pitch in
celebration, while New Zealand's
pair, Guptill and Jimmy Neesham, sat
disconsolate, scarcely able to comprehend what had happened.

This was a remarkable redemption
for Stokes, who in the 2016 World
Twenty20 final conceded four sixes
off Carlos Brathwaite to see defeat
snatched from victory, and who,
shortly before the Ashes tour in 2017,
had put his career in jeopardy having

been involved in a ugly fracas outside a nightclub in Bristol. Ever since, he had said that he owed his team-mates for their support and he paid them back with interest yesterday.

Nobody could quite believe what they had witnessed. Least of all Morgan, who was embraced by the players to a man at the conclusion of the game and who now, barely 30 minutes after the match had finished, walked on to the podium in front the old pavilion to receive the trophy. He did not have to wipe the sweat from his hands before receiving it, as Bobby Moore famously did before receiving the Jules Rimet trophy from the Queen in the middle of the Swinging Sixties. His nose was not bloodied, as Martin Johnson's was when the giant lock forward lifted the Webb Ellis Cup 16 years ago. His little finger, fractured on the eve of the tournament, was shorn of its protective bandages finally as he wrapped his fingers gleefully around the silver columns as he took possession.

It will be an image for the ages, the moment that the beaming, ecstatic Morgan consigned 44 years of failure to the history books. How light it looked, this trophy that had been specially minted 20 years ago, the previous time the World Cup had been held in England, but had seemed so heavy and burdensome to every England captain who had tried to claim it since. And who would have thought it – who could have thought it? – that the man to do it would be someone for whom the very notion of international cricket growing up as a boy in Ireland would have been little more than a pipedream.

It was a vintage World Cup final, the best there has ever been, and, my, it was tense. Maybe the day means too much, maybe the enormity of the occasion is inhibiting and maybe the pitch was too untrustworthy, slow and holding, for players to produce their free-flowing best, but with the destination of the game not clear until the last ball, it was gripping, totally gripping.

The finish of the 50-over portion of the match was so incredible it is hardly believable writing it even now. England required 15 runs off the final over, with Stokes playing a lone hand, and it was bowled by Trent Boult, who, moments before, had taken a catch on the boundary edge off Stokes that would have surely won the World Cup for his team had he not inadvertently stepped on to the boundary rope in doing so.

That drop, if it can be so called, came in the penultimate over when England required 22 runs from nine balls, and surely, had Boult not touched the boundary rope then, England's match was over, their dream done.

After two dot balls, during which Stokes refused runs to stay on strike, England still required 15 runs off four balls. Stokes, incredibly, got down on one knee then and swept the third ball from Boult into the Mound Stand for six, to tumultuous cheers. The next ball took the game out of reality and into realms of fiction, as Stokes drilled it to deep mid-wicket and diving into the crease to make his ground for a second run, deflected the ball with his bat to the boundary for six.

It was totally accidental, and Stokes immediately apologised by raising his hands, but the Laws of the game indicate that the boundary had to stand. Three runs required from two balls, then. Adil Rashid was run out, selflessly, trying to turn one into two by getting Stokes back on strike, as was Mark Wood off the final ball of the game. Match tied but, given the circumstances, it looked like an England victory was written in the stars, and how ironic in a tournament when the hosts had hit more sixes than the previous five World Cups put together, the one that mattered came via overthrows.

All this, too, after chasing a middling target of 242, the kind of score they would have knocked off blindfolded and without a second thought in a bilateral series but now looked more daunting, especially on a surface that allowed Colin de Grandhomme's slow nibblers to cause as many difficulties as thunderbolts from Lockie Ferguson.

It would have looked even more daunting had Jason Roy been given out first ball to Boult, as he could have been, when an inswinger hit him on the knee roll, causing a roar from the fielders that would have been heard in Hampstead. Not out, said the umpire Marais Erasmus, and the luck remained with England as Matt Henry passed the edge frequently during an outstanding new-ball spell that accounted for Roy eventually, caught behind by Tom Latham, but might have accounted for more.

The frustration of scoring on a slow surface was seen most of all in the innings from Joe Root, seven runs in 30 balls before his patience ran out,

and the way Morgan slapped a short ball into the hands of deep cover. It was only when Buttler, with a composed half-century, and Stokes came together with a partnership of 110 in a little more than 20 overs that England could think of victory again.

Spare a thought for Kane Williamson, who barely put a foot wrong throughout the tournament. He bravely took his chances, having won the toss on a cool, overcast morning, with the threat of rain only recently receded, by batting – Morgan was minded to bowl – and would have been relieved only to have lost one wicket in the opening ten overs, given how both semi-finals were decided by a rash of wickets with the new ball. Guptill was the solitary casualty here, and this after showing glimpses of his belligerent best when he upper-cut Archer over third man for six.

The key wickets of top-scorer Henry Nicholls and Williamson both fell to Liam Plunkett, who did what he has done so well for England since the 2015 World Cup, which is to say pick up good players at a key stage of the game. No seamer in world cricket has taken more wickets in the middle overs in that period than Plunkett and now he was too good for Williamson, first of all, who edged a rising ball that ran down the slope to the wicketkeeper, and Nicholls, who dragged on to his stumps, both balls delivered in cross-seam fashion, as is Plunkett's way.

It was a fine collective effort. Chris Woakes threatened with the new ball; Archer's five consecutive overs at the end with the old ball were Jasprit

Bumrah-like in their efficiency, but it was in the middle where the battle was won, when New Zealand found themselves restricted as they looked to push on. For this World Cup-winning team, there can be no finer emblem than Plunkett, a man who has endured his ups and downs and emerged, a dozen years after his first World Cup, triumphant at last.

................................................

PLAYER OF THE MATCH:
**Ben Stokes (England)**
PLAYER OF THE TOURNAMENT:
**Kane Williamson (New Zealand)**

---

# HOW THE SUPER OVER UNFOLDED

## England

**Batsmen:** Ben Stokes and Joss Buttler
**Bowler:** Trent Boult
1 Stokes slices over short third man into unattended area.
**Runs 3 Total 3**
2 Buttler hits the ball to deep square leg.
**Runs 1 Total 4**
3 Stokes clubs inswinging delivery to mid-wicket.
**Runs 4 Total 8**
4 Stokes slices full toss to backward point.
**Runs 1 Total 9**
5 Buttler hits yorker to cover. Nicholls slow to react.
**Runs 2 Total 11**
6 Buttler whips full toss to mid-wicket.
**Runs 4 Total 15**

## New Zealand

**Batsmen:** Jimmy Neesham and Martin Guptill
**Bowler:** Jofra Archer
1 Wide
**Runs 1 Total 1**
1 Neesham pushes to long off.
**Runs 2 Total 3**
2 Neesham clubs over mid-wicket.
**Runs 6 Total 9**
3 Neesham to legside again, Jason Roy misfield allows easy second.
**Runs 2 Total 11**
4 Neesham to leg, easy two.
**Runs 2 Total 13**
5 Bottom edge, scrambled single.
**Runs 1 Total 14**
6 Guptill to mid-wicket, run out by Roy's throw, attempting second.
**Runs 1 Total 15**

*With the scores still level, England won, having scored 26 boundaries – 24 fours and two sixes – to New Zealand's 17 (14 fours and three sixes) in the course of the match.*

## WHAT THEY SAID

'That was the best game of cricket you'll ever see. I'm pretty lost for words. All the hard work over four years, to get here and be champions of the world it's an amazing feeling. So much hard work has gone in, this is what we aspire to be.'

Ben Stokes

'My heart is still racing. It's one of the only tournaments I've ever won in my life.'

Jofra Archer

'To bat the way he did was incredible. Everyone watching at home will hopefully try to be the next Ben Stokes.'

Eoin Morgan

'If we lost, I didn't know how I'd play cricket again.'

Jos Buttler

'I don't even know quite how they won it – what was it? Boundaries or something?'

Kane Williamson

## KEY NUMBERS

### 3
New Zealand became the third team to lose successive World Cup finals

### 3
England's defeats in the tournament. Only Pakistan in 1992 lost that many games but still won the trophy

> ❝
> ## THE GREATEST
> ## GAME OF CRICKET
> ## IN HISTORY
>
> ANDREW STRAUSS,
> FORMER ENGLAND CAPTAIN

PHOTOGRAPH BY PIXEL8000

# THE TIMES

MONDAY JULY 15 2019 | THETIMES.CO.UK | NO 72899

ONLY £1.10 TO SUBSCRIBERS £1.80

# WORLD
# CHAMPIONS

### ENGLAND WIN AFTER SUPER OVER
### IN EXHILARATING FINAL

## ANALYSIS

STEVE JAMES

Frankly, it was a surprise that they did not ask Ben Stokes to bowl the Super Over too.

He seemed to be doing everything else. Despite barely being able to walk through the fatigue of the most intense of innings, you would not have bet against him nailing the yorkers.

This was Stokes' day. This was his repayment for what happened outside a Bristol nightclub nearly two years ago. This was confirmation that he is not only a truly great technical international batting all-rounder but also a cricketer of special character and temperament.

That it came against the country of his birth provided a story full of irony but that is a tale that has long since passed. Stokes has been an England cricketer for a long time now. Here, at Lord's, was where he proved what playing for England means to him.

The 28-year-old so nearly lost all that, so he has been trying desperately for almost two years to make up for the uncomfortable aftermath of that night in Bristol. This was the day all the work and all the maturing came to fruition.

And to think that he finished England's innings with 84 not out from 98 balls by slapping his bat in frustration and kicking it away.

Mark Wood had been run out at the other end and it meant the main match was tied and that the Super Over was to take place. Stokes could have done little else. He knew that he had to be there at the end, and had promised himself to do so, especially when he lost

Jos Buttler after a partnership of 110. His determination was palpable.

Maybe at the end of those 50 overs he was rueing trying to place the last ball, a full toss from Trent Boult, for two rather than smashing it. Maybe he was just rueing not finishing it there and then. Whatever the case, there was no doubt that he had to be the man who came out to bat in that Super Over with Buttler. 'As long as he wasn't too cooked,' Eoin Morgan, the England captain, said.

Stokes was up for some more time in the oven. He does not mind the heat, and he did not let his side, or his adopted country, down.

In truth he has not done so all tournament. He was there at the beginning for them and he was still there at the end. When England's nerves were jangling in the opening match of this tournament, against South Africa at the Oval, it was Stokes, with 89 with the bat, a couple of wickets and then a spectacular catch, who calmed them down. That was nothing compared to the tension here, but Stokes was still the same. He has been the same throughout the tournament. He has batted with quite incredible judgment and composure.

There were jitters aplenty in the England batting from the moment that Jason Roy was so very nearly leg-before to the first ball of the innings, but it was Stokes, in concert with Buttler, who showed the rest how to play on a slow and sticky pitch, where every ball had to be treated with some level of care but few were the sort of hand grenades that some batsmen made them appear.

It is said – with much justification – that Joe Root acts as England's glue in one-day international cricket. Now, Root is a quite magnificent batsman but Stokes has been the batsman to whom his team-mates have had to try to stick in the toughest matches. He has been both glue and dynamite.

It was the case here at Lord's in the group match against Australia, when he made 89; it was the case when he was left stranded on 82 not out against Sri Lanka at Headingley; and it was undoubtedly the case here. Those first two matches were lost but this one, eventually after a conclusion that will never be forgotten, was not. This was the one that mattered. Stokes deserved this.

He had one instance of remarkable luck, of course. For there was that moment in the last over when he was scurrying back for a second run, diving for the crease when the throw inadvertently hit his bat.

The ball raced away to the boundary. Had it not reached the fence, the batsmen would not have run. That is the game's etiquette.

Stokes raised his hands in apology. It was genuine. He did not even cast the merest glance towards the throw. It was horribly unfortunate for New Zealand but maybe it was just fate for England. Four years of bravery in changing the way they played brought this.

But it was still a moment that stretched credulity in a period of cricket full of them. Stokes had hit the previous ball for a proper six too. What an over, what a finish.

When Stokes eventually arrived in the middle for the Super Over – Buttler had to make his own way, while Stokes stood below the England dressing room balcony, beckoning for new gloves – he sliced the first ball over third man.

He would have been urging the ball to reach the boundary. If not, Buttler was always coming back for a third.

It was an immense test of Stokes' fitness. In between overs at the end of the main match he had been resting on his haunches, hardly able to speak to his partners, desperately trying to gather his breath. He suffers badly from cramp at the best of times, and at one stage in the field had reached for a calf muscle, so the threat of seizing up here must have been extreme.

All those hours on the training paddock and the treadmill were on the line here. He made it. Of course he made it.

Of course, he then had the power to smash Boult through the leg side for a four two balls later.

Sometimes Stokes has been urged to do less but he was training for such moments. They used to tell rugby union's Jonny Wilkinson the same but he was practising for that drop-goal in 2003. This truly was Stokes' Wilkinson moment.

He, too, is a national hero now.

# Sport

**History for Hamilton**
Record sixth British Grand
Prix in Silverstone thriller
Formula One, pages 52-53

**Djokovic's epic victory**
Federer loses longest final
after passing up match points
Wimbledon, pages 54-57

TIMES PHOTOGRAPHS MARC ASPLAND

# Glory boys

England win World Cup
for first time to join the
football and rugby heroes
of 1966 and 2003

## Ten-page special

Mike Atherton
Matt Dickinson
Steve James
Matt Hughes
Elizabeth Ammon

Jos Buttler is mobbed by, from left, Jonny Bairstow, Chris Woakes and Liam Plunkett, after completing the run out of Martin Guptill in a thrilling Super Over that sealed England's World Cup victory at Lord's

---

## Times Crossword 27,403

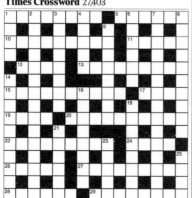

**ACROSS**

1 Piece of evidence vital, barrister reviewed case (8)
5 Briefly observe man in hat (6)
10 Force contained, one calmer? (9)
11 Bombardment, after withdrawal of artillery, lighter perhaps? (5)
12 Long throw has opener dismissed (4)
13 Undertake urban regeneration programme? Fraudulent practice (9)
15 Packing case shortly, soldier heading for old South American city (10)
17 Party hit (4)
19 Between two rivers, what was that German region? (4)
20 Marvel when one starts to hit problems in retirement, and soldiers on (10)
22 Container, and bags for pets (9)
24 Curious leader in parliamentary seat (4)
26 Boarding towards rear of ship, look up (5)
27 Soothing heart of fellow, time one loosened bandages (9)
28 Hat fitter making an adjustment (6)
29 Within plant, circuits failed again (8)

**DOWN**

1 Host, daft going topless (4)
2 Don't take the washing in, have some fun! (3,2,3,4,3)
3 Having abandoned parking, chap later travelling on the tube? (8)
4 Rev's sound study, maybe, in support of vicar at first (5)
6 African in old party, rather upstanding (6)
7 Figures, perhaps, in red book (8,7)
8 All, for example, hairline fractures? (10)
9 Poet: meddlesome man finally getting up after mid-morning? (8)
14 Country squire originally wearing creamy-white jacket? (5,5)
16 Rise in winners for Greek hero (8)
18 Requirement for the wet blanket (8)
21 Spirit one's necked (6)
23 Music centre: last of records on it (5)
25 Boss is a virile chap (4)

---

9 771742 498615

## COMMENT

MATT DICKINSON,
CHIEF SPORTS WRITER

Sick to the guts with tension, thrillingly alive with excitement, speechless at the sheer bloody drama of it all – the very best sport rips off the seatbelt, puts its foot on the gas and sends us all on the world's wildest emotional ride. And this World Cup final was as mesmerising sport as you would ever hope to witness.

It was almost unbearably tense to watch, so God only knows how the players managed to function. Everyone else at Lord's was a shaking wreck by the end of a contest that boiled down to a batsman's mad sprint, a fielder's throw and a wicketkeeper's composure. Jos Buttler must have stashed a secret supply.

England do not win World Cups very often but when they do, blimey, they make the nation suffer for its glory. After extra-time for Bobby Moore and England's footballers in 1966, and again for Martin Johnson and his rugby union heroes in 2003, a Super Over at Lord's made this the most beautifully spectacular way for Eoin Morgan's side to make history with the nation's first men's Cricket World Cup.

And there we were thinking that a penalty shoot-out in football – with all its promise of sudden death or immortality – was as much drama as can be packed into sport. You could ask whether this was the fairest system as, somehow, we went from England

needing 15 to win off the last over to New Zealand requiring 16 from six balls, but you could not begin to question that it served up scenes that made cricket suddenly feel, well, super cool, impossible to ignore.

From the shocked hush around Lord's when Jimmy Neesham hoiked Jofra Archer for six to the scream of joy around this historic ground when Martin Guptill was run out a few feet short of making the second run that would have won this game for New Zealand (perfectly deservingly, too), this was truly magnificent sport in front of a crowd that had spent a day lurching through hope, fear, doubt, dread and disbelief. And ecstasy by the end.

This time it was coming home; not that they were singing that in the Long Room, though they will have been in the nearby offices of the ECB. 'Who writes your scripts?' as Graham Gooch famously remarked to Ian Botham after another ridiculously improbable feat by the great all-rounder. The marketing men could not have imagined this better.

How amenable of Novak Djokovic to polish off Roger Federer in a five-set classic at Wimbledon just in time for anyone who had been gripped to the tennis to switch channels. At the start of the day, the ECB had been talking cautiously about an audience of four to five million being a decent figure for the first cricket game to be shown free to air in the UK since 2005. By the time of this climax in fading sun and long shadows at Lord's, it will have far exceeded every forecast.

This was the day when cricket would make itself available and it hoped, unmissable, to the whole country. This was not just about England's fate, but cricket's – how would it shape up against the competition on an afternoon when four televisions were needed to keep up with the sporting action.

Lewis Hamilton was winning the British Grand Prix and Geraint Thomas trying to stay on track in the Tour de France, but they were rendered peripheral by two classic occasions in different parts of London.

At Lord's, to think that for much of the day there were grumbles about the pitch from many in the press box, and not just because it was another one ill-suited to England's relish for big-hitting. If fours and sixes are meant to bring in the crowds, New Zealand going 15 overs without a single boundary meant that this final was initially played out to subdued murmurs.

England batted through more dot balls in the first 25 overs than in any match since they began rebuilding four years ago. The seats were slow to fill after lunch. It was a slow-burner, with an explosive end.

A crowd that had come above all with the hope of being able to say 'I was there' when England won the World Cup not only got to make that boast but also to tell tales of swashbuckling Ben Stokes. This correspondent has been lucky enough to witness many unforgettable sporting moments – the

Nou Camp in 1999, Istanbul in 2005, the Miracle at Medinah, Hamilton winning his first Formula One world title on the last bend of the last race, Super Saturday at London 2012 and a multitude of Olympic dramas – but this was as brilliant as any of them in the way it played with the emotions.

What a day not just for England, but for cricket. Modern sport obsesses about attention and legacy (perhaps modern media too). An event is not just to be won or lost but to transform the sport, to capture the next generation, to be converted into the paying punters of the future.

Organisations like the ICC and ECB are not so much 'governing bodies' as marketing departments, anxiously scanning the viewing figures, the sponsorship opportunities. A day like this, England at Lord's in a World Cup final, was prime box office.

This is a sport where, for pretty much the entirety of its existence, heroes have been shaped out of the great Ashes series – Len Hutton, Botham, Andrew Flintoff – but now offered something very different, and compelling.

As Bairstow had noted on the morning of the game, players like him had been 'inspired to take up cricket because of the marvellous feats of the 2005 England Ashes-winning team.' This was, he said, their opportunity and how, ultimately, they seized it.

It is unlikely that the viewing audience reached the peak from that golden summer of 2005 at more than nine million, or the 11.7m who recently watched England's women lose a World Cup semi-final to the United States.

For an organisation such as the ECB, which will launch The Hundred next year, though, in the hope of broadening an audience that, according to its own research, is 94 percent white, 82 percent male and 65 percent ABC1 with an average age of 50, there will be hope that this was not only a great triumph but a breakthrough. We shall see. If the way this game reached a staggering climax does not draw a crowd to cricket, nothing will.

# AFTERMATH

MATTHEW SYED

Character. That is the word that denotes the performance of Ben Stokes in the most pulsating game of cricket played in this or any other country. That is the word that captures how a 28-year-old all-rounder marshalled his considerable talents to construct the finest of innings as the pressure mounted, and the wickets fell, at the home of cricket.

They said that the scar tissue would never heal when Stokes was heaved for four sixes in the final over of the World Twenty20 final in Calcutta three short years ago. They said that he may never forget the ignominy wrought by the majestic hitting of Carlos Brathwaite. They said that, when a sufficiently big moment came once more, the memories would come back to haunt him.

'I thought, "I've just lost the World Cup." I couldn't believe it,' Stokes said in an interview with *The Telegraph*. 'I didn't know what to do. It took me so long to get back on my feet. I didn't want to get back up. It was like the whole world had come down on me. There weren't any good things going through my mind. It was just complete devastation.'

But, as Rudyard Kipling intimated, we are defined not just by how we triumph, but by how we respond to adversity. Since that T20 setback, not to mention the scandal in Bristol, for which the England player was banned from international cricket for eight months, Stokes has learnt critical lessons. According to those who know

him best, he has focused on cricket and, more importantly, recognised that being a superstar does not give one latitude to act like a lout.

His fitness has improved, a consequence of long hours in the gym and on the treadmill, but so too has his decision-making. He has played throughout this competition with finely calibrated aggression, demonstrating not just the swashbuckling belligerence of his previous incarnation, but a keen eye for the state of the game. Few could dispute that the synthesis of flamboyance and tactical intelligence has elevated a very good cricketer into the top rank of all-rounders.

And yet it was that final over of the 50 in which Stokes articulated his steeliness of character with such thrilling eloquence. Twice he refused a single when it may have been easier to take the run, thus bringing down the total, and passing the responsibility to Adil Rashid. Twice he held his ground at the striker's end, aware that he had not merely missed an opportunity to add to England's total, but was also intensifying the pressure on himself. Now, he had to deliver.

On the very next ball, Stokes stooped on to his knee to hit a six for the ages, 73 metres into the crowd, a shot that will always be etched in the national memory. With a slice of outrageous fortune on the next delivery, four overthrows being awarded after the ball deflected off the bat of Stokes, he went on to shepherd England towards the unprecedented tie that led to the Super Over. At that point, once again, he stepped forward to take responsibility.

Is this not the stuff of greatness? Is this not what Billie Jean King had in mind when she said: 'pressure is not a problem; it's a privilege.' Is this not the most conspicuous evidence of the journey that Stokes has travelled, not just as a cricketer but as a human being? Perhaps Eoin Morgan, the England captain, put it best. 'To come through it is extraordinary. He's almost superhuman. He has carried the team and our batting line-up. The atmosphere, the emotion that was going through the whole game, he managed to deal with that in an extremely experienced manner. Obviously everybody watching at home will hopefully try and be the next Ben Stokes. A lot of careers would have been ended after what happened in Calcutta. Ben, on numerous occasions, has stood up for us. He leads the way in training, in any team meetings we have, and he's an incredible cricketer. And today he's had a huge day out and we are thankful for that.'

We all know about Stokes' chequered past. He spent a night in the prison cells in 2011 after obstructing a police officer and got sent home for drinking late with a team-mate during the Lions tour to Australia in 2013.

He was acquitted of affray last year, but few who saw the pictures of that incident will have felt anything other than revulsion. Although he avoided a criminal conviction, the scandal denied England of his services for months, not least in the Ashes series.

I have never accepted, or fully understood, the notion that sporting success offers mitigation for moral failings. Do we really think that scoring a hat-trick, or hitting a sequence of sixes, excuses misdemeanours? And yet there are occasions when you can see a young person seeking to take responsibility, to learn from their mistakes. Stokes has not only sought but found a powerful version of redemption.

What seems certain is that this remarkable player is set to lead this England team forward, an example of the greatness that can emerge when ability and creativity are fused with discipline and dedication. From that astonishing catch in the first match against South Africa to his heroics in an unforgettable final, he has proved to be the backbone of this team. 'I'm pretty lost for words,' he said. 'All that hard work for four years and now to be stood here as champions of the world, it's an amazing feeling. There was no chance I wasn't going to be there at the end. It's moments like that you live for as a professional cricketer.'

's Elba,
a
**Exclusive interview**

INSIDE TIMES2

Deborah Ross
How I'd like to punish the Brexit MEPs

## become first British head of the IMF

doctrines. Mr Osborne will need the nomination of Britain's next prime minister to succeed. The *Evening Standard*, which he edits, recently endorsed Boris Johnson in the Conservative leadership race.

Although Mark Carney, the governor of the Bank of England could also be a candidate, Mr Osborne's allies believe that Mario Draghi, the out-

going head of the European Central Bank (ECB), may become his main rival because the governor is more closely focused on Canadian politics.

Supporters of Mr Osborne say that the former chancellor could win backing from both President Trump and President Xi. Mediating between the United States and China requires a politician rather than a technocrat,

they claim. They concede, though, that Brexit has made the appointment of a British candidate less likely.

The role of IMF chairman and managing director became available after Ms Lagarde was appointed to replace Mr Draghi as head of the ECB in the latest round of European Union appointments. The new head must be
Continued on page 2, col 3

### Not your call: bosses take smartphones from workers

Jack Malvern

Posting updates on social media and texting your friends at work could soon become a thing of the past as bosses confiscate smartphones to keep noses to the grindstone

Unions are warning that "a new front for friction" between workers and organisations is opening as managers feel that they cannot trust people to resist the temptation to post updates

While it is normal for retailers such as Tesco to make their employees put their phones in lockers, the practice is spreading to office workers.

A director of a marketing company in West Yorkshire recently ruled out recruiting candidates who would not hand over their mobile devices. Gerard O'Shaughnessy, of Business Marketing Services in Cleckheaton, said that he felt so aggrieved by people using phones during working hours that he confiscated them until lunchtime.

Café staff at the British Library must surrender their phones to their supervisor in case they are tempted to look at them between serving customers.

Mr O'Shaughnessy, 48, said that his company began confiscating its workers' mobile phones two months ago. "We've had girls have meltdowns when they've been told they need to put their phone in a box. Others have said it's almost breaching their human rights. It's almost like a separation anxiety," he said. "When we didn't have this policy in place people would be checking social media updates during staff meetings. Every customer I deal with tells me the same happens in their organisation with younger staff.

Strict phone policies have alarmed organisations such as Prospect, a union for clerical workers that represents some staff at the British Library. Mike Clancy, its general secretary, said: "Rigid controls over phone use, where no clear security and safety issues are involved, risks being real worker control, reflecting a culture that lacks trust." A British Library spokesman said that it was talking to its catering contractor Graysons about the matter.

result

The results olitics is in competition, difficult to of first past

Mark Sedwill, terday had a *Times* report ior civil ser- ler is not up to ntally" and has is losing his

anied by Jon Cabinet Office or 45 minutes in ce.

ank and detailed, views", a Labour e seriousness of and the evident d it was acknowl- nts in the meeting and Jon Trickett fully independent re trust and confi- ervice. They were endent element to stigation, that they ir updates on its it would report as hey made clear that he investigation will basis of its results." office spokeswoman discussion had been uctive". The investi- conducted by civil serv- o the events, and the shared with the first missioner, she said. ported at the weekend of Mr Corbyn was ge 2, col 3

in association with
**sky** sports **cricket**

High hopes Jonny Bairstow celebrates his century as England beat New Zealand
by 119 runs in Durham yesterday to reach the World Cup semi-finals. Pages 69-72

---

# England on the br

● Morgan's side outplayed by Australia at Lord's
● Captain denies claim he was scared of Starc

Elizabeth Ammon

England's World Cup hopes are hanging in the balance after a 64-run defeat by Australia at Lord's means that they may have to win both of their remaining two group matches to survive in competition.

Eoin Morgan rejected a claim made by Kevin Pietersen, the former England batsman, that he was "scared" of Australia yesterday, but the England side admitted that his side are low on confidence as they prepare to play India today and New Zealand next Wednesday.

England started their tournament as favourites but are in fourth place in the semi-final qualifying ... semi-finals — and two ahead of ... who have a

... made them ... four and ... of Morgan, ... mate, had ... 67

... in frustration after Mitchell Starc's yorker bowled him out for 89, the only innings of substance from an England batsman

DOWN

---

# THE TIMES
# Sport

## England restore fear factor

Fired-up Bairstow hits century to set up win
India and put hosts back on course for semi-

Elizabeth Ammon

The England captain Eoin Morgan said his side had "an outstanding day" after they kept their World Cup hopes alive with a 31-run victory that ended India's unbeaten run.

England bounced back from successive losses to Sri Lanka and Australia, and yesterday's win means that they are guaranteed a semi-final spot if they beat New Zealand on Wednesday at Chester-le-Street.

An exceptional 111 from the opener Jonny Bairstow, who had reacted to criticism after England's defeat by Australia by accusing people of wanting the team to fail, proved crucial in settling any nerves from the under-pressure hosts at Edgbaston.

"He [Jonny] does tend to get fired up a lot, and that suits him," Morgan said. "He likes a bit of fire in his belly, and I don't mind that when he comes out and plays like that. It's outstanding. It was
Continued on page 59

Bairstow takes the acclaim on reaching his 90-ball hundred in England

Times Crossword 27,391

## STATISTICS AND RECORDS

---

**w Syed**

es football part of
al-justice system

## FA exit for key strategy guru

**Matt Hughes Sports News Correspondent**

Dave Reddin, one of the key architects
of England's recent resurgence, is to
leave the Football Association after six
years. The head of strategy and team
performance has agreed a severance
package, the governing body confirmed yesterday.

The FA did not comment on the
reasons behind Reddin's departure but
he is understood to have clashed with
colleagues throughout his spell at St
George's Park and developed a
reputation as a demanding taskmaster.

The 49-year-old faced allegations of
bullying two years ago. He was accused
of presiding over a "climate of fear" but
he was then cleared of any wrongdoing
by the FA.

Reddin is understood to have experienced more difficulties in his relationships with key colleagues after those
continued on page 61

## Nadal criticises eeding policy

**art Fraser Tennis Correspondent**

ef Nadal has accused Wimbledon
respecting the world rankings by
t a special mathematical formula
etermine seedings for the men's
es — the only grand-slam
ament to do so.

seedings will be for the champion-
will be confirmed by the All
nd Club (AELTC) this morning,
the world No 2, will be seeded
behind his arch-rival Roger
r, who is ranked No 3 but will be
No 2 after winning the Halle
n Sunday.

Australian, French and US
imply replicate the latest world
which are based on the
52 weeks of results across all
for their seedings. Wimble-
ever, uses a formula that gives
on page 58

---

## WIMBLEDON

**Wimbledon 16-page guide**

Murray's return and how Konta can
win as tournament starts today
inside T2

## US accused in World Cup spying row

**Molly Hudson Lyons**

England and the United States have
become embroiled in a spying row
before their women's World Cup semi-
final after two plain-clothed members
of American staff were spotted in a
private area of the Lionesses' team
hotel in Lyons yesterday.

The FA is believed to be furious at the
unwelcome intrusion from the US, who
were scoping out the Fourvière Hotel
as a potential base for Sunday's final.
England face the US at Parc Olympique
Lyonnais tomorrow and the final will
also be played there.

England were training at a different
location 30 minutes from the hotel
while the two Americans were being
shown around by staff at their hotel.
The FA is said to be concerned that
the Americans went into rooms where
England have held team meetings.

They were not wearing any US-
branded kit and did not show their team
credentials to security on their way in.
Eventually the pair were spotted by a
member of the FA team.

The US coach Jill Ellis dismissed the
idea that it was arrogant to be scouting
a base for a final that her team may not
even reach, and to do it when their
semi-final opponents were staying
there. "I would assume everybody is
doing that — you have to plan ahead,"
Ellis, 52, said. "The only two people who
are thinking of planning ahead is my
administrator, because she has to book
all the flights and do all of that stuff, and
her boss. Everybody else, we don't
worry about that, so that is probably
who the two people [at the hotel] were.

"So, in terms of arrogance, that has
nothing to do with us, that is planning
and preparation for our staff."

Phil Neville, the England head coach,
said that it was poor etiquette and
insisted his staff would not have done
the same. "It'll have no bearing on the
game — I found it funny," he said. "I
Continued on page 55

ton, which boosted their World Cup semi-final hopes Pages 56-59

---

# Sport

**Now Wimbledon gets**
● Where Federer-Nadal w
● Serena storms into final
Pages 64-67

# One match from g

**England dominate Australia for shot at making history**

**Elizabeth Ammon**

England have the chance to win
their first World Cup after
hammering Australia by eight
wickets in their semi-final at
Edgbaston.

They will play New Zealand at
Lord's on Sunday, the first time
that they have reached the final
for 27 years, in a match that will be
broadcast on Channel 4 as well as
Sky. The pay-TV broadcaster
agreed to allow the match to be
shown free-to-air in a move that
they hope will allow the widest
possible audience to be inspired by
Eoin Morgan's team, should they
make history by winning at Lord's.

Morgan, 32, said: "It's the game I
love so it's great news that it's on
free-to-air." Reflecting on his side's
dominant performance with bat
and then bat, he said: "Everybody
out there on the field and even in
the changing room loved every
ball. There was no lack of
commitment, application and we
had a bit of a day out which is cool
when it happens like that,
particularly when the bowlers
bowl like that, it is awesome."

The only blemish on England's
day came when Jason Roy was
sanctioned by the ICC for showing
dissent to the umpires after being
continued on page 69

**World Cup final**
New Zealand

---

# THE TIMES

MONDAY JULY 15 2019 | THETIMES.CO.UK | NO 72899

ONLY £1.10 TO SUBSCRIBE

---

Check today's answers by ringing 0906
7577189 by midnight. Calls cost 80p per minute plus your telephone company's network
access charge. SP: Spoke 0333 202 3390.

# <u>2019 WORLD CUP STATISTICS</u>

## *LEADING RUN-SCORERS*

**648** Rohit Sharma (India)
**647** David Warner (Australia)
**606** Shakib Al Hasan (Bangladesh)
**578** Kane Williamson (New Zealand)
**556** Joe Root (England)
**532** Jonny Bairstow (England)
**507** Aaron Finch (Australia)
**474** Babar Azam (Pakistan)
**465** Ben Stokes (England)
**443** Virat Kohli (India)
**443** Jason Roy (England)

## *HIGHEST INDIVIDUAL SCORES*

**166** David Warner (Australia) v Bangladesh at Trent Bridge
**153** Jason Roy (England) v Bangladesh at Cardiff
**153** Aaron Finch (Australia) v Sri Lanka at The Oval
**148** Eoin Morgan (England) v Afghanistan at Old Trafford
**148** Kane Williamson (New Zealand) v West Indies at Old Trafford
**140** Rohit Sharma (India) v Pakistan at Old Trafford
**124★** Shakib Al Hasan (Bangladesh) v West Indies at Taunton
**122★** Rohit Sharma (India) v South Africa at Southampton
**122** David Warner (Australia) v South Africa at Old Trafford
**121** Shakib Al Hasan (Bangladesh) v England at Cardiff

# CENTURY MAKERS

## 5
Rohit Sharma (India)

## 3
David Warner (Australia)

## 2
Shakib Al Hasan (Bangladesh)
Jonny Bairstow (England)
Aaron Finch (Australia)
Joe Root (England)
Kane Williamson (New Zealand)

## 1
Babar Azam (Pakistan)
Carlos Brathwaite (West Indies)
Jos Buttler (England)
Shikhar Dhawan (India)
Avishko Fernando (Sri Lanka)
Faf du Plessis (South Africa)
Angelo Mathews (Sri Lanka)
Eoin Morgan (England)
Nicholas Pooran (West Indies)
Mushfiqur Rahim (Bangladesh)
KL Rahul (India)
Jason Roy (England)
Imam-ul-Haq (Pakistan)

# LEADING WICKET-TAKERS

Mitchell Starc (Australia) **27**
Lockie Ferguson (New Zealand) **21**
Jofra Archer (England) **20**
Mustafizur Rahman (Bangladesh) **20**
Jasprit Bumrah (India) **18**
Mark Wood (England) **18**
Mohammad Amir (Pakistan) **17**
Trent Boult (New Zealand) **17**
Shaheen Afridi (Pakistan) **16**
Chris Woakes (England) **16**

# BEST BOWLING

**6–35** Shaheen Afridi (Pakistan) v Bangladesh at Lord's
**5–26** Mitchell Starc (Australia) v New Zealand at Lord's
**5–29** Shakib Al Hasan (Bangladesh) v Afghanistan at Southampton
**5–30** Mohammad Amir (Pakistan) v Australia at Taunton
**5–31** Jimmy Neesham (New Zealand) v Afghanistan at Taunton
**5–44** Jason Behrendorff (Australia) v England at Lord's
**5–46** Mitchell Starc (Australia) v West Indies at Trent Bridge
**5–59** Mustafizur Rahman (Bangladesh) v India at Edgbaston
**5–69** Mohammed Shami (India) v England at Edgbaston
**5–75** Mustafizur Rahman (Bangladesh) v Pakistan at Lord's

# LEADING WICKETKEEPERS

**Dismissals**
Tom Latham (New Zealand) **21** (21 caught)
Alex Carey (Australia) **20** (18 caught, 2 stumped)
Shai Hope (West Indies) **16** (16 caught)
Sarfaraz Ahmed (Pakistan) **14** (14 caught)
Jos Buttler (England) **14** (12 caught, 2 stumped)

# LEADING FIELDERS

**Catches**
Joe Root (England) **13**
Faf du Plessis (South Africa) **10**
Sheldon Cottrell (West Indies) **8**
Martin Guptill (New Zealand) **8**
Chris Woakes (England) **8**

# HIGHEST TOTALS

**397–6** England v Afghanistan at Old Trafford
**386–6** England v Bangladesh at Cardiff
**381–5** Australia v Bangladesh at Trent Bridge
**352–5** India v Australia at the Oval
**348–8** Pakistan v England at Trent Bridge
**338–6** Sri Lanka v West Indies at Chester-le-Street
**337–7** England v India at Edgbaston
**336–5** India v Pakistan at Old Trafford
**334–9** England v Pakistan at Trent Bridge
**334–7** Australia v Sri Lanka at the Oval

# LOWEST COMPLETED TOTALS

**105** Pakistan v West Indies at Trent Bridge
**125** Afghanistan v South Africa at Cardiff
**136** Sri Lanka v New Zealand at Cardiff
**143** West Indies v India at Old Trafford
**152** Afghanistan v Sri Lanka at Cardiff
**157** New Zealand v Australia at Lord's
**172** Afghanistan v New Zealand at Taunton
**186** New Zealand v England at Chester-le-Street
**200** Afghanistan v Bangladesh at Southampton

# BIGGEST WINS

**10** wickets New Zealand v Sri Lanka at Cardiff
**150** runs England v Afghanistan at Old Trafford
**125** runs India v West Indies at Old Trafford
**119** runs England v New Zealand at Chester-le-Street
**106** runs England v Bangladesh at Cardiff
**104** runs England v South Africa at the Oval

# TEAM OF THE TOURNAMENT

Rohit Sharma (India)
Jason Roy (England)
Kane Williamson (capt) (New Zealand)
Joe Root (England)
Shakib Al Hasan (Bangladesh)
Ben Stokes (England)
Alex Carey (wk) (Australia)
Mitchell Starc (Australia)
Jofra Archer (England)
Lockie Ferguson (New Zealand)
Jasprit Bumrah (India)

# WORLD CUP RECORDS

*Overall World Cup records that were changed by the 2019 tournament. Top tens only.*

## LEADING RUN-SCORERS

2278 Sachin Tendulkar (India)
1743 Ricky Ponting (Australia)
1532 Kumar Sangakkara (Sri Lanka)
1225 Brian Lara (West Indies)
1207 A.B. de Villiers (South Africa)
**1186 Chris Gayle (West Indies)**
1165 Sanath Jayasuriya (Sri Lanka)
1148 Jacques Kallis (South Africa)
**1146 Shakib Al Hasan (Bangladesh)**
1112 Tillakaratne Dilshan (Sri Lanka)

## MOST RUNS IN A TOURNAMENT

673 Sachin Tendulkar (India) 2003
659 Matthew Hayden (Australia) 2007
**648 Rohit Sharma (India) 2019**
**647 David Warner (Australia) 2019**
**606 Shakib Al Hasan (Bangladesh) 2019**
**578 Kane Williamson (New Zealand) 2019**
**556 Joe Root (England) 2019**
548 Mahela Jayawardene (Sri Lanka) 2007
547 Martin Guptill (New Zealand) 2015
541 Kumar Sangakkara (Sri Lanka) 2015

*The highest individual score at the 2019 World Cup did not make the all-time top ten*

# LEADING WICKET-TAKERS

71 Glenn McGrath (Australia)
68 Muttiah Muralitharan (Sri Lanka)
**56 Lasith Malinga (Sri Lanka)**
55 Wasim Akram (Pakistan)
**49 Mitchell Starc (Australia)**
49 Chaminda Vaas (Sri Lanka)
44 Zaheer Khan (India)
44 Javagal Srinath (India)
**40 Imran Tahir (South Africa)**
**39 Trent Boult (New Zealand)**

# MOST WICKETS IN A TOURNAMENT

**27 Mitchell Starc (Australia) 2019**
26 Glenn McGrath (Australia) 2007
23 Muttiah Muralitharan (Sri Lanka) 2007
23 Shaun Tait (Australia) 2007
23 Chaminda Vaas (Sri Lanka) 2003
22 Trent Boult (New Zealand) 2015
22 Brett Lee (Australia) 2002
22 Mitchell Starc (Australia) 2015
21 Shahid Afridi (Pakistan) 2011
**21 Lockie Ferguson (New Zealand) 2019**
21 Brad Hogg (Australia) 2007
21 Glenn McGrath (Australia) 2003
21 Zaheer Khan (India) 2011

*No bowling performance at the 2019 World Cup features in the top ten*

# HIGHEST TOTALS

417-6 Australia v Afghanistan at Perth 2015
413-5 India v Bermuda at Port of Spain 2007
411-4 South Africa v Ireland at Canberra 2015
408-5 South Africa v West Indies at Sydney 2015
398-5 Sri Lanka v Kenya at Kandy 1996
**397-6 England v Afghanistan at Old Trafford 2019**
393-6 New Zealand v West Indies at Wellington 2015
**386-6 England v Bangladesh at Cardiff 2019**
**381-5 Australia v Bangladesh at Trent Bridge 2019**
377-6 Australia v South Africa at St Kitts 2007

*None of the lowest totals at the 2019 World Cup feature in the top ten*

# HIGHEST MATCH AGGREGATES

**714 Australia v Bangladesh at Trent Bridge 2019**
688 Australia v Sri Lanka at Sydney 2015
**682 England v Pakistan at Trent Bridge 2019**
676 India v England at Bengaluru 2011
671 Australia v South Africa at St Kitts 2007
**668 Australia v India at the Oval 2019**
**666 England v Bangladesh at Cardiff 2019**
661 West Indies v Zimbabwe at Canberra 2015
657 Ireland v Zimbabwe at Hobart 2015
656 England v Ireland at Bengaluru 2011

# ACKNOWLEDGEMENTS

As always, this book was far from being the work of one person. Mark Beynon of The History Press was fortunate to have a ticket for the World Cup final and emerged from the euphoria of that remarkable day at Lord's with the excellent idea of a compilation of *The Times'* coverage. The work was assisted by several people at *The Times*, including Tim Hallissey, the former Head of Sport; Alan Miller, of the sport picture desk; and Robert Hands, in the managing editor's department. Robin Ashton and Lily Carlton of the syndication department were also invaluable. My great friend and cricket lover Walter Gammie helped out with the short scores at the top of each report, while John Stern provided sound advice.

# ABOUT THE EDITOR

Richard Whitehead worked for *The Times* for 21 years after joining the newspaper in 1995. He held senior roles in a number of departments, including obituaries and books, as well as ten years on the sports desk. His previous archive books for The History Press are *The Times on the Ashes* (2015) and *The Times 50 Greatest Football Matches* (2019). He is now the Digital Editor of *Wisden Cricketers' Almanack*.